Popular Ideologies

Popular Ideologies

Mass Culture at Mid-Century

Susan Smulyan

PENN

UNIVERSITY OF PENNSYLVANIA PRESS

PHILADELPHIA

Published by
University of Pennsylvania Press
Philadelphia, Pennsylvania 19104-4112

Printed in the United States of America on acid-free paper

10 9 8 7 6 5 4 3 2 1

Library of Congress Cataloging-in-Publication Data

Smulyan, Susan.
Popular ideologies: Mass culture at mid-century / Susan Smulyan.
p. cm.
ISBN-13: 978-0-8122-4020-7 (cloth : alk. paper)
ISBN-10: 0-8122-4020-0 (cloth : alk. paper)
Includes bibliographical references and index.
Contents: Minstrel laughs: popular culture, race, and the middle class—The magic of nylon: the struggle over gender and consumption—Reorientation and entertainment in occupied Japan—Advertising novels as cultural critique: dry martinis, rare steaks, and willing women—Stories of *otaku* and *desis*
1. Popular culture—History—20th century. 2. Popular culture—United States—History—20th century. I. Title.
CB425 .S524 2007
973.9—dc22 2006050028

CONTENTS

INTRODUCTION

Escaping Popular Culture

THIS BOOK CONSIDERS how complex ideas of race, class, gender, nationhood, and consumption were created, expressed, and worked out in popular culture forms in the middle of the twentieth century. Whenever I've taught a survey of American popular culture, my students have ended the course saying, "Well, Professor Smulyan, we know you disagree, but we still think it's all just escape." Over thirteen weeks, I have explained how audiences found cultural expressions critical (protesters *died* in the Astor Place Riot), in part because ordinary people used popular culture to express and work out their most important thinking. I have discussed how cultural producers used entertainment and consumption to construct and reinforce hierarchies of gender, class, and race. Yet my students preferred to regard such cultural forms as empty of ideology, as a way to escape thought. For many reasons I can't overcome my students' resistance, perhaps most importantly because the culture industries, with resources infinitely greater than mine, have always worked hard to mask their functions. But I set out to look for instances where the ideas expressed by popular culture were so strong, and so integral to the popular culture itself, that no one could dismiss them. I found the clearest examples in the middle years of the twentieth century, when popular culture went through a series of key changes.

Each of the case studies takes up a crucial paradigm of mid-twentieth-century U.S. history: the intertwined nature of racial and class formation, the construction of gender, the internationalization of American culture in the postwar world, and the critique of consumption. In Chapter 1, I look at amateur minstrel shows presented around the country through the 1950s. Amateur minstrelsy raises, in the context of middle-class formation, all the issues present in the other cases. Just as popular culture helped constitute a white working class in the nineteenth century, the changing nature of popular culture helped the middle class define itself in the middle of the twentieth. I contend that the change from popular to mass played a role in class formation as the middle class struggled to delineate itself as consuming, white, gendered, and American in a particular way. Between 1920 and 1960, commercial publishers sold amateur performers guides to presenting minstrel shows. These books offered songs, skits, instructions about how to produce a minstrel performance, and directions about how to "black up." This widespread amateur theatrical tradition, based on a commodified set of directions, provided a moment when it was possible to see the working of racial and class ideology within a popular culture form.

The second case study examines the invention of nylon. The DuPont Chemical Company, using an elaborate research and development process, invented nylon to replace silk in women's stockings. The invention process included the scientific discovery of superpolymers; the technological innovations needed to produce, spin, and weave thread made of polymer; and the marketing of the new fiber to hosiery manufacturers, store managers, and women consumers. Beginning with the expanded markets for stockings brought by the short skirts of the 1920s, the story of nylon continues with its discovery in the 1930s, its engineering for use in stockings in the 1940s, and its marketing in the 1950s. In each part of the invention process, the attributes of nylon were gendered as DuPont scientists and engineers built ideas about femininity and women's bodies into the fabric. As lives changed through the prosperity, hard times, and war work of the mid-century, women's roles were reinscribed in this new product. Nylon, like minstrel shows, had ideas embedded in its very structure.

In the third chapter, I consider Hollywood films shown in Japan during the Occupation as part of the Allied goal of "teaching democracy" to the defeated enemy after World War II. Despite the best efforts of Occupation officials to provide a coherent message, the Hollywood movies chosen for exhibition showed the difficulty of using commercialized popular culture for propaganda purposes and the ideological confusion attached to any specific piece of popular culture. The slipperiness of the specific message contained in a particular film may help explain why my students so easily dismiss popular culture as "just escape." Equivocation is one method by which commodified entertainment hides its ideology. The U.S. government failed to establish the educational value of any individual Hollywood film during the Occupation. But, by insisting on its own commercial, privatized, yet still government-supported film industry as the only model, the United States taught the Japanese a lesson about capitalist control of communications while protecting the Japanese market for American films. Thus, the ideology conveyed by American commercial films depended not principally on the content of the films but on the business arrangements made to import such films into Japan. The power of the U.S. government to impose its film industry on the world, while pretending that American films were ideologically neutral, became an important building block of America's international cultural expansion after World War II and an important step in the transformation of cultural forms from popular into mass.

Finally, I look at a spate of novels set in advertising agencies and published in the 1950s. These books presented a popular critique of mass culture, following that provided by the so-called New York intellectuals and the Frankfurt School. Written by authors active in the advertising industry and ranging from the melodramatic to the comic, the novels enjoyed tremendous popularity. Acting as Roland Marchand's "apostles of modernity," advertising industry professionals warned their readers of the sterility and dangers implicit in the mass culture of consumption being sold by postwar advertisers.[1]

The case studies in this volume explore different ways in which ideology gets included in popular culture and the varying relationships of the cultural producers and consumers to the ideas expressed. Amateur minstrels took notions of racial superiority for granted and, like my students, saw their plays as ideology-free. Yet, in retrospect, the instructions on how to put on a minstrel show seem almost overdetermined in their ideas about race. Like the amateur minstrels, the DuPont scientists and marketers didn't examine their ideas about femininity while building them into the molecular structure of nylon and into the advertising and presentation of the new fabric. But the consumers who protested the quantity and quality of nylon stockings believed that women could have stockings that were both strong and sheer without compromising gender identity. The Occupation authorities and the U.S. government agreed that films could teach democracy, but expressed their ideology most effectively not through the polysemic Hollywood films, as they had hoped to do, but in the film distribution system set up to bolster American capitalism in new international markets. The advertising novelists set out to write popular books that told their own stories and became social critics in the process, expressing a coherent critique of mass culture, advertising, and consumption. The message that cultural producers sought to send, even when they were not conscious that they were sending a message, was not always the one received by audiences and consumers. But popular culture carried ideology despite its being unexamined or unintended by its producers. And, as the century progressed, the power of the producers grew.

Who puts the ideas into popular culture? I examine four different groups that expressed themselves through this medium. The groups—participants in amateur theatricals, a large corporation, the federal government, and popular intellectuals in the form of best-selling writers—differed in their access to power, their cohesion, and the kind of ideas they wanted to share. I don't want to ignore the contribution of the audience or consumers, nor the struggle over meaning that ensued when popular culture expressed strong ideas. But I do think that the nature and intensity of meaning-making by the audience varied widely and must be continually called into question. In this book I am, most interested in those groups or institutions that had power (racial, gendered, economic, national, social) over other people and in how they expressed that power. Studying the amusements of ordinary people brings an understanding of such expressions of power, their construction, and their influence. In many ways, this book moves between intellectual and cultural history, spending more time on the producers of popular culture than on the audiences. Like many cultural historians, I'm interested in the culture industries and how they function.

The book takes up mid-century changes that occurred as popular culture became less open to audience input and more an expression of powerful institutions. The intertwined relationship of popular culture and the culture of consumption, growing since the 1920s, may have brought us to a "mass" culture by the 1960s. "Mass" is a contested term that gets explored further in the last chapter, but in his book, *American Culture, American Taste*, Michael Kammen makes a compelling and detailed case that leisure and entertainment had changed by the 1960s. Kammen calls the leisure activities of the 1920s-1960s "commercialized popular culture" and calls what follows "mass culture." In *Time Passages: Collective Memory and American Popular Culture*, George Lipsitz also noted important changes in popular culture after World War II as the mass media expanded and Lipsitz focused on the indeterminacy of popular culture in its subject, form, position, and reception.[2] The changes described by this book are ones of scale, commercialization, simultaneity, and internationalization. These transformations, which took place largely between 1920 and 1960, had implications for the ways people use and are used by the commercialized culture they enjoy. This process, which Kammen calls an alteration from popular to mass, is also the subject of this book. The case studies trace the beginnings of a commodified mass culture, whose possibilities Lipsitz describes for the postwar period, to the early twentieth century. I have always used the term "popular" for the forms I teach, because too often "mass" culture has been used to denigrate a form sight unseen. But the mid-century changes my case studies describe, when added to the detail of Lipsitz's and Kammen's descriptions, may force me to alter my nomenclature for cultural forms after about 1950.

The book examines four decades that represent a mix of peace and war, prosperity and depression, and active and passive enjoyment of popular entertainment. These forty years turned out to be crucial ones in the culture of consumption, as it flourished before and then survived the Great Depression and a world war. Popular culture also changed dramatically, in scope and reach, with the introduction of broadcasting and the growing importance of American film outside the borders of the United States. The increasing financial role of consumer product advertising throughout the period also proved critical in the evolution of the commodified mass culture with which we are so familiar.

Examining four case studies over fifty mid-century years seems a long way to go to refute my students' contention that popular culture is "just escape." But I take their objection to the course seriously. U.S. college students are the best possible readers of popular culture, intimately familiar with its history and its many genres, and possessing the time and skills to undertake its study. I wondered why such sophisticated audiences believed the onslaught of commodified music, television, film, books, and products helped them "escape." In the following case studies, I look at the ways in which American popular culture skillfully hides its ideology. If my students can't see it, I want to know why not. I'd contend that none of us can escape the importance of popular culture, although we might very much want to.

Studying Popular Culture

Rejecting the notion that popular culture provides an escape, I believe that a study of popular culture leads to important insights. Such study happens both outside and inside the university, and most scholars of popular culture came to it in a tangle of intellectual, political, and personal experiences. The reform movements of the 1950s, 1960s, and 1970s—the Civil Rights movements, the antiwar crusade, the women's liberation movement, the struggles for gay rights—had important cultural components and included people who wanted to work, both intellectually and politically, to understand *and* to move ordinary people. So those who worked for social change and wanted to make alliances with others who were less active looked to popular culture as a place to meet (literally and figuratively) and, in addition, hoped that they could use popular culture forms to share their ideas about social change.

It is true that portions of the Left, working at the same time, believed that popular culture was a capitalist tool designed to oppress students and anyone else working for change. But many of us were television kids, born in an age of rock and roll, and our outlooks on popular culture were formed indelibly by the fact that we liked mass-mediated forms of entertainment. How could the television programs we'd grown up with, and the songs we'd fallen in love to, prove to be tools of the capitalist hegemonic order? Older Marxist scholars taught us that popular culture oppressed us, but such forms were also crucially important to how we understood our lives. Scholars began to work in dialectical ways, as we had been taught, to explain how popular culture was produced and made to appeal to large groups of people. Popular culture at once confined and liberated, maintained the status quo and promised utopias, promulgated and spread stereotypes of minorities and women and gave many Americans their first glimpse of ordinary people of color and working women struggling hard for better lives, and made fun of African Americans and let others hear their voices.

As my friend Paul Buhle wrote in an introduction to an early and important collection of essays about popular culture:

> By the 1970s and 1980s, in what may be known as the "age of the cassette," critics who had reached early middle-age were self-conscious products of that mass culture, with special reasons to believe in its social influence. Their identities had been formed and transformed by the television they watched, the top-forty music they heard, even the comics they read. Advertising, that symbol for everything corrupt in mass society, had actually conspired with the decisive sexualization of popular music and with the cachet of recreational drugs. Television had brought the horror of America's Vietnam engagement (and its effects, such as the 1968 Democratic convention) into the living room. "Celebrity," the synthetic creation of hero status, had given the counterculture a Bob Dylan or a John Lennon

> to pronounce vague but emphatic alternatives to the apparently collapsing system.[3]

Issues vividly raised in the 1960s and '70s had resonance for us when we looked at popular culture: scholars formed in those decades studied popular culture in order to understand the people, including ourselves, who participated in and made it. Integral to this project is an examination of how best to study such material. My own work takes place within the discipline of history, in the subfield of cultural history, but within an interdisciplinary set of methodologies necessitated by my objects of study.

Cultural history is about how and which ideas get transmitted and discussed, and why. If social history considers what ordinary people did, cultural history examines what ordinary people thought and why they thought it. While social historians looked to scholarship in sociology for methodologies, cultural historians often looked to anthropology. Anthropologists find evidence of how culture operates in rituals, objects, and cultural expressions. Popular culture, in the forms of rituals, objects, and expressions, provides important sources of evidence for cultural historians as they work to unravel the intellectual history of ordinary people. But cultural historians (like anthropologists) found such sources difficult to use, particularly in looking at the twentieth century. Given the way commodified culture was produced, how did it "reflect" the ideas of its audience? If audiences were passive viewers, how did popular culture explain what ordinary people thought?

Most scholars have rejected the shaping versus reflecting dichotomy as well as the passive versus active binary as ways of explaining popular culture. These scholars suggest, in addition, that rather than providing an "escape" from the hard problems of everyday life, popular culture was and is where people engaged, both passively and actively, with important issues. At the University of Birmingham's influential Centre for Contemporary Cultural Studies (CCCS), beginning in the middle 1960s, researchers struggled to find ways of thinking about popular culture that illustrated the constructed nature of culture, used interdisciplinary methods, drew on neo-Marxist theories, and pushed forward a political agenda. Referring to the ideas of Althusser, and particularly those of Gramsci, to consider culture and the role of ideology, these scholars self-consciously worked in the tradition of Richard Hoggart, Raymond Williams, and E. P. Thompson. The researchers maintained a lively interest in the leisure activities of the British working class and often focused on the media.[4] The work of Stuart Hall proved particularly influential for scholars working in a U.S. context. In his important essay, "Notes on Deconstructing 'The Popular'," Hall described popular culture as a "site of conflict." Hall's conflict model considered popular culture a place where cultural work got done with the audience as active participants using popular culture for important political purposes, rather than as "cultural dopes" waiting to be indoctrinated.[5] American scholars have applied Hall's ideas about popular culture as a site of conflict with interesting results.

Hall's conflictual approach helped center issues of race and gender in ways that other models for studying popular culture did not. Robert Toll's early book, *Blacking Up: The Minstrel Show in Nineteenth Century America*, should have pointed the way for more work in this area, but very few people followed his lead. His work was important because he talked about two issues that were intertwined but that scholars often separate. Toll described the racist content of minstrel shows and showed how and why such racism became part of the American theatrical tradition. Then he went a step farther and examined how this racist content, and the racist ideology that supported it, affected black performers. So Toll examined the interactions between the content of a popular culture form and the society in which it appeared but also considered the users of popular culture—in this case, African Americans—not only as subjects of popular culture but also as participants.[6]

But even as the idea of popular culture as a "site of conflict" explained so much, I came to see students' insistence that popular culture was "just escape" as a complaint about the way I had used the Birmingham school's description of popular culture as a struggle over meaning. In its more naive applications, such an idea left little room for exploring the power dynamics of a commodified cultural exchange. While television audiences can, and did, make meaning out of half-hour sitcoms, they had little power to influence the format or content of the shows they watched. In a related issue, more important for this project, the idea that meaning came out of a struggle downplayed examination of producers' imposition of a strong ideology in favor of examining the struggle over that ideology once it was presented. In the push to bring the audience into focus as significant contributors to the meaning-making happening in popular culture, scholars sometimes downplayed the role, and the real strength, of the cultural producers.

Many of the scholars at Birmingham came out of sociology and remained interested in qualitative audience surveys as a research tool.[7] Scholars in the United States, particularly those working in a literary reader-response model and those in communications, used this method to good effect, but historians continued to struggle to find out "what the audience thought."[8] Because such historical forays into audience research were time-consuming and difficult, other areas of popular culture research languished. Privileging the audience left the equation lopsided, especially when audience members had little power. I remain committed to the concept that the meaning of any cultural expression is made in the interaction among the different groups and objects (producers, texts, audiences), but I have found that that formulation, as it is often applied, downplays issues of power and content. In commodified culture, different players have different stakes and different abilities to present their ideas. An analysis of commodified versions of popular culture must take those differences into account. Michael Denning contends that popular culture doesn't exist outside commodification, that "mass culture has won; there is nothing else . . . all culture is mass culture under capitalism."[9] Such pervasiveness makes it difficult to find a focus for a study of popular culture, especially for a study that might foster social change. As Janice Radway notes, Denning suggests

> that any cultural studies animated by the desire to foster intervention must therefore ask how cultural commodities are actively, continuously, and redundantly articulated to historical blocs and, by understanding that process of articulation as precisely an open-ended, undecided cultural struggle, seek to understand how certain articulations still might be challenged and changed.[10]

Cultural historians, especially in the United States, have been increasingly conscious of the way popular culture changes and the dangers of using the same methods to study earlier and later forms. Kammen's definition of mass culture as "nonregional, highly standardized, and completely commercial," and his comparison showing popular culture "*more often than not*" as participatory and interactive while mass culture "*more often than not*" is privatized and passive, remind us that a study of the way popular culture becomes mass may require more than an examination of audience actions to completely understand the process of change.[11] The question of how to undertake a mass culture study dedicated to producing the possibility of social change remains open, but I believe that examining expressions of power is crucial. This study takes up that issue both by looking at the moments when cultural expressions took steps toward mass culture and by focusing on powerful cultural producers.

The Birmingham Centre for Contemporary Cultural Studies pushed scholars to consider issues of agency, how culture is constructed through the interaction of audience and texts, and the idea that hegemony is always struggled over. But sometimes, in the search for ways in which audiences were not "cultural dopes," the ways in which they *were*—and colluded in making themselves—dopes became harder to remember. Hall wrote that "hegemonizing is hard work" and capitalist society works unceasingly to ensure that the meaning made by audiences contributes to the hegemony constructed by the powerful. Seeking out moments when the audience made oppositional meaning, I worry that we've often overlooked the meaning-making engaged in by powerful culture producers and the ways they enlist the audience in that project. James Carey has written that British cultural studies "could be described just as easily and perhaps more accurately as ideological studies for they assimilate, in a variety of complex ways, culture to ideology."[12] While continuing an interest in conflict and in culture, as well as in how culture functions to support hegemony, I want particularly to examine ideology.

Recently cultural historians have rethought their affinities with intellectual historians. While intellectual historians traditionally paid attention to the thought of intellectuals, cultural historians proudly considered the thought of ordinary people to be as important, as intellectual, as the writings of a nation's political leaders. But cultural historians have begun paying closer attention to the culture producers with the most influence, those best suited to get their products into the hands (and eyes and ears) of consumers. Rather than seeing this as a repudiation of a "bottom-up" form of history, cultural historians make the case that, in an increasingly commodified system, it remains impossible to understand the audience, and their agency, without understanding the economic and political context in which popular and mass cultures are produced. James Cook has termed this "The Return of the 'Culture Industry' Concept," and has gone so far as to recuperate Adorno in his search for a way of studying the business and intellectual arrangements of nineteenth-century popular culture, particularly P. T. Barnum.[13]

In the juggling act that is popular culture scholarship, some historians have kept all the balls in the air while examining commercialized forms. They have balanced issues of oppression and agency; ideology and culture; the constructed, hegemonic nature of popular culture and its conflicted reception. In the three books discussed below, the authors share an interest in the relationship between politics and commodified popular culture that might be called mass culture. While examining different constituents (sometimes producers, sometimes audience members), these books all describe the possibility of a transformative popular culture. I have found these books to be the best models for the work I want to do.

In *Where the Girls Are: Growing Up Female with the Mass Media*, Susan Douglas, drawing on the work of Jürgen Habermas and on feminist film theory, showed how female audiences used and were abused by pop music, movies, television programs, magazines, and advertising from the 1950s to the 1990s. Douglas painted a nuanced picture of the mass media that revealed female listeners and viewers as both agents and manipulated masses, receiving messages that portrayed women in contradictory ways, as, for example, at once narcissistic and masochistic. Using herself as an example of audience reaction, Douglas wrote that "the mass media are both our best allies and our most lethal enemies." Portraying women as agents, but without neglecting the oppressive aspects of the mass media, Douglas also traced the economic basis of popular culture, to make an argument about politics and how political movements interact with popular culture. Douglas asked how the Women's Liberation movement began and how women were able to imagine social change given the oppressive popular culture young women encountered.[14]

In *The Cultural Front: The Laboring of American Culture in the Twentieth Century*, Michael Denning wrote about a group of people who expressed political ideas through popular culture. Denning claimed that "the communisms of the Depression triggered a deep and lasting transformation of American modernism and mass culture, what I will call the **laboring** of American culture."[15] Denning considered culture not as an empty arena in which different groups worked out an ideology but as a forum in which ideas were expressed, debated, and modified and where the forum was also shaped and changed, depending on the ideas. Denning looked directly at what he called "commercial culture" and how it is formed, and he insisted that such culture is a vehicle for important ideas. Furthermore, he didn't privilege the audience as the sole arbiter of whether popular culture contained ideas and what those ideas might be. I share Denning's interest in how cultural studies and cultural history are conducted and appreciate his contention that the "critical American Studies of the postwar years was scarred by the intellectual repression of the Cold War, and in many ways it represented a retreat from the cultural history that had been pioneered by Popular Front scholars."[16] Denning examined one important group of artists and how they used popular culture to express their political views and, in the process, shaped now-familiar forms of mass culture. Although I look at groups at the opposite end of the political and power spectrum, Denning's method, and his thesis that progressive artists shaped American culture, have guided my work.

Like Denning and Douglas, George Lipsitz has written extensively and importantly on popular culture. In *Dangerous Crossroads: Popular Music, Postmodernism, and the Poetics of Place*, Lipsitz looked at popular culture transnationally, paying particular attention to how different groups communicated musically with others separated from them by race or national borders. Lipsitz used the concept of place to tie together a wonderfully wide range of examples. While not ignoring conflict, in this book Lipsitz puts the "site" back into Hall's idea that popular culture is a "site of conflict." Balancing the local with the international, Lipsitz's insights into the importance and meaning of a global popular culture seem important to me. In what follows, I try to locate important moments in the twentieth century when this transnational popular culture began. Like Denning, Lipsitz focused on those who produce the primary works of popular culture, the musicians themselves. Pulling together the ideas of place, politics, and commercialized popular culture, Lipsitz wrote: "By playing on the contradictions between national states and the capitalist economies they sustain and support, popular musicians have sometimes successfully used commercial culture as a vehicle for political agitation and education."[17] With his fascinating readings of the ways such political action happens, Lipsitz made a case that popular culture studies (like popular culture itself) is, at base, political.

My students read works by Douglas, Denning, and Lipsitz, but because they refused to believe in the oppressive nature of popular culture, in the crucial fact that hegemony is constructed through it, they failed to see the opposition between cultural production and reception uncovered by these authors. While Douglas focused on reception and Denning and Lipsitz on popular culture producers, I explore, in the work that follows, the use the powerful have made of popular culture, rather than the way audiences and progressive authors of popular culture texts have expressed their radical ideas. But I don't want to lose the sense of optimism (no matter how guarded) found in the texts by Douglas, Denning, and Lipsitz. Even while examining the difficulties commodified culture presents to such a politics, I want to keep the idea that popular culture is used by audiences to protest their oppression and by producers to express their views. I look to these texts as models of method and outlook, as well as of careful and incisive scholarship.

Keeping these good models in mind, in writing this book I chose to focus on the concept of ideology for a number of reasons. I could have chosen hegemony, culture, or discourse, for example, as operative terms, but because I remain interested in issues of power and in twentieth-century American popular culture, which is often mass-mediated, ideology became most important.[18] Terry Eagleton, in *Ideology*, made the simple but crucial point that the concept of "ideology" was itself part of a capitalist (or at least industrial, class-based) system. My students resisted the idea that popular culture contains ideology, at least in part, because such an idea is deeply Marxist.[19] Only with capitalism and the formation of a bourgeoisie do people notice competing ideas of how the world works. Lawrence Levine's work on American interpretations of Shakespeare after the Civil War and other late nineteenth-century forms showed this well. As capitalism and its accompanying class formation advanced, clashes over popular culture increased so that different classes could set themselves apart by their popular culture choices.[20] The ideologies that underlay class formation were expressed and constructed through and within popular culture forms. These case studies show that such clashes continued in the twentieth century as the middle class sought a privileged position as consumers.

For Eagleton, ideologies are "unifying, action-oriented, rationalizing, legitimating, universalizing, and naturalizing."[21] Hegemony, according to Eagleton, existed in forms other than discursive, whereas

> Ideology refers specifically to the way power-struggles are fought out at the level of signification; and though such signification is involved in all hegemonic processes, it is not in all cases the **dominant** level by which rule is sustained. . . . Hegemony is also carried in cultural, political, and economic forms—in non-discursive practices as well as in rhetorical utterances.[22]

The examples I explore exist as discursive words and images, as the performative and narrative parts of culture. The critics, philosophers, and historians who have used the concept of ideology, especially since Marx, have been those interested in communication, just as I am in this project, where I examine consumer goods, theater, film, and novels and how they communicate ideas.

One of the best descriptions of the usefulness of ideology in looking at communications remains that of John B. Thompson, as outlined most fully in his *Ideology and Modern Culture: Critical Social Theory in the Era of Mass*

Communication. Thompson rethought the theory of ideology in the light of the development of mass communications because, as he explained,

> the writers who have concerned themselves with problems of ideology have failed to deal adequately with the nature and impact of mass communication in the modern world. . . . They were inclined to regard the development of mass communication as the emergence of a new mechanism of social control in modern societies, a mechanism through which the ideas of dominant groups could be propagated and diffused, and through which the consciousness of subordinate groups could be manipulated and controlled. Ideology was understood as a kind of "social cement" and mass communication was viewed as a particularly efficacious mechanism for spreading the glue. This general approach to the relation between ideology and mass communication is one which I shall criticize in detail.[23]

Thompson's text carefully described and dissected the notion of ideology. His description of a scholarship based on this definition of ideology sounds like what U.S. cultural historians have been practicing for a decade, with an emphasis on studying producer, the text, and audience simultaneously.[24]

Thompson's definition of ideology as "meaning in the service of power" proved especially important. Critics have compared Thompson's use of ideology with other scholarship that instead used the word "discourse." Scholars who use "ideology" talked about domination and the role of the powerful, while those who invoked "discourse" usually discussed people who were oppressed.[25] Thompson himself noted: "I wish to prise the concept of ideology apart from the search for collectively shared values, redirecting it towards the study of the complex ways in which meaning is mobilized for the maintenance of relations of domination."[26] Because I study the powerful, members of the dominant groups and institutions, ideology becomes an important concept. My case studies range widely in the political purposes to which popular culture is put and illustrate the ways in which power is spread through a number of institutions, but my examples cluster to the right of the political spectrum, certainly to the right of those explored by Denning in *The Cultural Front*. Because of the nature of the material I have examined, I believe that scholars of popular culture need to keep ideology in the equation, especially when thinking about those popular culture producers who occupied powerful positions in class, racial, gendered, and national hierarchies.

The concept of ideology allows me to look at mass-mediated communications while emphasizing how powerful groups and institutions (white middle-class people, DuPont, the federal government, best-selling authors) made meaning. In addition, ideology served as a way to think about how scholarship interacts with social change. Thompson wrote that "the interpretation of ideology implies a critical potential: it opens a path for a critical reflection, not only on the everyday understanding of lay actors, but also on the relations of power and domination within which these actors are enmeshed."[27] Stuart Hall believed that "The *problem* of ideology is to give an account, within a materialist theory, of how social ideas arise. We need to understand what their role is in a particular social formation, so as to inform the struggle to change society and open the road towards a socialist transformation of society."[28] In this work, I concentrate on ideology rather than on hegemony, culture, or discourse because the concept of ideology allowed me to look at forms of communication, consider domination and power, and think about the possibilities for social change.

In the four chapters that follow, I look at the producers of popular culture and how they have expressed ideology, and at the consequences for their audiences of those expressions. I've looked at the changes, over the middle forty years of the century, as popular culture became a commodified mass culture. Popular culture, by definition, contains many meanings, so different audiences can interpret and find pleasure in any particular form. Such indeterminacy makes it a particularly slippery ground for scholarly interpretation. And we have to do it while juggling.

CHAPTER ONE

Minstrel Laughs: Popular Culture, Race, and the Middle Class

Burnt Cork and Melody: Learning from Amateur Minstrels

A 1953 INSTRUCTION book for amateur minstrel performers, *Burnt Cork and Melody*, noted that "despite the fact that all professional minstrelsy had practically vanished, there was never a night when a minstrel show was not being given somewhere in our country."[1] During the first sixty years of the twentieth century, white middle-class men, women, and children across the United States joined together to put on minstrel shows. A large industry supported these amateur minstrels with books of instructions, music, and jokes; costumes, wigs, "bones," and burnt cork makeup; and sometimes professional directors to organize the amateur productions. One of the most prolific writers of amateur minstrel materials, Arthur LeRoy Kaser, wrote that amateur minstrel shows had become "so very popular" that "if one is not given occasionally in a community everybody wonders why." According to Kaser,

> a minstrel show is one of the best entertainments for amateur groups. One reason is that the preparation and presentation are not too difficult; another reason is that it gives an opportunity to use the various types of talent in the community; and a third reason is that in a well-performed minstrel show there are not dull moments—it is all meat.

Finally, minstrel shows provided "clean fun with nothing to offend the most fastidious."[2]

Why were amateur minstrel shows popular, nonoffensive, and yet "meaty" during the first half of the twentieth century? I want to suggest that the "meat" represented the ideology contained in the performances. Audiences and performers didn't articulate the ways in which they participated in the racialized formation of a middle class, but their enjoyment illustrated that the shows explored issues interesting to them. In local minstrel productions, everyday people enacted racial otherness, performed class solidarity, and took their place in a newly commodified, and increasingly mass produced, world of leisure activities.

The instruction books often reported that community groups found minstrel shows "easy" to produce. The audience agreed about the ideas being promulgated in the shows and found further ease in the racial masking during which white middle-class people constructed, expressed, and reinforced their racialized class positions while not taking responsibility for their actions. As one book aimed at high school students noted,

> Boys and girls who might not otherwise get the valuable experience of appearing before the public may find their chance in the minstrel show. Almost any type of novelty can be inserted in its flexible form. The black-face make-up hides self-consciousness and encourages the young performer to express himself.[3]

The shows provided a common space to express and work out ideas that might not have been so "easy," "fun," or nonoffensive with other performers or audiences. The lack of material that might "offend" referred to the ways in which amateur minstrels presented female sexuality, participating in the separation of theaters into middle-class spaces welcoming to women and working-class spaces for men.

The amateur minstrel shows borrowed from nineteenth-century professional minstrelsy but with important differences. A nineteenth-century minstrel evening was divided into three acts, the first a series of jokes and songs delivered by a small group of performers seated in a semicircle, the second an "olio," which resembled a vaudeville show with a variety of acts, and the third a short play. The twentieth-century books explained the tradition and offered help with the first and third parts, generally leaving local groups on their own for the variety acts. Communities found it easy to fill the variety section with individual performers, who rehearsed on their own and appeared for the performance. Groups found it more difficult to envision, practice, and perform the first parts and the plays. The instruction manuals focused on the popular minstrel "first parts" and showed community groups how to produce them easily. Performers sat together on the stage, in a semicircle, with individuals standing up to deliver an occasional joke, story, or song (all provided by the textbooks) while the master of ceremonies ran the show. Minstrel "first parts," according to the twentieth-century books, always included "end-men" in blackface and a master of ceremonies, often called by his nineteenth-century name, "the interlocutor."[4] *How to Put On a Minstrel Show*, published in 1921, advised that "the selecting of the end-men is a very important factor in the First Part" and noted that they "must be men who will not lose their heads during the performance, but who can keep perfectly calm and self-possessed during the show" because "these are the men who tell the jokes and on whom, together with the Interlocutor, depends the success of the show."[5] Over the century, most amateur minstrel shows shrank to include only the more distinctive "first parts," and later books focused on them.

The cultural history of amateur minstrelsy is relatively easy to discover, although its social history remains hidden. By the turn of the century, publishers offered books of minstrel songs, jokes, and plays for community groups who wanted to put on a minstrel show, and an examination of these texts provides a cultural history of the form. These minstrel books, along with materials prepared for other amateur theater groups, appeared in the catalogs of major play publishing companies. The publication of amateur minstrel show books peaked in the 1920s and 1930s, but it began about 1900 and continued into the 1950s.[6] While it is a bit difficult to get a good count of amateur minstrel show materials, there are plenty to examine.

The amateur minstrel instruction books differed greatly in their length and level of detail. Some included technical instructions for putting on a performance, suggesting committee structures and publicity gimmicks, as well as how to arrange the stage, costumes, and makeup, while others were simply scripts for minstrel "first-parts."[7] Many texts presented a painstaking level of detail. Even if amateur groups followed only a tenth of the directions given, examining the "perfect" show outlined in the instruction manuals gives the cultural historian a lot of material with which to work.

The social historian is not so lucky. I first found out about amateur minstrel shows from college students who, after reading about professional minstrels, told me of family members who had been in minstrel shows at church or as part of a club. The students wanted me to absolve their relatives of racism by agreeing that attitudes had changed. I tried to explain the structural nature of racial hierarchy, its effects, and our collective responsibility, but they had a more personal relationship to the story than my abstract explanations could accommodate. I looked for evidence to help us think about this particular form and found very little. While amateur minstrel shows occurred often around the country, the records are scattered throughout local historical societies. Also, amateur minstrelsy was part of a shameful history of racial oppression, and many communities believe that such activities are best forgotten. While historians may disagree about how to approach the histories of oppression (African slavery and Japanese American internment, for two other examples), keepers of local records agree that such recent, and disturbing, historical materials should not be made available to outsiders. One rural Wisconsin town may have had the longest-running amateur minstrel production in the country, but, despite an introduction from the head of the local high school's social studies department, the elderly town historian did not want to discuss the subject, and the story had been carefully left out of the town's bicentennial history.[8]

Amateur minstrelsy may be the perfect example of the strengths of cultural history, not only because the social history record proves difficult to access, but because the audience, performers, and even authors were the same. Amateur performances thus provide special insight into ideological formation. Since actors and audience members swapped places in the middle of performances, we don't have to wonder whether audiences agreed with what happened on stage. Amateur minstrel shows perpetuated a "common sense," taken-for-granted ideology and provide excellent historical evidence of the construction and consideration of such ideology. In addition, amateur theatricals were widely popular in the early twentieth century, as huge numbers of Americans participated, and deserve study in their own right. When a writer in *Harper's Monthly*, Merrill Denison, examined the phenomenon in 1938, he found that "last year more than 70,000,000 people in the United States attended more than 250,000 shows of one kind and another put on by amateur groups throughout the country."[9]

Twentieth-century amateur minstrel shows helped the middle class see itself both as white and as able to purchase leisure activities. With these productions, middle-class, small-town whites announced a position of economic superiority (since many performances raised money for charity), and the performers signaled that they could afford to buy things to amuse themselves (because the performances depended on instruction books and other purchased products). By tying the middle class to consumption, amateur minstrel shows also served as a crucial bridge between popular and mass culture. Amateur productions showed how amusements became further commodified, codified, and national as publishing companies sold a "system" that provided everything needed for a minstrel show production. Finally, the move from participatory shows, given by and for communities, to standardized performances, taken from a book written by a professional producer, illustrated the beginnings of the change from popular to mass culture.

But the lengthiest directions in any amateur minstrel book concerned how to black up. Any explanation of amateur minstrels as creating a consuming middle class, ready to be part of a mass audience, must always return to the ways in which race structured and expressed these processes. In chillingly racist detail, the books described the preparation and use of either actual burnt cork or commercial makeup. One early book described how amateurs could fabricate their own burnt cork:

> get a number of dry corks—a pail full—place them on an old piece of sheet iron to keep the dirt and sand from them. Pile them on a few shavings or splinters. They will burn easily. When they crack open like popcorn, put them in a pail. Let them remain dry.
>
> When you wish to make up, dip your hands in water, wet your neck and ears, then wet your hands, shaking them around in the pail of corks, then rubbing them on your face. By repeating this you will be thoroughly blackened. As you will have only the dust of the cork, no grit, you should have a small baby's brush to brush the dust from your face and back of your hands. This gives them a polish.[10]

Most of the books also included elaborate descriptions of how to remove the makeup. Books disagreed on the "proper" minstrel way to make up lips and eyes to look more or less grotesque. *The Five Star Minstrel Book*, published in 1938, warned that only amateurs felt "that the lips must be painted a vivid red," while no professional "burnt cork comedian" painted his lips because "the effect is very unhappy and complicates considerably the removal of the make up."[11] The books aimed at women minstrels agreed that many women did not like to black up and suggested that only a few of the company do so.[12] The minstrel books tried to present blacking up as easy, a simple activity, and that simplicity quickly gave the middle-class white person a chance to cross boundaries and investigate the construction of racial categories.

Minstrels who hated the mess of blackface could choose other forms of racial masks also offered by minstrelsy. Wigs played important roles, with the books advising, "always use a black kinkly wig"; "if wigs are available so much the better"; and "acceptable minstrel wigs can be manufactured from large, black stockings, but the genuine article may be obtained at so reasonable a price that this is seldom necessary."[13] Many of the books discussed how a show could be costumed cheaply, noting that the minstrels needed only to wear clothes of "more or less ludicrous design and color" and cautioning, "do not let your show suffer from lack of color and ridiculous costumes."[14]

While much of the material in the amateur minstrel shows came straight from vaudeville—punning, jokes about families, male-female relationships, and city life—most shows also contained stories, jokes, or running commentaries on the stupidity of African Americans.[15] These stories provided additional ways for the performers to create, teach, and reinforce racial hierarchy. Historian Melvin Patrick Ely demonstrated that when Freeman Gosden and Charles Correll, later famous as radio's "Amos 'n' Andy," directed amateur minstrel shows, they sometimes toned down vaudeville's ethnic humor in order not to offend members of local theater groups, but they could count on the white performers and actors to enjoy portraying and watching foolish African American characters. Local elites showed that they were good sports, with secure places in the community, by blacking up and acting foolish. Ely noted that the fun of this activity "depended on one simple, widely shared assumption: that the black man was an inferior and often ridiculous figure." Ely further suggested that in amateur minstrel shows the mannerisms employed by the performers were the signifiers of race more than the blackface itself.[16] As John Lawrence's *Ladies' Minstrel First-Part*, published in 1929, explained, "it will add to the effectiveness of the song if the endwoman singing the boy's part is dressed in the exaggerated costume of a young darky lady-killer."[17]

If many of the jokes and songs found in amateur minstrels shows came from vaudeville, the concept and format came from nineteenth-century professional minstrelsy. The historical authority conferred by nostalgic references to minstrel shows' beginnings helped make the shows popular, but the ways in which the two centuries of minstrelsy operated connected them on deeper levels as well. Historians David Roediger and Alexander Saxton have carefully outlined how working-class whites used professional minstrelsy in the nineteenth century to construct their racialized class positions, while Eric Lott has explained the ways such performances psychologically assisted whites in perpetuating racial hierarchy.[18] Just as professional minstrels played a part in working-class formation in the nineteenth century, amateur minstrels assisted in solidifying the self-identification of the middle class in the twentieth.

Professional minstrel shows flourished in nineteenth-century America, whether as traveling troupes visiting small towns or as permanent shows located in big cities. Robert Toll described brilliantly the changes in the form and content of these shows over the century and outlined their relationship to the debates about slavery and race taking place around and through them. Toll carefully noted the presence of both black and white performers, usually in segregated shows, often performing for segregated audiences.[19] Historians have long contended that professional minstrelsy died with the nineteenth century, although a careful postmortem remains to be done. In part, newer forms (burlesque, vaudeville, and eventually film and radio) superseded the minstrel show; in part, the form may have run its course, with minstrels finding it difficult to innovate enough to satisfy an ever restless commercial audience.[20]

At the end of professional minstrelsy, the black performers and their shows and the white performers and theirs took different directions. Black minstrels influenced Broadway musicals as well as small traveling blues shows.[21] White minstrelsy continued on in vaudeville (and from there moved into film and radio) as well as among amateurs. The three other branches of twentieth-century minstrelsy—black musical theater, traveling blues shows, and vaudeville minstrels who later appeared in films and on the radio—provided a context for amateur minstrels, the twentieth-century minstrel form with the largest number of participants. If the amateurs lived in a large city or in the South, they knew that African Americans sometimes used the minstrel name and performed some of the same forms (so-called coon songs) for both integrated and all-black audiences. Vaudeville, films, and radio provided white amateur minstrels with readymade and long-lived stereotypes and ideas about how minstrels should look and act, and the amateurs showed their commercial cousins that an audience still existed for minstrel materials.[22]

Amateur minstrel shows may have begun on college campuses, with male students imitating a form that was already on its way out and thus provided little professional competition to the college minstrels. In the 1890s, the Brown University Minstrels (sometimes called the Brunonian Club) toured as far west as Chicago and as close to home as Mystic, Connecticut. An 1893 account explained the attraction of putting on a show when it noted that "after the performance at Mystic the young ladies of the town gave a reception and dance to the young men, and all left Mystic voting it a jolly place."[23] Camaraderie and a chance to meet the opposite sex remained at the heart of all amateur theatricals and proved an important factor in the choice to present a minstrel show rather than something else since minstrel shows involved simple performances requiring minimal rehearsal and thus allowed more time for socializing than more complex productions.

In addition, as industrialization continued, college students (training to become new managers) had a particular interest in securing, extending, and shoring up their middle-class positions and were among the first to see how minstrel shows could help. The Brown minstrels needed performances that would attract suitable young women to their performances and to the parties afterward. Minstrel shows provided the perfect vehicle. Blacking up allowed the students to show that they had learned to be "easy" with their status and proved that they could provide genteel entertainment acceptable for women. An advertisement from the Providence Opera House for the 1890–91 season announced that the Brown University minstrels would give two performances and noted that "the comedy part of the entertainment differs sufficiently from professional minstrels, to make it attractive and laughable but not in the least objectionable."[24] The middle-class theater needed to manage sexuality, in part to set itself apart from working-class entertainment, in part to make performances appealing to middle-class women. Both because of the racial material and because the casts were single-sex, amateur minstrels avoided presentations of sexuality. Brown students found minstrel shows easy, fun, and appealing to just the audience they sought; at the same time the students could present themselves as members of the white middle class.

The instruction books and articles about amateur minstrels never talked about other amateur productions as precursors but always described their relationship to the older tradition of professional minstrelsy. In his work on nineteenth-century minstrels, Eric Lott explained that this repeated story about the beginning of minstrelsy was a form of white concern over the appropriation of black cultural forms. Lott wrote:

> It was in the rather obsessive accounts of minstrelsy's origins that these anxieties were most extreme. . . . [E]ven offhand contempora-

> neous narratives of the minstrel show's origins attempted to legitimate or resolve pressing ideological questions raised by their subject. For all positions on the origins and make up of blackface minstrelsy implicitly or explicitly rely on a theory of the racial politics of American culture.[25]

The twentieth century's nostalgia about minstrelsy, like the nineteenth century's "obsessive" interest in the form's origins and history, also operated as an explanation of racial politics that posited benevolent whites and passive African Americans.[26] In addition, the twentieth-century interest in the origins of minstrelsy helped explain that all commodified cultural forms have their origins in "authentic" and more personal expressions of an earlier age. A minstrel show prologue from 1933 asked, "ladies and gentlemen, will you come with us this evening as we turn back the clock of time and transport you for an hour, to the days when minstrelsy was in flower?"[27] One article noted, "many a boy has heard his father or grandfather sing some of these old-time melodies" while another spoke of minstrelsy as a "distinctively American form of entertainment that for more than half a century held a warm place in the affection of the public" but lamented that "the old-time minstrel-show is disappearing before the all-conquering film."[28] In one of several books for women minstrels, the performers were given a song to the tune of "Turkey in the Straw":

> Oh, we'll crack some jokes, and sing some, too;
> And we'll bet you like it before we get through.
> We're all amateurs, but what if we are?
> Couldn't have more fun if each was a star.[29]

The amateur minstrels knew that they operated in a newly commodified culture with the beginnings of a cult of celebrity. Yet their historicity, which allowed the mass culture to hide while making significant inroads, remained one of the reasons for the popularity of amateur minstrel shows and another reason they operated so well as a site of ideological expression. The amateur productions, while expressing and constructing a range of ideological positions on race and class, also served as a bridge between popular and mass culture.

The Burnt Cork Entertainer: Minstrel Shows as Mass Culture

Amateur theatricals, amateur minstrels in particular, played a transitional role in the history of commodified and mass popular culture. Historian Daniel Czitrom has noted that before electrical communications, communication and transportation were the same. For entertainment (a particular form of communication) and transportation that equation remained true into the twentieth century.[30] The earliest forms of commodified popular culture did reach the masses as vaudeville, minstrel shows, and circuses traveled the country on "circuits" and began to entertain a national audience. In the late nineteenth century, with the increasing number of entertainers, theaters, and performing companies, show business became too complicated for individual theater managers and performers. Managers joined together to offer series of dates to performers. At the same time, performers and their agents tried to get the best possible schedules. Soon circuits of theaters controlled by a handful of business entrepreneurs took control of the popular stage. Vaudeville producers like B. F. Keith and E. F. Albee began to clean up "variety," an early form of vaudeville, and experimented with continuous shows. Even before the turn of the twentieth century, Keith and Albee had expanded their operations, and by the 1920s their United Booking Office controlled more than four hundred vaudeville houses. After that, performers signed with Keith-Albee (who received a percentage of their earnings) or paid them a substantial fee if they wanted to work in Keith-Albee theaters.[31] The idea that popular culture appealed to a national audience and that its appeal could be rationalized, centralized, and made to turn a profit had important consequences when the next technologies to "carry" popular culture came along—film, radio, and then television.

At the same time, theatrical entertainments became more respectable. Robert Allen, in his book on burlesque, *Horrible Prettiness*, noted that the rise of vaudeville came as theatrical managers severed their connections with working-class culture and working-class sexuality in order to appeal to the middle class. Theater producers reworked vaudeville from earlier forms to attract "respectable" audiences.[32] At the same time, and as part of the same process of incorporating the middle class into their audiences, theaters became nonparticipatory. The working-class protestors in the Astor Place Riot of 1849 complained about the introduction of new, more decorous theaters and theatrical styles, as well as about the lack of audience control over what happened on stage. With industrialization increasing throughout the nineteenth century, leisure was more set off from work, daily life became more commercialized, and the differences in classes became more pronounced.[33] Entertainment forms both constituted and expressed the changes in class formation and class consciousness. As class lines hardened, the upper classes began a spatial separation of recreational forms and also described and participated in their own amusements to set themselves apart from workers. By the beginning of the twentieth century, some theatrical audiences had thus been constructed as national, middle-class, and nonparticipatory, with content provided by centralized and commercialized producers. But the audiences for these live entertainment forms existed serially, not simultaneously. The introduction of film, and then of radio, changed the serial nature of the national audience as everyone experienced the same performances at the same time.[34] Amateur minstrelsy illustrated the halting and partial steps of these processes of nationalization, commodification, and class stratification.

Amateur minstrel shows proved an important phase in the building of mass culture. Amateur minstrels performed locally at a range of venues and times, with programs geared to local events and people, and with the performers and the audience the same people. A 1924 magazine article about amateur theatricals noted that the audience was "made up of three classes: the friends of the cast; the enemies of the cast, and those who would like to be in the cast, but aren't."[35] In many ways, the amateur minstrel shows represented a "folk" form (in the midst of a newly commercial world), with the play growing out of the interaction between performers and audience, who could change places at any time. One article noted that amateur theatricals became more popular at the same time as movies and radio because "there is no conceivable way in which" local clubs "can bend either movies or radio to their modest fiscal needs," so "it seems probable that there will be an amateur theater as long as there remain social groups to put on plays and friends and neighbors willing to spend two bits or a dime to go to see them."[36] Amateur theatricals filled a gap as mass culture became more impersonal and audiences became part of a national audience, rather than local groups.

Despite their local and participatory nature, the amateur minstrel shows used nationally marketed books that explained how to produce a minstrel show and provided the content of the shows in excruciating detail. Most of the content came from vaudeville, that ultimately middle-class form of entertainment carved out of burlesque and variety. The amateur shows drew on vaudeville rather than minstrelsy for their materials, because vaudeville had incorporated much of minstrelsy, including blackface acts. In addition, vaudeville was an intrinsically middle-class and respectable entertainment, while minstrel shows carried a tinge of the risqué and working class. Amateurs would be reassured by the vaudeville, and thus highly respectable, materials found in the instruction books. At the same time, minstrel shows provided the historicity and nostalgic aura that allowed for an exploration and construction of race that so fascinated white Americans.

An examination of the authors of amateur minstrel books proved the strong link to vaudeville that was apparent in the materials themselves. Prefaces and introductions celebrated the books' authors as theater professionals who now offered their tricks to the amateur. Fitzgerald Publishing Company explained on the inside front cover of *The Old Maids' Minstrel Show* that

> any new entertainment written by Arthur LeRoy Kaser is good news for amateur groups. Most of them know from experience that he is a "theatre-wise" author with a shrewd sense of entertainment value. This is one of his best efforts—funny, easy to produce, and a welcome addition to the scanty list of good minstrel material for the ladies. We feel sure you are going to like it.[37]

Kaser, in fact, produced a large number of minstrel show books for amateurs, along with huge amounts of other amateur theatrical materials. Born in the Midwest in 1890, Kaser dabbled in vaudeville, even performing a blackface act, before serving eighteen months in the infantry during World War I. Kaser turned to writing full-time when marriage and the birth of a child pushed him to find a more stable source of income than performing in vaudeville.[38] By the late 1920s he published 1,500 pages of stage material each year. He was prolific and fast, and publishers found it easy to work with him. One story recounted his visit to the Walter H. Baker publishing company in Boston. Baker described a book he needed and asked Kaser if he would like to write it. Kaser replied, "I believe I would. . . . Where's a typewriter?" During the 1930s, Kaser wrote less because ill health forced him to take work as a carpenter rather than spend days at the typewriter, but he continued to write until his death in 1956. Of the 436 separately issued publications in his bibliography, about a third were minstrel materials. The rest included vaudeville sketches, plays, and various ethnic humor items, all intended for amateurs.[39] The minstrel shows shared content and worldview with the amateur plays, ethnic monologues, and vaudeville acts that Kaser also wrote. Minstrel shows filled with vaudeville material gave publishers a good product—one with a historical gloss that included familiar, and safe, jokes.

The minstrel instruction books provided more than comfortable content. In their prime, the minstrel publishers sold a complete minstrel show in several pieces, all purchasable from one company. The instruction books provided national and homogenized content to individual communities. Sold as "easy to use," these minstrel show systems made local productions part of a commercialized and national arrangement that allowed for some local autonomy while connecting people to larger trends.

Advertisements inside the books described the pieces available to amateurs to make their minstrel show better and easier. Sophie Huth Perkins, in the introduction to *Mirandy's Minstrels*, recommended using the "musical program at the beginning of this book" with "Denison's Ladies' Minstrel Opening Chorus and Finale" and noted that "orchestrations, if required, are available for all the numbers listed." Finally, she explained that "for women's organizations that are inexperienced in minstrel work, much invaluable help may be derived from the minstrel manual 'How to Stage a Minstrel Show.'"[40] Many books included ads for burnt cork, minstrel ties, collars and dickeys, tambourines, bones, clappers, wigs, and posters.[41] An advertisement in *Baker's Minstrel Joke Book*, published in 1928, summarized what the publishers were selling:

To
Make
Your
Minstrel
Show
Howlingly
Funny
Use
Baker's Minstrel Joke Book
To
Make
It
Tuneful
Use
Baker's Opening Choruses and Finales

And
Baker's Song Programs
To
Open
It
Right
Use
Baker's Minstrel First Parts
To
Lend
Variety
Use
Baker's Minstrel Afterpieces
For
Fill
In
Bits
Use
Baker's Minstrel Monologues
And
Make
Up
Your
Minstrel
Men
With
Baker's Burnt Cork and Wigs.[42]

Publishers could supply everything an amateur needed to present a successful minstrel show, and, in addition, they explained how to fit the pieces together.

To convince potential customers that a minstrel show would be easy to produce, the publishers presented detailed instructions. Harold Rossiter, in *How to Put On a Minstrel Show*, from 1921, included such categories as "Getting the Talent," "Arrangement of the Stage," "Selection of Songs," "How to Use Bones and Tambos," "Costumes for the First Part," "Starting the Show Promptly," "Time for the Members to Arrive at the Hall," "How to Make Up," and "Advertising the Show." Other books contained equally specific directions.[43] The information provided seemed detailed to the point of inanity. Kaser informed readers that they should give minstrel shows in the winter because the summer might be too hot and because "in this day and age and people take advantage of the automobile to get out in the open on hot summer nights."[44] Potential minstrels probably bought the books for the jokes and songs and found certain of the instructions more useful than others, but the packages worked to reassure first-time impresarios. Publishers promised familiar content, ease of use, and a system of books and materials that took amateur minstrels one step on the way to a centralized, commodified, and national popular culture.

In one of his publications, Kaser referred to another way in which amateur minstrel shows participated simultaneously in both the local and the national. In 1929, Kaser wrote that

> these books will prove a salvation for the many amateur minstrel troupes which lack the personal counsel and guidance of an experienced director. Thoroughly professional in style, yet entirely practical for amateurs and give big opportunity for localized jokes. Written to order especially for troupes wishing to stage an expertly routined show at a nominal cost.[45]

As Kaser intimated, other options, besides a do-it-yourself approach, existed for wealthier communities and groups. Beginning with the historical pageants that preceded amateur theatricals, professional directors traveled the country staging shows for local communities.[46] Companies that provided costumes, plays, sets, and publicity, in addition to directors, grew quickly, and the popular press often described the perils and pratfalls of the traveling directors.[47] Some traveling directors specialized in minstrel shows. *American Magazine*, describing the "King of the Minstrel Circuit," explained that Tom S. Howell of Emporia, Kansas, "travels the country over bringing back those minstrel days by putting on shows with local talent and using his own know-how and equipment."

Howell had been in the metal products business and put on several local shows for charity. When he "saw the interest in this strictly American type of entertainment, it dawned on him that this could be his career."[48] More important, two radio pioneers began their own careers as traveling minstrel directors. In 1928, when Freeman Gosden and Charles Correll went on NBC as Amos and Andy, portraying black men newly arrived in Chicago from the South, they used their experiences in professional minstrelsy and vaudeville and as directors of amateur minstrel shows to create one of the first continuing national narrative radio shows.[49] Gosden and Correll met in 1918 working as directors/coaches for the Joe Bren theatrical company based in Chicago. The company provided professional directors and written minstrel materials for civic and fraternal organizations. The Bren coaches spent about a week in a town, organizing and rehearsing a minstrel show starring local people for the financial benefit of a local organization.[50] Gosden and Correll's participation in amateur minstrel shows illustrated the link between the different forms minstrelsy took in the twentieth century, as well as that between amateur theatricals and the mass culture that broadcasting helped solidify.

In his book, *Blackface, White Noise: Jewish Immigrants in the Hollywood Melting Pot*, Michael Rogin noted that the "transformative" moments in American film grew out of minstrelsy and that "all organized themselves around the surplus symbolic value of blacks, the power to make African Americans represent something beside themselves."[51] One could extend Rogin's analysis to make the case that all American popular, and mass, culture was born in race, in the minstrel show, including broadcasting (with "Amos 'n' Andy") and music (drawing from black sacred music and the blues). Historians Eric Lott, David Roediger, and Alexander Saxton have explored nineteenth-century professional minstrel shows as a site where members of the white working class investigated African American culture while expressing racial difference and class solidarity.[52] In the amateur minstrel shows of the twentieth century, the middle class, working through both the implications of a newly created mass culture and their own identity in the emerging culture of consumption, returned to racial formation as the central trope in American culture. Participating in amateur minstrelsy, local communities both moved toward a mass culture and resisted it and created themselves as white by masquerading as black. As they participated in the move toward a mass culture, amateur minstrels cared deeply about their middle-class positions and worked to identify the middle class as racialized and consuming.

Frills and Frolics: Minstrels in the Remaking of the Middle Class

Advertisements for amateur minstrel materials, as well as the titles of such books, give clues as to who publishers thought used the materials and the way they tailored materials to many different groups. In the early twentieth century, the middle class began to see itself as large but always as racially marked. The inclusion of varied kinds of people in the minstrel show universe illustrated the wide reach of the middle class. An advertisement for *The Minstrel Encyclopedia* noted that "this book is especially suited to High Schools, Colleges, Lodges and Church clubs, as the material is clean from start to finish, the book containing no suggestive or offensive material." The ad also listed other minstrel materials available from the same publisher, including

> Moonlight Cabaret Minstrels: For large stages, colleges, clubs and society events Corn-Fed Cut-Ups: A white-face minstrel show for a bunch of rubes in the grocery store Fraternal Minstrels: With several songs especially written for Elks, Moose, Shriners, Masons, Y.M.C.A., K. of C., etc. also suggested endings for each organization Patriotic Minstrels: For American Legion Posts, Boy Scout shows or High Schools Impromptu Minstrels: For small stages, only nine men required.[53]

Titles of shows indicated their potential audiences and performers. The *By Heck Minstrels* was aimed at "farm folks." *Frills and Frolics* was described as "A Musical Melange for Ladies' Minstrels." *Bandanna Junior Minstrel First-Part*, *Kiddie-Kutups Minstrels*, *Jolly Pickaninnies Minstrels: A Complete Minstrel Program for the Grades*, and *The High School Minstrel Book* were designed for children to perform.[54] Amateur minstrelsy appealed to a wide range of white people, thus constructing a racialized position for the middle class.

Class, however, remains difficult to parse in the United States. Loren Baritz, in *The Good Life: The Meaning of Success for the American Middle Class*, wrote that "searching for the American middle class is a little like looking for air. It is everywhere, invisible, and taken for granted."[55] Despite the fact that many have referred to the United States as a middle-class country, the question of how that ideology formed and reformed, and then got adopted and expressed, remains difficult to decipher. Stuart Blumin, in *The Emergence of the Middle Class: Social Experience in the American City, 1760–1900*, showed convincingly and subtly that the middle class had formed, at least in the cities, by the middle of the nineteenth century. Blumin wrote:

> However broad the bourgeois consensus may have been in comparison to European societies, it did not preclude the formation of dis-

> tinct classes within American society. The all-encompassing American bourgeoisie, then, may well have been a class after all—the power of its values serving to reinforce rather than to destroy social class boundaries.[56]

Blumin acknowledged the difficulty in locating a middle-class consciousness, in the Marxist sense, in part because middle-class ideology privileged "atomism," was "built around values that reduce the likelihood of its manifestation in politics," and expressed "awareness of its common attitudes and beliefs as a denial of the significance of class."[57]

The charitable goals of most amateur minstrel shows remained one of the simplest ways to view them as expressions of the middle-class positions of the participants. Examining clippings and letters kept by the publishers, one article explained that amateur productions came together for economic reasons because "putting on a show . . . remains one of the surest methods of raising funds for almost anything," including "instruments for the school band, a new rug for the minister's study, or woolen bed socks for the deserving Eskimo."[58] Often the shows existed before the fundraising impulse. In *Staging the Amateur Minstrel Show*, Kaser wrote that there needed to be a good reason for putting on the show. He noted that "getting up a minstrel show just for the fun of it is very liable to turn out a money loser" because a show without a purpose meant that "the sale of tickets will doubtlessly be limited to friends and relatives of the performers, and unless each performer is well supplied with relatives and friends there will be many empty seats." On the other hand:

> A minstrel performance given for the benefit of orphaned children, charity purposes, and the like, if well advertised, will always be well attended, because everybody, as a rule, is humanitarian, and to give a good cause and be entertained at the same time is considered a very good investment by the common run of Americans.[59]

Middle-class people wanted to express their economic status publicly, and amateur performances allowed them to do so.

Middle-class ideology also expressed itself in terms of taste and gentility, often seen as the provenance of women. In her work on middlebrow culture, Joan Rubin found a middle ground between "high art and popular sensibility" in such institutions as the Book-of-the-Month Club, radio programs on reading, and the "great books" curriculum. Rubin showed how the middle class, in constant formation as urbanization, immigration, and industrialization changed the outlines of the American class structure, used culture to construct itself as genteel and educated.[60] Amateur minstrels could be seen as analogous to such activities as Book-of-the-Month, providing entertainment rather than uplift but expressing class ideology in much the same way. Rubin also connected the middle class to consumption when she wrote that "middle-class Americans in the mid-nineteenth century scrambled to purchase replicas of luxury items (carpets, upholstery, watches) in order to mimic the upper echelons of society."[61] As a culture of production lost ground to a culture of consumption, the middle class eagerly sought to become the consuming class with a favored place for women in the consumption process, just as they had previously held a special role in matters of gentility and taste.

Publishers of minstrel show books often boasted that they provided clean and nonoffensive material, joining with other purveyors of amusements who believed that they could change their class position by including women in their audiences, in part by managing what appeared on stage. Amateur theatricals posed problems for the middle class in the presentation of sexuality. Blackface allowed for the inclusion of sexuality in a genteel way that maintained the illusion of the stage and allowed the audience to enjoy the sight of their friends acting foolishly. As many magazine articles suggested, the big issue for amateur theatricals was "the kiss."

An article entitled "What Every Amateur Actress Ought to Know," published in *Ladies' Home Journal* in 1913, reported that girls involved in a love scene should "rid it of all sentiment by attaching no significance to the 'business,'" but also noted that "the usual lovers' kiss need never be given on the stage," and proceeded with lengthy instructions so that the actors could seem to be kissing without making physical contact.[62] For *Century* magazine, the issue of the stage kiss was part of the larger problem of suspension of disbelief, since "it is hard for the audience to get away from the personalities of people who are well known to them, and whom they meet in their every-day existence. . . . 'Did he really kiss you?' is an embarrassing question for the leading lady whose family is out in front."[63] Both the actors and the audience found great enjoyment in the idea that people they knew had permission to act foolishly on stage. But there were limits to middle-class foolishness, and sexuality proved to be one of them.

A 1911 story published in *Colliers*, "The Thespians: The Story of a Chorus Girl's Experience with an Amateur Dramatic Company," took up the issue of cross-class friendship and romance as well as the role of race as an acceptable way to perform sexuality. According to the story, the lead in the local play went to a nice rich girl who had just broken her engagement to a popular but poor boy. Preparation for the show went badly, particularly because the theater wasn't available for evening rehearsals since the owner had booked a comic opera group for a week. The amateur director suggested that the leading lady perform a wild dance as her big production number, but the sad leading lady and one of the chorus girls from the comic opera became friends. The chorus girl, knowing the situation, suggested that the leading lady sing a minstrel song instead. She explained:

> Oh, it's just a simple little song about a colored wench calling for her man to come back to her; but, you see, even if she was a colored wench and he was just a common roustabout, he **was** her man. That was all she cared for in the world, and she wanted him back terribly bad.[64]

The leading lady took the advice of the chorus girl, sang the song, made a huge hit, and, because of her sincere rendition of the minstrel song, got her boyfriend back. The minstrel song and her portrayal of a "colored wench" allowed her to express sexual feelings onstage in way she couldn't have without racial masking.

In minstrel shows, the use of racialized masks might have made the issue of sexuality more difficult, given taboos on interracial romances and on the expression of African American sexuality without strict controls. But amateur minstrels used the historical excuse that old-time minstrels had performed in single-sex troupes to evade the issue of performative black sexuality. Most of the amateur minstrel materials presented all-male or all-female companies—only the shows designed for children or young people had co-ed casts.[65] Kaser "strongly advised" that directors use either an all-male or an all-female cast because "a director has plenty of trouble with one or the other, but when they are mixed his troubles are increased a hundredfold."[66] While many of the jokes and songs enacted gender roles, with the male minstrels presenting a range of misogynist ideas and the female minstrels making fun of men as well as participating in oppressive stereotypes of women, the minstrel format (especially when confined to the "first part") had very little interaction that could be sexualized.[67]

"The kiss" disappeared as a problem in minstrel shows although it remained an issue for middle-class formation. When the U.S. government took American culture to Japan, after World War II, the acceptability of kissing scenes in movies became an issue for the Japanese. While the American middle class had, gradually, accepted a certain level of sexuality in mass culture, in part by separating the audience from the performers, the importance of foreign markets meant that such an understanding needed to be exported. As explored in Chapter 4, part of the ideology imposed by the United States on Japan during the Occupation focused on how to connect the middle class with mass culture.

Amateur minstrel shows helped begin the transformation of popular culture into mass culture for the white middle class, suitable for men, women, and children from a variety of groups. In the process, the middle class began to see itself, and to be, the dominant part of an American national identity. Michael Rogin wrote about "motion picture blackface," which appeared on Hollywood movie screens at the same time as local amateur groups enacted the same tropes and structured the same racialized identities. Movie minstrelsy, according to Rogin, "inherited the function of its predecessor; by joining structural domination to cultural desire, it turned Europeans into Americans."[68] Amateur minstrels also helped turn the white middle class into the very definition of America. The *Cotton Blossom Minstrel First-Part* published in 1950 featured a patriotic song that began, "We are so patriotic that we're all assembled here; To sing the praises of the land that we all hold so dear" and continued:

> Where Old Glory waves there are no slaves;
> We'll never tolerate oppression,
> And our liberty, shall ever be
> Our most valuable possession.[69]

Americans were here defined by their historical position—past slavery—as well as by their possessions.

Minstrelsy, and the middle class, also took their place as quintessentially American. As *Burnt Cork and Melody* put it in 1953, "today this, the only form of theater which is truly American, is steadily being revived by amateur groups, in night club and, of course, on the radio and television." The same book noted that Negro dialect "may be used at the director's and cast's discretion, but it is respectfully suggested that anything offensive or derogatory be carefully omitted."[70] This 1953 warning about causing offense is the first sign that either publishers or amateur minstrels noticed anything problematic about their projects. Minstrel shows were so much a part of the American landscape that the Federal Theater Project of the Works Progress Administration (WPA) both produced minstrel shows and urged community groups to produce them throughout the New Deal.[71] During World War II soldiers presented amateur shows for each other because "the Minstrel show is well designed to accommodate the miscellaneous talent an army camp is likely to provide at any given time."[72] On the home front, publishers rushing to provide minstrel material with wartime themes published a *We're-in-the-Army Minstrel First Part* and an *Uncle Sam Minstrel First Part.*[73] Minstrel show books published in the 1950s presented patriotic songs, fewer performers in blackface, and fewer jokes, but contained all the other elements of early shows.[74] Whites heard little criticism of the minstrel show until the Civil Rights movement began in the early 1950s.

Only when race and nation began to clash, when the nation's racial attitudes had an impact on foreign policy, and when middle-class people began to believe that racial tolerance might help secure economic advantages in the world did minstrel shows become problematic. As the Cold War deepened and the United States sought the allegiance of developing countries, particularly in Africa and the Middle East, the oppression and stereotyping of African Americans became a foreign policy issue. In particular, the government enlisted African American musicians for international tours to present African American culture as an important component of American life. These "jazz ambassadors," as Penny Von Eschen called them, played the music of African Americans for the world and served as living refutations of the minstrel stereotypes. Minstrel shows became an embarrassing reminder that the attitudes of ordinary Americans had not progressed, and, like other racisms, these attitudes became obstacles to a Cold War victory.[75] Despite the interest of the U.S. government in eliminating racism, the individual complaints that actually stopped local minstrel shows came from African Americans and integrated antiracist organizations.

Divided by class and region, African Americans had long found it difficult to unite against representations of themselves in entertainment. Many African Americans hated minstrel shows throughout the two centuries they were a mainstay of American entertainment, but others found them either amusing and authentic tributes to African American culture or of little importance in the landscape of American racial oppression.[76] As a target, amateur minstrel shows presented problems. The amateurs presented shows for only a few nights each year, sometimes in small towns with few black residents, and the most powerful members of the white community were performers and audiences for the shows. The ephemeral nature of the amateur shows, their widespread presentation, and the local and immediate power of their producers over the protestors made them difficult to organize against.

When African Americans did target minstrel shows, they did it on the basis of their own intertwined middle-class status and national interests. The early Civil Rights Movement, with its emphasis on representation, schooling, church-based action, and the importance of U.S. presentation of a good example to the rest of the world, saw amateur minstrel shows as a useful target and used a middle-class approach to protest them. Beginning in 1950, local chapters of the National Association for the Advancement of Colored People (NAACP), Urban League, and Catholic Interracial Council attacked particular amateur minstrel performances as well as minstrel shows in general. The Portland, Oregon, Urban League outlined the problems with minstrel show performances, noting that they defeat "the purpose of schools, and churches to educate for participation in a democratic and moral society."[77] At about the same time, the New York Catholic Interracial Council and the *Catholic Interracialist* issued general condemnations of minstrels. One author noted that "there is little of malicious intent and purpose in the minds of amateurs who choose the minstrel show as requiring the least skill and experience," but added that "these thespians should be constantly reminded that the minstrel is by its very nature an insult to Negro citizens" and spoke against the "grave moral wrong of prejudice."[78] Another article, entitled "Blackface Minstrels: 10 Reasons Why They're Not So Funny," ended with a familiar call to end racial prejudice at home so that the United States could "secure the triumph of our ideals in a world threatened with atomic extinction if we fail."[79]

During the 1950s local groups worked to ban individual minstrel shows. One New Jersey NAACP chapter explained in a letter to the editor of the local paper that while minstrel shows have a "grand tradition" and can be "excellent fun . . . as a vehicle for good-natured lampooning of local personalities," the "jokes of the blackface funnymen are not funny to sensitive Negroes, whether they are presented on a local stage or on a national radio network."[80] In Hudson, New York, the NAACP chapter and the American Legion fought bitterly over the Legion's minstrel show. At one point, the American Legion demanded the NAACP membership lists, and the NAACP and its friends in the New York state legislature compared this to tactics used by the White Citizens' Councils in the South.[81]

By the 1960s many people had decided that objections to blackface minstrel shows merited consideration, and amateur minstrelsy died out. Amateur groups presented minstrel shows sporadically, throughout the next thirty-five years, but organized protests followed most performances.[82] Ironically, college campuses, where amateur minstrelsy was born, presented some of the last amateur shows.[83] As college populations and racial attitudes changed, students used minstrel shows as a form of rebellion against "political correctness" rather than as the status-affirming entertainments of earlier generations.

During the first half of the twentieth century, amateur minstrelsy served as a way for the middle-class white men, women, and children who participated to construct the racial, gender, and national aspects of their class positions. In 1934, Arthur LeRoy Kaser described "the present-day minstrel show" as "a versatile vehicle, a potluck meal where anything really good may be slipped in." The show's wide appeal, "enjoyed equally by opera enthusiasts and sideshow patrons," required "time and hard work."[84] Some of that hard work went into inserting ideology into a popular culture form.

The racist stereotypes played out by middle-class white people on the amateur stage implanted constructions of racial inferiority deep in the middle-class consciousness and proved to be one of the bases for the reformation of the middle class in the twentieth century. Amateur minstrel shows became one way for the middle class to articulate and understand its class positions. College students, with their ongoing investment in the status hierarchy, early used minstrel shows ideologically to express and construct a middle-class consciousness. The amateur minstrel instruction books that drew primarily on vaudeville writers and materials also illustrated the interest of the amateur minstrels in their class positions. As Robert Allen wrote, "the rise of vaudeville is but another chapter in the history of the consolidation of the American bourgeoisie."[85] In choosing to produce an amateur minstrel show, rather than another form of theater, middle-class whites aligned racial stereotyping with good taste and gentility. The large range of groups targeted by the amateur minstrel instruction books illustrated the way in which all whites were included and all blacks excluded from the middle class. The use of minstrelsy to raise money for good causes, at the same time requiring the purchase of materials to use for entertainment, aligned the middle class with the newly emerging culture of consumption. Finally, the nationalism expressed in the minstrel shows helped make the middle class congruent with the nation, reexpressing the United States as a middle-class preserve where class lines were unimportant since all white citizens shared the same class position.

My examination of amateur minstrelsy grounds the case studies that follow in an examination of the formation of a consuming middle class. Each of the other chapters takes up the status anxieties of the white middle class in the twentieth century. Facing a new mass culture, members of the middle class sought to reimagine their lives and their relationship to society. Amateur minstrel shows represented a site where the performers and audience alike considered the ways in which whiteness and class intersected. The invention of nylon raised the issue of how gender would be consumed and expressed in maintaining a middle-class life. The exportation of films to "teach democracy" to the Japanese after World War II showed a society attempting to work out how to be American and middle-class consumers in a changed world. The importance of a nationalist agenda to middle-class life remains important to examine. Finally, the advertising novels addressed the issue of middle-class individuality and how it could be maintained in the face of mass culture. Several scholars (Stuart Blumin and Kenneth Ames in particular) have discussed the ways the nineteenth-century middle class thought about, and expressed, its status through material culture.[86] My case studies suggest that, in the twentieth century, such ideological concerns and struggles can be read not only in objects but also in the production of plays, in the marketing of films and consumer products, and in popular novels. Popular culture, as broadly defined to include consumer products, their marketing and their consumption, became the site of struggle as the middle class continually set itself apart as white, American, individualistic, and gendered.

In titling this chapter "Minstrel Laughs," I thought of Arthur LeRoy Kaser's note, in his 1927 book of the same name, that "instead of being a volume of miscellaneous crossfire from which to pick and choose," his book gave "an exact procedure to be followed in staging" an amateur minstrel show. Kaser's belief that he could explain how to make people laugh, how to help people escape, mirrored the DuPont Chemical Company's idea that it could manage what, how, and why women bought a particular product. Both Kaser and DuPont had particular ideas to impart to their audiences. While the amateur minstrel shows bridged a popular, participatory entertainment and the commodified forms that followed, the story of nylon stockings showed another step in the process, as new inventions constructed ideas about gender that could be mass marketed.

CHAPTER TWO

The Magic of Nylon: The Struggle over Gender and Consumption

Elasticity, Luster, and Strength: The Invention of Nylon

MOST STORIES OF nylon begin in 1928, with the DuPont Company's hiring of Wallace Hume Carothers, a young organic chemistry professor, to work in its new research laboratories. We are told that Carothers, assisted by other chemists working for DuPont, invented nylon during a series of experiments between 1928 and 1930, but that statement isn't true or doesn't tell enough of the story. The story continues with DuPont's announcement of nylon at the New York World's Fair in 1938 and then with the first sales of nylon stockings in 1940, and later with the reintroduction of nylon after World War II. Every new technology or product of technology must be conceived in thought as well as in physical terms, and each invention involves more than the first discovery.[1] DuPont and the consumers who used nylon, the advertisers who promoted it, and the scientists and engineers who produced it, all played a part in inventing it. Jeffrey Meikle in *American Plastic: A Cultural History*, David Hounshell and John Smith in *Science and Corporate Strategy: DuPont R&D, 1902–1980*, and Yasu Furukawa in *Inventing Polymer Science: Staudinger, Carothers, and the Emergence of Macromolecular Chemistry* carefully outline a social, scientific, and technological history of nylon. I want to build on their work to look at the invention of nylon as a series of cultural events that constructed ideologies of gender, race, and nation.[2]

The "invention" of nylon falls into two halves. The scientific experiments, engineering designs, and production of the first stockings belong in the first section. So too do the naming of the material and its first announcement in 1938. The second phase began when nylon stockings became available for purchase in 1939. From then on, public relations professionals, the advertising industry, and consumers continued to invest stockings with meaning. DuPont played an enormous role in both parts of the invention, even though it didn't manufacture nylon stockings for public sale. DuPont invested and profited hugely in nylon but never became a stocking manufacturer. Yet DuPont worked hard to solve the technical problems faced by stocking companies and advertised and marketed nylon stockings to consumers. As its scientists, engineers, salesmen, and public relations staff invented nylon, physically and intellectually, DuPont gave it meaning. In addition, as the company interacted with the women who bought nylon stockings, DuPont constructed what it meant to be gendered humans as well as gendered consumers in the twentieth century.

Nylon, and the work done by DuPont in its technology and marketing, show the ways in which consumption came to be the language of popular culture, a way of seeing and knowing. The gendering of consumption, with middle-class women becoming shoppers, began in the nineteenth century but specialized products, like nylon, reinscribed gender as a consumer good and the new consumer goods reconstructed gender. Postwar advertising made nylon, and the ideology it contained, available to large numbers of consumers. Beginning before World War II and continuing into the postwar period, DuPont's domination of a single market, its positioning of women as middle-class consumers, and the mystification of women's use of nylon stand as important steps in the formation of mass culture.

I'm also interested in how DuPont accomplished its ideology-making. DuPont described nylon stockings through a wide range of oppositions. The tension between such opposites provides one of the "sites of conflict" where, Stuart Hall says, popular culture gets produced.[3] Conflict can be taken literally (the "riots" women participated in to obtain stockings when they were in short supply) or figuratively and intellectually (the tension between technology and culture).

DuPont's use of oppositions to explain and sell nylon presented stark contrasts to make the unpalatable palatable by insisting that the company's choice was the lesser evil. Oppositions gave consumers the illusion of choice and allowed DuPont to continue the fiction that large corporations "negotiated" with consumers. Finally, much of the marketing of nylon reinforced already strong cultural ideas. DuPont listened to consumers to understand which cultural values they currently found salient and then sold those back to them. These tactics grew from, and succeeded because of, DuPont's power with respect to the female consumers who bought stockings. DuPont engineered a product that would appeal, within limits, to women consumers and then sold it to them. But the ideology is in the details of how and why DuPont developed and marketed nylon stockings to women. In cultural terms, how did DuPont invent nylon?

Wallace Carothers, usually named as nylon's inventor, probably didn't set out to make a better stocking, but he was quickly drawn into DuPont's marketing plans. In his book on the development of superpolymers, historian Yasu Furukawa wrote that Carothers, despite later DuPont mythmaking, "did not intend to produce an artificial fiber when he started his study of polymerization in 1928, for, as he later remarked, 'I do not think we . . . had definitely in mind at all the idea of making a fiber, but we did want to make a molecule as large as we could get.'"[4] Furukawa admitted that, within twelve days of the first synthesis of superpolymers in the spring of 1930, Julian Werner Hill, working in Carothers's lab, observed that superpolymers could be drawn from a solution into fibers with the characteristics of silk.[5] From that moment on, scientific experiments, engineering explorations, and advertising worked to ensure that the fiber made from superpolymers would have specific properties. In both the patent application, filed 3 July 1931, and the first scientific paper describing the new material, Carothers and Hill noted that

> the fibres prepared from the materials of this invention not only have a high degree of strength, pliability and luster but they are superior to any artificial fibres known hitherto in the fact that their wet strength is substantially equal to their dry strength and in the fact that their elastic recovery resembles that of natural silk and in certain instances is even better than natural silk.[6]

DuPont worked tirelessly to make sure that the finished fiber, which came to be called nylon, had silk's elasticity, luster, and strength.

The story of Carothers, Hill, and the others involved in the laboratory experiments that led to nylon has been told and retold by historians and by DuPont. Historians of science and technology saw the chemical exploration of polymers that led to nylon as an important moment in the development of research and development laboratories, tied to a larger fight between applied and pure science, and this struggle had important consequences for science in a corporate consumer culture. In its own accounts, DuPont often appeared as the voice of reason, arrayed against the unreasonable scientists who selfishly sought to explore all of science rather than using their talents to produce useful products. Such oppositions helped DuPont present its own search for a profitable product as a service to the community. The scientists and DuPont both sought a fiber with elasticity, luster, and strength, but seeing the process as oppositional aided DuPont's publicity machine.

From the beginning, DuPont thought of the new artificial fibers as replacements for silk, particularly for silk stockings. In the first press coverage of nylon, both the trade and business press wrote that the unnamed artificial fiber "may replace real silk in its one great remaining market, hosiery," and described elasticity, luster, and strength as the synthetic fiber's main characteristics.[7] *Newsweek* reported that there were huge profits in silk importing because of the millions of pairs of stockings sold each year. Another article noted that women's hosiery "accounted for 3.1%" of the average department store's total sales and for "10% of its total profit."[8] DuPont wanted nylon to act like silk because silk, when made into women's stockings, had proven itself a profitable product.

DuPont, and the country at large, also saw the new fiber as a useful competitor with a major Japanese import and positioned nylon not only as a rival to silk but as an anti-Japanese commodity.[9] A spate of newspaper articles from 1938, reporting the announcement of several test plants for artificial silk, bore nationalist headlines. "Major Blow to Japan's Silk Trade Seen," said the *New York Times*, while the *Beaumont (Texas) Journal* called nylon "A Blow to Japan" and the *Chicago Tribune* headlined that the new material was "Expected to Replace Silk from Japan."[10] Science News Letter noted the foreign policy consequences of the discovery by insisting that, with the new product, "America . . . will be one step nearer freedom from foreign domination of its silk requirements."[11] *Time* magazine reminded its readers, "there are only a few major raw materials of which the United States does not have its own supplies. Such are rubber and tin. Such also is silk."[12] The *New York Telegram* concluded that "it looks as if the laboratories might be about to steal a march on the foreign offices by imposing economic sanctions on the Orient's aggressor."[13] DuPont included a nationalist component, along with elasticity, strength, and luster, in nylon's characteristics.

Principally, though, DuPont chose elasticity, luster, and strength as qualities nylon needed because of the material's intended use in women's stockings. Each of these words, chosen to describe nylon, contributed to the primary opposition in stocking manufacture, that between covered and uncovered. Wearing stockings, a woman's legs would be both covered (by her stockings) and uncovered (by her clothing). Stockings also needed attributes that called attention to the leg without obscuring the view.

Each of nylon's attributes contributed to these oppositions. By elasticity, the scientists and engineers meant that the fibers could be repeatedly pulled longer and then return to a shorter length. Because of their elasticity, nylon stockings would stretch when put on but then hug and outline the leg, presenting its contours to the public gaze. Luster became important because the first artificial fibers lacked silk's shine, an attribute necessary to call attention to the leg. Later, luster also referred to the color and sheerness of the stockings knit from nylon. Shine, color, and sheerness reinvigorated the contradiction between covered and uncovered. Viewers needed to be able to see the leg, through the fabric, for the desired effect. Sheerness also connoted the softness, expense, and luxury that products designed for women incorporated. Strength addressed the contradiction between seen and unseen, since nylon stockings needed to be strong enough to be wearable yet sheer enough almost to disappear. But strength also came to have meaning as an important marketing tool and concession to consumers. Women hoped that the new fiber would save them money by providing longer-lasting stockings. DuPont sought strength within limits.

Women's legs had long been important elements in sexual and gender identification. The curves of women's legs proved crucial markers in the concept of feminine beauty, based on painter William Hogarth's idea that curves are more pleasing than straight lines. Throughout the nineteenth century, most women hid their legs under skirts, and both sexes considered legs powerful erotic objects. At the same time, some women shortened skirts to show their legs at different times and for different reasons. Some sports, like ice skating, included short skirts in their costumes; feminists advocated dress reform that would have bared ankles and shown the limbs in bloomers; some working women such as waitresses wore slightly shorter skirts than middle-class women.[14] More important, perhaps, historian Robert Allen carefully described the ways in which female performers' display of their legs served as both "ordination" and "insubordination" of femininity.

In his book, *Horrible Prettiness: Burlesque and American Culture*, Allen presented the history of the theater in the United States as a "struggle over the appearance of women onstage" and reported that "ultimately, it was a struggle *over* women's sexuality, played out through public debates over the length of ballet dancers' costumes." Ballet dancers were the first nineteenth-century women to display their legs, clad in wool or cotton tights, in public. Allen writes of the ballerina: "Her costume foregrounded the materiality of the body, flaunted the physicality of women, revealed the outline of that secret half of the female body that sentimental fashion kept hidden. The very lengths that fashion went to conceal the lower body invested in its veiled and partial revelation enormous sexual energy.[15]" Ballet survived because its identification with the upper class helped mask its open sexuality. Burlesque performers, who in the mid-nineteenth century also wore short skirts and tights, were said to be in the "leg business." Allen described with great subtlety how the structure and content of burlesque both contained and expressed female sexuality.

By the beginning of the twentieth century, then, some women displayed their legs at specific moments, and in the first decades of the new century these moments became more frequent. Women's sports became more active and called for looser and shorter clothing, while the beginnings of beauty pageants and women's long-distance swimming competition brought briefer bathing suits into wider acceptance. Women's participation in the workforce before and during World War I brought clothing that enabled more activity. As both a cause and an effect of these changes, fashionable dress underwent important modifications.

Fashion historians talk about the S curve of women's dress at this time, with the Gibson girl being the look's popular representation. Historian Elizabeth Ewing described the S curve as featuring a "lavish bust and impressive hips," all hidden and accentuated by long, full skirts over strong corsets.[16] Around 1908, Paris and then American fashions changed to a "straight line," with new underwear designed to make the new look possible. Women's own rebellion against corsets played some part in this change.[17] The new straight line and less constricting underwear made shorter skirts easier. Skirts went up in the 1920s, down a bit to mid-calf in the early '30s, and then started climbing again. Ewing suggested that the manufacture of full-fashioned hosiery, designed to fit the leg with dropped stitches to make the ankle narrower than the top, began in the United States, while the first factory in Great Britain to make such stockings, out of silk and rayon, opened in 1928, just about the time DuPont hired Carothers.[18]

DuPont, then, entered the women's stocking market very early in its existence. Women didn't need full-fashioned hosiery, stockings that clung to the leg to outline it, while they wore long skirts. When DuPont began work on nylon, most women had worn short skirts for only about ten years. But ideas about the importance of women's legs as defining sexual features both predated short skirts and continued as skirt lengths rose.

When research began in earnest on how to make a fiber from superpolymers, one particular polymer became the focus of research, based on the cost of raw materials and the probability that it would produce a better finished fabric. The 1935 Report of the Chemical Department at DuPont explained that the "successful development of a synthetic fiber of outstanding properties" was the aim of this research. The polymer chosen for development "possesses all of the important desirable properties of other polyamides that have been examined" and "excels all the commercial textile fibers in strength and, furthermore, is unique in possessing excellent elastic recovery."[19] The report explained that three big problems remained. DuPont needed a spinning technique, processes to prepare large amounts of material, and a way to control costs. The solutions chosen for each of these problems continued to be predicated on a finished product with the proper elasticity, finish, and strength for use in women's hosiery.

The engineering and chemical problems encountered in making nylon thread into stockings were formidable. In 1936, the Chemical Department report explained that:

> Difficulties have been encountered, however, in spinning fine denier, high filament-count yarns such as required for hosiery, and attention is being centered on improving the design of the spinning cell and working out the necessary spinning conditions.[20]

And the problems multiplied. For example, silk had a natural finish that protected it from snagging while it was being spun and woven. Chemists had to devise a coating for nylon that would protect it while it was being handled and then had to figure out how to remove the coating before sale. The stockings made from nylon had a funny color, and none of the known dyes worked well. The nylon stockings need to be "boarded," steamed into shape, or they wrinkled too much. The nylon thread abraded the spinning mechanisms. At the time, the number of problems and their difficult solutions made each one seem insurmountable.[21]

DuPont chemists and engineers focused on making nylon into stockings, not toothbrushes or synthetic wool or any number of other possibilities, and by building several test factories, collaborating with stocking manufacturers, and solving the problems as they came up, they produced acceptable nylon stockings in a remarkable five years. As one memorandum put it,

> In my opinion all our effort should be directed toward the large potential outlet, namely full-fashioned hose. If there are by-product uses, that's fine; but do not let them interfere with or delay getting to the main objective. . . . As I see it, we are on the No. 1 tee and we ought to shoot the No. 1 hole first.[22]

Everyone at DuPont understood the goal. Writing of the first test factory, G. F. Hoff, a DuPont chemist who served as the liaison between the Rayon Department and the Chemical Department, noted "the necessity of harmonizing the viewpoints of research and sales" in order that "all of us may be together and understand the objectives." Reiterating what had been understood from the beginning, Hoff stated that: "Our most important problem is to demonstrate that we can make yarn acceptable for full-fashioned hosiery . . . with respect to strength, elasticity and luster."[23]

Trade reports showed that DuPont monitored the first independent nylon hosiery factories for the same qualities that had been its focus from the beginning. Yet as DuPont brought nylon stockings to the market, the manufacturers raised different issues. Manufacturers of the new stockings worried about the position of nylon stockings in the market, how they would be priced, and primarily whether they would be so durable as to decrease sales. A DuPont representative, writing to company executives, reported:

> We explained to these gentlemen our plan to go into the fine thread, sheer field where quality is the consideration and not price. This relieved their minds some for they had been greatly worried that long wearing qualities would cut down consumption of hose.[24]

The early positioning of nylon stockings as an expensive, sheer, and not particularly long-lasting alternative to silk stockings reinscribed ideas about women consumers as more interested in sheerness than in durability and as easily deceived. DuPont continued to present women consumers and their desires in this way during and after World War II.

When DuPont announced the invention of nylon, at a New York World's Fair Forum for Women, the contradiction between sheerness and durability took center stage. Using familiar language, DuPont Vice President Charles Stine (the person who hired Carothers) announced:

> This is the newest of the synthetic fibers, the development of which has occupied the attention of my colleagues for a number of years. Though wholly fabricated from such common raw materials as coal, water and air, nylon can be fashioned into filaments as strong as steel, as fine as the spider's web, yet more elastic than any of the common natural fibers and possessing a beautiful luster.[25]

But the *New York Herald Tribune*'s account of the event noted that when Stine said that the filaments would be "strong as steel," one woman "on the platform applauded, and the whole audience, visualizing stockings strong as steel, joined in."[26]

From nylon's introduction, DuPont worked to both boost and contain consumer expectations about the fabric. The difficulty in naming the new product—called Rayon 66 during the development process (the number referred to the specific polymer chosen for development)—illustrated the difficulty of this equivocal job. At one point the marketers suggested and then enforced the name Fiber 66 to denote the material's difference from rayon and thus overcome consumer resistance to the earlier product. In the two years leading up to the women's forum at the World's Fair, a range of people in DuPont, from the president on down, attempted to come up with a name for the new fiber. One favorite contender was Duparooh, which was an acronym for "DuPont pulls a rabbit out of a hat." But Duparooh didn't fit all the important criteria outlined in an early memo:

> since one of the chief commercial users of Fiber 66 will be the same as that of silk and rayon, any generic name selected therefore should probably be easy to pronounce and be a combination of syllables which would tend to be suggestive of delicacy and appeal to the imagination.[27]

The final name combined syllables from the words "new" and "rayon" and took into account alternate pronunciations and previous trademarks. While perhaps more delicate than Duparooh, nylon ran into trouble with Japanese businessmen who heard the rumor that nylon stood for "Now You Lousy Old Nipponese" and referred to the competition between nylon and silk.[28]

The naming of nylon then was part of its invention, part of its marketing, and part of its structuring through a series of oppositions.

Nylon had ideas about femininity, and to a lesser degree ideas of race and nation, built into its molecular structure. Nylon took the physical and intellectual form it did because of normative ideas about feminine sexuality as expressed in fashion, as well as because of the part played by the United States on the world stage. DuPont developed nylon for use in women's stockings, and within three weeks of its first mention in lab notebooks, scientists and engineers began designing the new material as elastic, sheer, relatively durable, and competitive with Japanese silk. Elasticity and sheerness related to how both the culture and DuPont constructed women's bodies as objects on display. DuPont knew that nylon stockings needed to be more durable than silk in order to sell, but not so durable that consumers needed only one pair. DuPont thus contained consumers' impact on the product within narrow boundaries. Nylon's invention as competition for a Japanese product shows that ideas of race and nation, as well as those of gender, were engineered into a particular consumer good.

With the introduction of nylon, marketers joined scientists and engineers in designing stockings to outline women's legs and make them available for viewing. In order to protect profits, DuPont marketers presented women consumers with a Hobson's choice: fashionable fragile stockings or thick but long-wearing ones. Finally, DuPont blamed consumers who questioned the alternatives. In the marketing phase of nylon's invention, the opposition between sheerness and durability would become an important structuring narrative.

But DuPont had always structured nylon through a series of oppositions. While the opposition between oppression and agency structures ideology, the first structuring opposition for nylon would be between technology and culture. Both technological and cultural aspects must be considered to understand the laboratory creation of nylon; both operated at all times, and each influenced the other. During nylon's first, or chemical, invention phase, the opposition between technology and culture was often described as pure versus applied research. In the engineering phase, the primary opposition for thinking about the fiber involved the contradiction between women's legs as both covered and uncovered. Other oppositions swirled around the early invention of nylon. These replicated and extended the technology versus culture and the covered versus uncovered oppositions and included a long list of other oppositions: research versus development, science versus technology, organic versus inorganic chemistry, organic versus physical chemistry, the myth of the lone inventor versus research and development laboratories, natural versus man-made products, Japan versus the United States, and consumers' wishes versus producers' profits. The intellectual and cultural work involved in thinking through and around these oppositions helped build the ideology embedded in the new invention.

In the marketing phase of invention, DuPont would come to depend even more heavily on oppositions to provide meaning for nylon. The oppositions worked to produce both ideology and a marketing plan as DuPont defined the role of women consumers in a culture of mass consumption.

Denier, Gauge, and Sheerness: The Marketing of Nylon

DuPont's invention of nylon happened several times, and each component of the invention contained within it ideas about gender. Chemists in the research and development laboratories at DuPont invented nylon as a material out of "coal, water, and air," while engineers, employed by DuPont and by hosiery manufacturers, ensured that stockings made of nylon used the material's "elasticity, luster, and strength" to best advantage. Next, the marketers at DuPont, and their allies in the popular press, presented stockings made of the synthetic to women consumers in a way that gave new meanings to nylon and to consumption. Nylon's invention included each of these processes—chemical synthesis, engineering construction, and market positioning. While inventing nylon, DuPont both reinscribed femininity and reinvented the relationship between women and consumption.

During the introduction of nylon stockings to women consumers, DuPont and its customers struggled over who got to define consumption. DuPont maintained its power in the relationship through a deflection of responsibility, from itself to the consumers and through a manipulation of the opposition between sheerness and strength. Women wanted sheer, strong stockings, and DuPont told them that they could have one or the other. DuPont entered the fight with more power, but, as George Lipsitz (explicating Gramsci) noted, the maintenance of hegemony always requires a struggle. In the marketing campaign for nylon stockings, we can see that struggle.[29]

Nylon stockings became part of the key paradigm of the twentieth century, a paradigm that scholars have dubbed the "culture of consumption." Any twentieth-century product, introduced into a culture of consumption, must be marketed, and corporate decisions about that marketing process contribute to the product's meaning, its invention in an expanded understanding of that term. Modern marketing techniques, already well established when nylon stockings were introduced, meant more than the advertising of a new product, although advertising played a key role. Marketing included naming the product, creating a demand for it, branding it and promoting strong brand identification, distributing it, researching consumer desires, setting prices, maintaining relationships with retailers, and continuing public relations (unpaid advertising) efforts.[30] Because DuPont did not make nylon stockings, marketing (rather than simply advertising) became a crucial part of their success. Nylon didn't exist without the marketing of nylon, and its marketing was part of its invention.

As a product aimed at women, stockings presented DuPont with a marketing challenge. From the beginning of the culture of consumption, interactions with women consumers have been fraught with tension and uncertainty. Manufacturers and advertisers (who usually took over much of the marketing) found women consumers confusing, in part because of the conflict between women's position as shoppers in the public marketplace and their role in the domestic, private sphere. As the consumer culture took hold in the twentieth century, it needed to reconcile these two seemingly opposite aspects of women's cultural work. Moreover, advertisers complained that they didn't understand women's minds and often hired women consultants to help. In truth, understanding any consumer proved a continuing problem for manufacturers and their representatives, but it was a problem that was often laid at women's door as the consumer began to be constructed as female. Manufacturers found women consumers culturally confusing and, at the same time, blamed women for all problems with consumption.[31] The fights over nylon stockings proved an important battle in this ongoing conflict.

The ideology built into stockings included ideas about gender held by both producers and women consumers, as well as ideas about how female consumers did and should behave. It would be too easy to posit nylon as an example of either coercion or emancipation. The assertion that men invented nylon to oppress women by treating them as sexual objects, on display for men's pleasure, is too simple. The idea that women consumers, acting as free agents, influenced DuPont's production and marketing of nylon stockings is also too simple. Nylon might be seen as a test case for scholars who believe that consumers influence the products presented to them for purchase. Issues of power, which people have it and what they do with it, become key. When producers take into account some small measure of women's wishes, real consumer resistance or a significant change in the product becomes more difficult. Moreover, genuine emancipation involves more than having a large corporation take female preferences into account.[32] Nylon contained, in its material design, complex ideas about gender, and the ways in which DuPont presented nylon stockings to consumers and treated consumers also contained important ideas about gender.

Examining DuPont's marketing of nylon stockings may be the best way to understand the interlocking stories of power, gender, and consumption presented by stockings. DuPont publicists, and the reporters for newspapers and women's magazines who covered the stocking story, created nylon just as surely as did the scientists in the research and development laboratories. Women consumers remained the other important characters in this tale of consumption. Jeffrey Meikle wrote that DuPont, uncertain about how to market nylon, took into account the negative responses of women consumers and changed the company's selling strategy. Domestication occurred, according to Meikle, at the moment when women showed more interest in run-proof hosiery than in stories of scientific and technical prowess. Meikle asserted that women consumers pushed DuPont to change its presentation of nylon.[33] I agree, but I argue that DuPont gave women a different presentation of nylon rather than stronger stockings and that DuPont continued to blame women consumers for nylon's faults.

The marketing of nylon stockings began four different times: the introduction of nylons in 1939 and 1940, the prewar embargo on silk and the wartime disappearance of nylon, the domestic reintroduction of nylon after the war, and the postwar abundance of stockings and other nylon products. The first three moments are marked by the scarcity of nylons and women consumers' reaction to that scarcity. The events that occurred at moments of scarcity were labeled "nylon riots."

At such moments, the argument between DuPont and the consumers seemed to be over supply. Women wanted more stockings than were available. That reading overlooks the real fight. Customers wanted a sufficient supply of dependable stockings that were reasonably sheer. Stocking manufacturers, principally DuPont, blamed consumers, as consumers and as women, for the fact that stockings didn't last. Women, according to DuPont press releases, advertising, and articles in the popular press, had unreasonable expectations and no understanding of how stockings were made and labeled, and didn't take proper care of their stockings. DuPont portrayed women as frivolous fashion-seekers, choosing sheer stockings over more practical thicker ones and then complaining that the stockings tore easily.

DuPont understood the fight but deliberately chose to misrepresent it. In 1947, Warren Beh, DuPont's director of nylon sales, addressing a hosiery merchandising forum at the Waldorf-Astoria, said, "American women . . . have almost universally expressed themselves as wanting sheerer and sheerer hosiery, but they also want dependability and at a reasonable price."[34] Beh understood what women wanted, but DuPont remained unwilling to meet this consumer demand. DuPont responded only to women's demands for more stockings and ignored their requests for stronger ones. In part, DuPont reacted to nylon's early history of shortages; it marketed nylon to conform to traditional gender roles, and it felt a technological push to continue to "improve" nylon to be as sheer as possible. All these responses combined to produce sheerer but weaker stockings, about which women consumers often complained but which they were taught, by marketers and advertisers, to accept.

After the introduction of nylon at the New York World's Fair in 1938, stockings made of it didn't become available for several years. In October 1939, DuPont began test-selling some nylon stockings in its home town of Wilmington, Delaware. In language that became familiar in media descriptions of stocking sales, *Time* magazine reported that the doors opened at the "lingerie shops and department stores" that sold nylons and "Wilmington women rush in like so many hens at feed time."[35] The sales began as a way of gauging consumer satisfaction but quickly focused on how to sell a few pairs of stockings to the large number of customers who wanted them.[36]

From the beginning, strength joined scarcity as the most important issues in consumer satisfaction. The introduction of nylon had included information about its strength relative to silk. The first press release about the national availability of nylon stockings noted that "well-made nylon hose have no superior."[37] Magazine coverage pushed the claims, with *Life* noting that nylon stockings were "preceded by tales of fantastic durability" and that consumers found "hose, as sheer and sheerer than silk, which wore infinitely better." *Good Housekeeping* cautioned that "we cannot predict . . . how long a single pair will wear," but concluded, "none of the pairs we wore developed a hole from abrasions; the final failure, even after several weeks, was always due to a snag or cut. This is remarkable."[38]

DuPont and the manufacturers of the stockings began selling women's nylon hosiery nationwide in May 1940, with warnings about their durability. In a news release, DuPont wrote that its "only claim regarding the wearing qualities of nylon stockings has been that 'on the average, nylon stockings will wear at least as long as other fine quality hose of equal weight and workmanship,'" but reported that "from the standpoint of beauty, well-made nylon hose have no superior."[39] *Newsweek* noted that

> department and specialty stores were jammed with buyers who snapped up nationally advertised Nylon hose. . . . The most frequent question was "Will they run?" The answer was they would if the thread was broken, but that Nylon boasted of "superior weaving qualities."[40]

From the beginning, DuPont tried to have it both ways, warning customers that nylon was not "run-proof" but also telling them that it was a strong and superior material.

Consumers couldn't buy nylon stockings for long. During the summer of 1941, the federal government commandeered all stocks of silk, 90 percent of which had been used to make stockings, to produce parachutes and bags for explosives. The resulting "stocking panic" brought hordes of women into department stores to grab the silk stockings left on the shelves. News reports suggested that nylon might take the place of silk in stockings, but noted that there wasn't enough nylon to produce the large supply of stockings required.[41] Within six months, the government also diverted the production of nylon to wartime needs. As one "embittered manufacturer of women's hosiery" noted, "we could figure a way to knit them of grass one day, and the next day there would be a priority on grass."[42]

Interestingly, women blamed DuPont rather than the government for the shortages. From the beginning, consumers distrusted the competing ideas DuPont had spread about nylon's miraculous nature and strength. In language reminiscent of 1930s consumer protests, one woman wrote to *Business Week*:

> Women were given a glorified hose several years ago, and that is what they want now. Nylon hose came, conquered and disappeared within a short time and now women are rebelling good and strong. . . . Is it just one more racket? Nylon is made from AIR, WATER, and COAL . . . [and] isn't there plenty of these ingredients to con-

tinue making nylon, and if it is machinery, why can't they alter old machinery?[43]

A reply by a *Business Week* editor, "a woman and a stocking-wearer," explained that DuPont now used all available nylon in war production, assured the correspondent that making nylon was more complex than the phrase "coal, water, and air" suggested, and promised that rayon stockings would improve.[44] In reaction to the shortages, DuPont and popular culture presented nylon's strength as important to the war effort, represented women as desperate for stockings, and described bare legs as possibly fashionable. All of these characterizations would have important postwar consequences.

Women had few stocking choices during the war. DuPont and other companies, along with the government, explained the importance of nylon to the war effort. Articles in the popular press, along with DuPont's wartime publicity and advertising, touted nylon's strength and praised women's sacrifices. A B. F. Goodrich Rubber Company advertisement, "We Borrowed Their 'Nylons' to Make Tires for the Navy," featured a picture of a woman's legs and described nylon as having "such great strength that it is possible to build tires with less rubber."[45] Bomber tires remained an important image. One article explained that the tires, "containing strong sinews of nylon . . . have given a good account of themselves in a year of action in the Pacific War Zone" while parachutes made of nylon had "such lightness and strength that ten pounds" could "support a soldier and his equipment."[46]

Throughout the war, articles also appeared (most at DuPont's instigation or at least with its help) that described, in the words of a *New York Times* headline, "Post-War Jobs for Nylon." The story explained that industry would use nylon because of its exceptional strength even in small sections.[47] Often these articles picked up on DuPont's insistence that nylon would be found in many products other than stockings, each stronger than the next. A *Collier's* article, "Your Life Tomorrow," described nylon screens "more durable than the finest metal ones of today," nylon string to "tie up better bundles," "an unbreakable elastic tow rope," and sailboat rigging that will "outlast hemp rope by many years."[48] DuPont responded to the shortages by explaining nylon's importance to the war effort because of its strength, and by promising a postwar plentitude of durable nylon products.

Wartime popular culture presented women as desperate for stockings. One cartoon showed a woman applying for a job in a parachute factory because "I understand you'll be the first to convert to nylons and I want to avoid the rush," while another, entitled "The Most Dangerous Branch of the Service," showed European women with scissors chasing a downed parachutist yelling "nylon!"[49] According to the popular media, women's desperation over the nylon shortage too often drove them to the black market. An article in *Reader's Digest* noted, "No mere man can fully understand the power of nylon stockings over women's minds, hearts and consciences. But a lot of men are busy exploiting this feminine weakness."[50] After the war, DuPont would elaborate these images of women as hysterical consumers to insist that women didn't know what they wanted and were mostly concerned with the supply of stockings.

The barelegged craze was the third wartime phenomenon with important postwar consequences. Much evidence points to the fact that women simply went without stockings during the war and found it easier and cheaper. Edith Efron wrote, in a *New York Times Magazine* article entitled "Legs Are Bare Because They Can't Be Sheer," that "women began to reject all substitutes and appeared barelegged on the streets, in night clubs, at work—in unseasonable weather." Efron noted that "Hosiery professionals are torn between secret relief that bare legs will relieve the crush at stocking counters . . . and secret dread that women will come to enjoy the freedom of bare legs and refuse to return to their formerly stockinged state." In the end, the article responded to hosiery manufacturers' worries that going without stockings would become a postwar trend. The article insisted on the need for stockings to "mold the leg" and found that need to be more than frivolous fashion. Better-quality and cheaper stockings would be available after the war, and the "glorification of the American leg" would become "an important factor in our economy."[51]

Much of the postwar marketing of nylon stockings, including DuPont press releases, newspaper articles, and advertising, as well as feminine discontent with both the supply and quality of stockings, came out of the wartime presentation of nylon's strength, the popular depiction of women as desperate stocking-seekers, and hosiery manufacturers' worries over bareleggedness. Reconversion from military to domestic production produced another wave of so-called nylon riots. On 22 August 1945, DuPont announced that the changeover from nylon war production to "peace time applications" would happen the following week. DuPont would make enough yarn for "360,000,000 pairs in a year—11 pairs for each woman in America."[52] But despite such rosy predictions, nylon stockings remained in short supply for several years, with large numbers of women competing at store counters for a few pairs of stockings.

Responding to women who "rioted" for more stockings, DuPont laid out a marketing strategy that it continued to use in times of plenty. DuPont presented itself as helping alleviate the shortages, denied that shortages existed, and presented women as desperate yet frivolous consumers who contributed to the problem. Finally, when women sought better-quality stockings that might mean less corporate profit, DuPont presented increases in the supply of nylon stockings as the end of the problem. Women emerged from the struggle over nylons with stockings that consumers claimed were inferior to prewar hosiery. The nylon riots, both pre- and postwar, marked the continuing erosion of power away from women consumers to the large corporations that controlled production.

The media gave the postwar shortage of nylon stockings a lot of attention. Newspapers, magazines, and cartoons depicted lines of women waiting for stockings and the various mechanisms used by stores to ration stockings. Such writings continued the discourse of women's desperation that began before the war and was carried throughout. In December 1945 the *Los Angeles News* headlined "1200 Cheer as Nylons March In," and the next month the *Syracuse Post Standard* headed its story, "10,000 Jam Nylon Line: Two Hours in Snow Pays Off." By February 1946, the *St. Louis Post Dispatch* described "how St. Louis Dealers are coping with this national feminine frenzy" and the *Minneapolis Star Journal* blared, "Screaming Mobs Rush Dayton's Nylon Sale."[53] Macy's took out an advertisement in the *New York Times* that read, "Yesterday Macy's sold 50,000 pairs of nylons. . . . An Apology to those who didn't get theirs. . . . Sorry—for the present we have no more nylons!"[54] The stocking supply didn't improve through the spring as *Women's Wear Daily* described the "Headaches of Selling Hard-to-Get Goods" and worried that the "public" was "Seen Revolting Against Hosiery Lines." *Hosiery and Underwear Review* talked of "That Nylon Nightmare" and pleaded "Heaven Help Our Hosiery Buyer." In June, an article in the *Pittsburgh Press* reported, "Nylon Mob, 40,000 Strong, Shrieks and Sways for Mile."[55]

Comedic depictions of the nylon shortages focused on women's desperation but gave practical reasons for the long lines for hosiery. A short poem, appearing in the *New York Times* in February 1946, presented the problem humorously:

> Rising, roaring cavalcade,
> Marching on in grim parade,

"Salesman, man the barricade!"
Whistles blast, and sirens wail,
Hold the fortress, never quail.
"Nylons, ladies, are on sale."
Up and at 'em pile on—
Faint Heart never won fair nylon.[56]

Cartoons made the same point. In a Gladys Parker cartoon, a young woman told a fortuneteller: "Never mind the guy you see me with. Tell me, am I wearing nylons?" while many others presented bedraggled women coming back from hosiery sales or doing crazy things to obtain stockings.[57] These cartoons culminated in a *Popeye* strip in which Popeye asked Olive why she wanted nylons. Olive replied, "Ain't I a woman?? Every woman wants nylons!" Popeye asked, "Will ya stop lookin' if I shows ya one that don't??" and took Olive to meet Minnie the mermaid who had no legs.[58] But the humor also pointed out that more than female vanity was at stake. The *Chicago Daily News* contribution to nylon poetry explained:

Take my sweets and fats away;
Take my white bread—make it gray;
Take my cocktails—take my cheese—
But clothe my limbs before I freeze!

The newspaper reported: "Chicago's women are clamoring today—not for nylons—but for any kind of stockings to protect themselves against wintry breezes."[59]

Two 1946 cartoons depicted DuPont's worst nightmare—that women would tie the shortages to the company that made nylon. In one, at a stocking counter with a "no nylons" sign, a woman customer explained to the salesgirl, "I wrote to the DuPonts and they simply can't understand why you're all out of them." Another took place in an office marked "Dupont & Co. Nylon Division." The customer said to the man behind the desk, "I represent a group of women who have agreed to do without other nylon products so you can concentrate more on stockings."[60] DuPont, with some justification, worried that the anger of women consumers over the scarcity of stockings might reflect poorly on the company and result in fewer stocking purchases.

Hosiery manufacturers and DuPont had made cheerful predictions about the postwar stocking supply and so had fostered some of the disappointment caused by the shortage. As early as April 1943, a DuPont press release assured consumers that "once the word is given" nylon plants will shift from "parachute to stocking yarn, not in months or weeks, but rather in a few days."[61] A May 1944 article in *Cosmopolitan* made the same point in answer to the question, "When will nylon casings be available for the legs for which American women are so justly famous?" The article reported that "All that needs to be done is to change . . . small perforated disks about the size of a half dollar, called spinnerets, and the yarn will go spinning out to hosiery manufacturers." The author assured readers that "within sixty to ninety days thereafter nylon hose should be back on the counters."[62] When such optimistic predictions proved inaccurate, the National Association of Hosiery Manufacturers admitted that

> A normal, prewar supply of women's hosiery will not be available to the market or to the consumers during 1946, even after steady production of nylons has been established. At no time during this year may the American woman expect to be able to purchase all that she may desire.

The press release blamed bottlenecks in the stocking mills as well as a lack of nylon being shipped by DuPont.[63] One cartoon pointed to the continuing broken promises about the ending of the shortage, as a woman looks at six different signs in successive cartoon panels:

> Some Nylons by September 1945
> Plenty of Nylons by Thanksgiving
> Plenty of Nylons by Christmas!
> Nylons by the first of the year
> Plenty of nylons by Easter
> 6 Pairs of nylons to every woman pledge by July OPA's goal.[64]

Women saw the nylon shortages as a string of broken promises.

DuPont itself blamed the "psychological situation attending any shortage," which brought an "extraordinary demand for . . . nylon hosiery," but pointed out that it was building a new plant which would provide "ample production" and referred questioners to bulletins from the National Association of Hosiery Manufacturers.[65] Another cause of the problem was that women could not and did not want to return to either silk or rayon stockings, and so demand for nylon outpaced planned production.[66] DuPont blamed hysterical consumers and the hosiery manufacturers for the problem and pointed out that it was working to correct it.

DuPont also continued simply to deny that the problem existed. Warren Beh told the Ninth Hosiery Conference, in April 1946, that DuPont had predicted that postwar supplies of nylon would be three times that of prewar capacity and had "more than met that forecast."[67] The next year, Beh again explained to an industry group, "basic demands for nylon stockings may already have been met in the 18 months since V-J Day" and by February 1948 reported:

> we forecasted . . . a year ago that 1947 would see a considerable increase in the supply of nylon yarn and . . . the possibility that an abundant consumer supply might be reached sooner than expected. . . . The aforementioned comparisons bear ample witness to the forecast of yarn supply, while the availability of nylon hosiery in retail stores today speaks for itself.[68]

By March 1947 DuPont announced, with some truth, that "the acute shortage of nylon hosiery is now a thing of the past," and picked up a theme that had appeared as well in earlier press releases. "Manufacturers," the news release said, "are beginning to turn their attention to new styles and colors to broaden their lines."[69]

Despite shortages and consumer irritation, DuPont presented nylon as the best material for stockings and itself as the benevolent provider of this new, exciting material. Before, during, and just after the war, DuPont's problem in defining nylon was the issue of shortages. Women could have decided that nylon stockings were not worth the trouble of waiting in line and continued "barelegged." By not answering many of the complaints and pretending that the problem didn't exist, DuPont left the idea in the public mind that nylon was a desirable commodity that hysterical women consumers desperately sought. In many ways, DuPont used the "nylon riots" to stand in for a much more important fight, the one women consumers attempted to engage in over the quality of the nylon stockings presented to them. The fight over quality had greater consequences and so DuPont repeatedly pointed to the concern over supply to show both that the company listened to consumers and that consumers were hysterical. The popular press portrayed women as hysterical over a supply problem that was, in retrospect, quickly solved and then implied that the quality issue was the same—imaginary.

In addressing the question of whether stockings could be stronger, DuPont used many of the same tactics as it had in dealing with nylon shortages. It raised expectations and then portrayed disappointed women consumers as the cause of the problem, denied that the problem existed, and presented its attempts at constructing meaning as a consumer education campaign, replete with scientific terms.

Women believed that postwar hosiery tore more quickly than prewar nylon stockings. As early as 1942, the letter to *Business Week* cited earlier said that "women all over are saying the manufacturers found that the nylons lasted too long for their own convenience," while a 1946 *Women's Wear Daily* article, "Public Seen Revolting Against Hosiery Lines," described complaints about hosiery supply and quality, calling for action before the "spread of the Bare-leg fad" and before "consumers sour on stores and manufacturers."[70] Complaints about quality did not end with a more plentiful supply of nylon stockings. A representative of a stocking manufacturers trade group went on a Philadelphia radio station in 1949 to "answer kicks on hose quality."[71] In 1950, a *Good Housekeeping* magazine survey reporting on stockings explained that

> People say "They're not so good since the war," and "Of course they're being manufactured cheaper to make us buy more," and "They used to wear like iron and now they fall apart in six wearings." So *Good Housekeeping* decided to investigate.

The *Good Housekeeping* article told women, "if it seems to you that nylon stockings aren't wearing as well as they used to, you're not alone. Nearly half the women in the country would agree with you."[72]

It was no wonder that women were surprised by the fragility of their stockings. DuPont had followed up wartime propaganda about nylon's strength with a series of advertising campaigns that featured the toughness of nylon as one of its main selling points. A 1948 campaign listed nylon's attributes, showing it in a variety of products, with the headline, "If it's nylon it's nicer . . . and oh so . . ." followed by a set of words that, in different advertisements, included "tough," "strong," and "long wearing," as well as "light," "holds its shape," "fast drying," and "easy to wash."[73] Another ad explained, "it all started with a stocking—a stocking sheerer, lighter, lovelier—and stronger—than any woman had known before" and went on to explain new uses of nylon.[74] Other versions of this advertisement, headlined "Nylon gives you something extra," explained that products made of nylon gave "extra value" in "strength, long wear, lightness, easy washing, elasticity, fast drying, toughness, flame resistance, resistance to moths and perspiration."[75] Women who had read articles extolling nylon's role in the war, descriptions of nylon's postwar promise, and postwar advertisements promising strength, long wear, and toughness understandably thought that nylon stockings would wear as promised.

DuPont responded to the contradiction—its own advertising and marketing portrayed nylon as strong while consumers found stockings to be weak—by both denying that it existed and blaming women consumers for any problems with stockings. Consumers, DuPont asserted, did not understand stockings or how to take care of them. Most important, women's frivolous and fashionable demand for sheer stockings meant that the blame for failed expectations, for any failed stockings, belonged to the consumer. Women wanted sheer stockings that were long-lasting, and DuPont sometimes told them that this was possible, sometimes told them that they couldn't have both, and always told them that they needed education in science and in how to take care of stockings.

After the war, DuPont, and those who wrote articles from DuPont's press releases, campaigned to convince consumers of the absolute trade-off between sheerness and strength. Consumers wanted sheer stockings and therefore had to accept the blame if hosiery did not wear well. DuPont representatives and hosiery manufacturers told Judith Crist, then a reporter for the *New York Herald Tribune*, that "nylon thread itself has, if anything, been improved in tensile quality since the war." But, a department store buyer explained to Crist, "women don't realize that they are buying much sheerer stockings than before the war."[76] This argument continued to be made, repeatedly, through the 1950s and into the 1960s. A 1951 headline in the *New York World-Telegram* proclaimed "Nylons Don't Last? Of Course Not! Women Demand Them Sheer—Fragile, That Is—and Get Them That Way."[77] Sylvia Porter, writing in the *New York Post*, replied to a letter to the editor that declared that, "after the Army-McCarthy row is settled, the committee should continue sitting and investigate why women's nylon stockings tear and run so easily." Porter wrote that there was no "plot": that the fault belonged to women who didn't understand that sheer stockings ran more quickly than thicker ones.[78] In a self-fulfilling prophecy, *Vogue* magazine declaimed in 1954, "since 90% of all stockings bought now" are sheer, "then it seems logical to conclude that one of the things women want most in stockings is sheerness."[79] *Kiplinger's* warned, "before you waste breath putting all the blame on the nylon hosiery industry," women should know that "the industry can produce figures to show that you think only about glamour when you go down to the stocking counter, and don't give a thought to durability until the first run comes."[80] In 1957, *National Business Woman* magazine explained that, despite that fact that women complained about stockings, "today's stockings" were not "poorer" but "*sheerer.*"[81] As late as 1964, one newspaper reported that, "as consumers, we demand sheerer and sheerer hosiery, but often we don't exercise care to make these filmy beauties last."[82] This campaign constructed nylon as a strong material that women, perversely and foolishly, wished to make weak.

DuPont built on this idea, and continued to invent stockings, by instructing consumers in the engineering and technology that went into stocking manufacturing. This education campaign positioned women consumers as both ignorant about stockings and responsible for the fact that nylon hosiery did not last. The educational campaign had two parts: explanations of how to fit and care for stockings and a presentation of technical terms that described the sheerness of nylon stockings.

Women's magazines and reports of home economists had long published articles on how to care for silk stockings, which everyone agreed were quite fragile, and then for the rayon stockings that appeared during the war.[83] The articles described the thickness of silk stockings by talking about "thread" (the number of threads twisted together to make the yarn) and "gauge" (the number of stitches per inch and a half), and suggested that women buy stockings that suited their activities—thinner stockings for evening, thicker for daytime wear. Other tips included buying the correct size, buying more than one pair at a time, and being careful in handling and washing stockings.[84]

While much of DuPont's description of nylon differed little from discussions of how to buy and wear silk and rayon stockings, DuPont presented nylon as more scientific, newer, and more complex than the materials that had come before. DuPont advertising and press releases talked about choosing, caring for, and wearing stockings but spent most of their time explaining the terms "denier" (analogous to "thread" in silk stockings) and "gauge." Just after the war, DuPont began to teach consumers the terms "denier" and "gauge" to explain why stockings didn't last. Referring to the yarn and stitches used in fabricating stockings, DuPont said that denier described the thickness of the yarn (a high number was a thick yarn; a low number, a thin one) while gauge described how many stitches were in an inch an a half. DuPont took out advertisements ("Is the lady getting the run-around on hosiery or is she getting the dope on denier?") and produced a sound-slide show to explain denier and gauge to retail saleswomen. During the slide show, "why some women have the mistaken idea that today's nylon stockings do not wear as well as earlier types is logically explained in a typical over-the-counter scene" because shoppers find the hosiery terms "confusing."[85]

In articles about hosiery, women's magazines explained over and over again that in order to understand stockings and why they tore, women had to understand denier. One article noted "But look here, you'll say, nylon is known to be super-strong. You can tow airplanes with it. That's true, but not with 15-denier wisps. And right here we'd better settle this business of denier."[86] DuPont executives and their allied hosiery manufacturers patiently explained that, before the war, nylon stockings were woven of 20-, 30-, and 40-denier thread and that, after the war, women primarily bought 15-denier stockings.[87] An understanding of denier, according to this marketing campaign, explained the perception that stockings had become more fragile.

But an understanding of denier and gauge raised an interesting question. Why couldn't DuPont make stockings with a low denier (thin yarn), but a high gauge (densely knit) or with a high denier (thick yarn) and low gauge (loosely knit) that would be both sheer and strong? The bigger question remained: Could DuPont have made stockings stronger?

While the historian and the consumer might agree that the question of strength was the most pressing, DuPont and stocking manufacturers continued to treat the issue as secondary and of little interest. In 1950, the National Association of Hosiery Manufacturers hired Elmo Roper to compile a statistical report on consumer buying of women's hosiery. Roper identified the most important "challenge" for the stocking industry as "maintaining and strengthening the belief that stockings are essential to good appearance." The most serious consumer problem was that of "bareleggedness," the tendency for some women to go without stockings. The survey reported that only 1 percent of women said they never wore stockings but two-thirds said they sometimes went without stockings. On the other hand, "slightly more than half of those interviewed" complained about "poor wearing qualities." Yet the report about the survey results contained no suggestions for answering consumer complaints but discussed instead how to convince women of the absolute necessity of always wearing stockings.[88] The postwar success of the campaign against "bareleggedness" can be seen in a 1957 *Consumer Reports* article that noted: "In the wonderful world of fashion there are occasions when it is bad taste to be bare-legged but quite right to wear stockings to try to achieve the effect."[89] DuPont and hosiery manufacturers worked hard to maintain demand for stockings, an ironic effort given that the demand for nylon stockings outpaced supply for the first fifteen years of their existence.

Nylon was scarce during its early history. Sheerness could be seen as a reasonable response by manufacturers to scarcity. Thinner stockings called for less nylon, so their manufacturers could meet ever-increasing demands for nylon stockings. Consumers complained both that there weren't enough stockings and that the stockings tore too quickly. DuPont paid attention to only one of these complaints, focusing from the beginning on issues of supply and demand rather than on the quality of the product.

Fearing a drop in demand, hosiery manufacturers continually worried that DuPont would invent nylon so strong that women would buy fewer stockings. Just after the introduction of nylon stockings, a 1941 *Harper's Magazine* article noted:

> So popular have the new Nylon stockings been that the available supply of the fiber has not yet caught up with demands and numbers of hosiery manufacturers have taken advantage of the situation; retailers have followed suit, jacking the price of stockings from $1.35 to $1.50. They had best take their profit quickly for Nylon outwears silk, and one of our largest retail stores has predicted that hosiery sales—an important source of revenue—are likely to be reduced to a fifth of their present volume in from three to five years.[90]

Outside observers saw sheerness as a form of obsolescence. As *Business Week* wrote of the postwar hosiery manufacturing industry, "For the past year it has been promoting ultra-sheer hosiery. Object: to regain some of the turnover it once enjoyed with the much more fragile silk hose."[91]

In retrospect, DuPont believed that complaints about quality came with the introduction of 15-denier hosiery, which became widely available in stockings just after the war. While developing an even sheerer stocking, 12-denier, in 1953, DuPont worried that "consumer complaints might possibly mount" as they had with 15-denier hose. There are hints in internal memos and in press releases that DuPont suggested that 12-denier nylon be more closely knit on high-gauge equipment, which produced better "wearability."[92] Nylon stockings might well have been made stronger, as women consumers suggested, but DuPont worried more about other supply and demand problems and ignored women's complaints about strength. In part, DuPont believed that women, as a gender and as consumers, lacked the technological knowledge and technical skill to make substantive suggestions about nylon stocking construction. All manufacturers found consumers perplexing, and DuPont showed that women, and especially women as consumers, existed to be taught the proper way to understand and use products.

Conflicts within popular culture, such as the fights over stockings, often occur when one group wrests power from another. The 1849 Astor Place Riot, a fight over differing theatrical interpretations of Shakespeare, in which working-class audience members died trying to maintain control over the New York City theater about to be taken over by the rising middle class represents an important moment in the history of class formation.[93] Women's protests over the supply and strength of nylon stockings represent a moment when female consumers complained about the power of corporate manufacturers. Coming just after the Depression when women consumers had asserted their rights, these protests scared DuPont. By manipulating a series of oppositions, DuPont instilled nylon stockings with the ideology of corporate control of production and consumption and also reinforced already existing ideas about femininity. DuPont solved the problem of supply and told women consumers that they should be satisfied, ignoring the problem of fragile stockings by blaming consumers for it. Women could have either strong or sheer stockings, not both. The carefully constructed ideology of women as hysterical and in need of instruction rather than as enraged consumers, of women as frivolous fashion-seekers rather than as political protesters, would have important consequences in postwar American life.

Coal, Air, and Water: Object as Ideological Text

Introducing the first wholly synthetic fiber, the DuPont Company declared that nylon was made out of "coal, water and air." This chapter showed that DuPont included other ingredients in its formula for nylon. Objects, just like other cultural productions, can embody ideology, and DuPont built an ideology of gender and of consumption into nylon during its three phases of invention—chemical, engineering, and marketing. In this instance, ideology worked through a series of oppositions that DuPont presented to scientists, engineers, and consumers. DuPont held the power and manipulated the oppositions in order to create the illusion that the corporation had taken outside ideas into account. Ideology also operated to reinforce strong cultural values, particularly about gender. Ideas of how women should look and behave as well as an evolving corporate relationship with women consumers were part of nylon from the beginning.

Nylon contained ideologies of gender and consumption from its inception. DuPont developed nylon for use as a silk substitute in women's stockings by assigning the problem to chemists working in one of the first corporate research and development laboratories. The invention of nylon involved a change in the way corporations interacted with scientists, and the fascinating story of what happened in DuPont's new labs is full of intrigue, madness, and suicide. But nylon's "invention" involved more than a new mixture of chemicals; it also included changes in the technology of textile production, and marketing innovations, all of them carefully orchestrated by DuPont. In each step of this complicated "invention," DuPont embedded ideas about gender that also illustrate the ways gender ideology defined the twentieth century's culture of consumption. Nylon also illustrates the relationship between the culture of consumption, with its emphasis on marketing and advertising, and a commodified mass media.

Cultural historians have long used objects as texts to provide evidence for how ordinary people thought and lived. Drawing on the work of anthropologists (as social historians draw on the scholarship of sociology), cultural historians have read objects. But historians who routinely used material culture already knew both that objects were best read in context and that twentieth-century objects, created by corporations for profit, called for different methods and contexts in order to be understood. Museum curators have refuted the idea that "objects talk" in favor of a deeply contextualized examination of objects, not simply to explain how the object came into being or how it was employed or how it worked but to use the object to better understand the culture in which it was produced.[94] Steven Lubar's work on a nineteenth-century pin machine showed how ideas about skill, industry structures, and cultural norms became embedded in industrial design.[95] Nylon provides a case study of how a mid-twentieth-century object can be seen as expressing ideology. Mass-produced material culture quickly became part of popular culture. Products aimed at children provide some of the best examples. We remember a moment when Pokemon lunchboxes, Barbie dolls, and Game-boys clearly illustrated the mix of technology, gender norms, transnational interests, and marketing strategies invested in objects available to all at the same time. This particular ideological mixture began with the introduction of nylon.

DuPont produced nylon in a culture of consumption that began in the late nineteenth century in the United States and expanded as the twentieth century continued.[96] For historians of popular culture, consumers present some difficult issues. On the one hand, consumers are comparable to audience members. Like an audience, consumers paid to participate (by shopping) in the popular culture, they played an important role in a for-profit enterprise, and they seemingly influenced the products offered for sale. I would argue, however, that consumers have even less agency than most audience members.[97] Some historians stress the importance of consumers in actively shaping production. A number of case studies, for example, illustrate the political savvy and influence of organized women shoppers, particularly during certain time periods and often as part of organized labor.[98] Other new work discusses consumer influence on the design of products.[99] The presence of active consumers, protesting and influencing, is an important part of the story. In developing and marketing nylon, DuPont reasserted control over consumption. A range of consumers in the 1930s protested prices and quality, and, for a moment, it looked as if the balance of power between producers and consumers might be significantly shifted. The nylon riots, and DuPont's reaction to them, showed DuPont's power in dealing with consumer demand.

As part of developing new products, corporations manipulated consumers to keep them from insisting on any changes that might lessen profits. In his wonderful account of the introduction of nylon included in *American Plastic: A Cultural History*, Jeffrey Meikle wrote that DuPont responded to the concerns of female consumers who "quickly devised their own agenda for the new synthetic."[100] Meikle explained that

> While the company promoted nylon as an unprecedented synthetic material emblematic of the new world of wonder-working chemists, housewives and salesclerks whose enthusiasm for "nylons" quickly became apparent, actually mistrusted DuPont's rhetoric and reinterpreted the new material in an informal domestication process that left the company scrambling to keep up.[101]

Meikle usefully described a process whereby DuPont kept consumer interests and needs in mind, but I insist on seeing the glass as both half full and half empty. DuPont, to a small extent, changed its marketing of nylons in response to consumers, but the product stayed the same. When disappointed women complained about frequent runs in nylon stockings, DuPont did not send nylon back to the laboratory for improvement. Instead, with the help of advertising and public relations experts, DuPont explained that women's expectations of nylons were too high. DuPont contained consumer influence on nylon within narrow boundaries.

For much of their early history, nylon stockings were a scarce commodity. The so-called nylon riots in which women lined up to purchase stockings were important moments in consumer history, analogous to the shift of power represented by the Astor Place Riot during the nineteenth century. During the nylon riots, women sought to demonstrate consumer power, but DuPont and the popular press presented women consumers as desperate and frivolous, interested in fashion more than in quality, in quantity rather than in science. The fight over nylon can be seen as a conflict, between producers and consumers, over who would hold the power in a consumer society.

DuPont presented nylon as technological and therefore difficult for women consumers to understand. Advertisements and the media described nylon as magically made of "coal, air and water" and defined terms (such as "denier" and "gauge") that women needed to understand before becoming knowledgeable consumers. During this mystification process, DuPont, and the women's magazines that printed its press releases, explained that the lack of quality and durability were the fault of unsophisticated consumers who didn't understand the new miracle fiber. I don't think women believed this, but, despite their individual disbelief, DuPont's ideological campaign successfully portrayed incipient female rebellion over low-quality stockings as riots for more stockings.

Neither DuPont nor women consumers were alone in their concerns about what the new culture of consumption meant. In the 1950s, worries over the role of consumption in everyday life, and as a constituent of mass culture, surfaced within the advertising industry. In addition, the role of men in a commodified mass culture that positioned middle-class women as key players concerned many. Individuality, and the power of any particular consumer, became one of the main ideas taken up by intellectuals after the war. The last chapter explores these intertwined concepts as developed in a group

Figure 1. Harold Rossiter, *How to Put On a Minstrel Show* (Chicago: Max Stein, 1921), front cover. Instruction manuals such as the one pictured here provided community groups with the music, jokes, and directions needed to stage a successful amateur minstrel show.

MINSTREL PROPERTIES AND REQUISITES

REAL BURNT CORK MINSTREL

"CREST" BURNT CORK

This is not a grease or paint but "burnt cork." The kind that is used by professionals, prepared from the best ingredients, perfectly harmless, applied easily and is removed with soap and water. Three sizes, 35c., 50c. and 75c per box.

"CREST" WASH-UP SOAP

Quick change cleanser from black to white instantly. Nothing better made. Price, 25c per package.

MINSTREL TIES

Another novelty that we exclusively make up for the special accommodation of our patrons. As seen in the illustration, they are just the thing to match the Minstrel End Collar and to materially aid the appearance of the first part. Made of first-cass goods, in Red, White, Yellow, Green, Tan, Purple, Orange, Black and Blue. Special attached neckband and catch that is easy to adjust. Price, $1.00.

MINSTREL END COLLARS

An absolute necessity for all "end men." We make a particular specialty in the manufacture of these collars and guarantee their quality. They are made from the best 3-ply linen, laundered and ready for use. Being thoroughly washable, they are good for many performances, and will well withstand perspiration and hard wear. We can supply all sizes, from 14 to 17½, including half sizes, by return mail. Price, 75c. each.

BOSOMS OR DICKEYS

For Minstrel End or Comedians.—These are reliable Dickeys made of "Linene." All ready for instant use. Price, 25c. each.

TAMBOURINES

8 inch $1.50
10 inch 2.00

BONES

Rosewood, 7 inches .... Per Set $ .75
Ebony, 7 inches .... Per Set 1.00

CLAPPERS

Metal Hammer—Double .... Per Pair .20

MINSTREL AND OTHER WIGS

Our Wigs have always given satisfaction. They are made of the best materials, and fit well and easily. Please note that we do NOT RENT Minstrel Wigs. All prices given here include postage. Extra well made Negro Wigs for Minstrel Circle, $1.50 each; Plain Negro Wigs for Minstrel Circle, per dozen, $15.00; Negro Wigs with parting, $3.00 each; Eccentric Wigs for End Men, $4.00 each; Negro Crop for Monologists, $5.00 each.

There is no style of wig we cannot supply. Describe wig you want and character for which it is required, together with size of hat you wear, and we will quote you prices by return mail. We also sell Moustaches and Eyebrows for any style character. Crepe Hair in all shades. Price, 35c. per half yard.

M. WITMARK & SONS NEW YORK

Figure 2. Gene Arnold, *Gene Arnold's Complete Modern Minstrels* (New York: M. Witmark, 1933), inside back cover. Publishers sold a complete system of minstrel materials, including posters, costumes, wigs, and makeup, to amateur minstrels. Performers could perpetuate ugly stereotypes easily when one company supplied all the necessary materials.

Figure 3. Jack Mahoney, *Mahoney's Modern Minstrels: A New and Original Complete Minstrel Show* (New York: Central Music Publishers, 1945), front cover. Amateur minstrel shows, and the publications that sustained them, continued into the 1950s. The cover art for this 1945 book showed minstrels constructing the same racial hierarchies throughout the first half of the twentieth century.

Figure 4. Tom Sims and Bill Zaboly, "Popeye," *Philadelphia Inquirer*, 14 July 1946. This cartoon conflated femininity with nylon stockings and commented on the acute stocking shortage. Olive Oyl imagined all women wanted nylons, shopped for them at the "Salon de Femmes," and relented only when faced with a woman with no legs, Minnie the mermaid, who didn't need stockings. Accession 500 Series II Part 2, Rutledge Papers 1942–1946, Hagley Museum and Library; used with permission of King Features Syndicate.

Figure 5. "Your Legs Are Lovelier in Nylons," 13 May 1957. Advertisements for nylon stockings promised the same qualities of elasticity, luster, and sheerness that scientists and engineers had designed into the new synthetic fiber. Nylon stockings needed to outline, and call male attention to, women's legs. Accession 903, DuPont Company Records, Series II Part 2, Rutledge Papers 1950–57, Hagley Museum and Library.

Figure 6. "If It's Nylon It's Nicer . . . And Oh So Tough," 1948. Ads described nylon as tough and led consumers to believe nylon stockings would wear better than proved true. When women complained, DuPont blamed them for not caring for hosiery properly. Accession 903, DuPont Company Records, Series II Part 2, Rutledge Papers 1947–1949, Hagley Museum and Library.

Figure 7. Deanna Durbin, playing the Hollywood film's title character, starred as *His Butler's Sister* and married the Broadway producer who owned the Manhattan penthouse pictured here. Durbin and her movie performed several varieties of ideological work during the Occupation of Japan, drawing Japanese fans of the young star back to American films, valorizing working women, and highlighting American consumer goods through its luxurious setting. *His Butler's Sister*, Dir. Frank Borzage, Perfs. Deanna Durbin, Franchot Tone, Pat O'Brien. Universal Pictures, 1943. Courtesy of Universal Studios Licensing LLP.

Figure 8. *Madame Curie* featured Greer Garson and Walter Pidgeon, pictured here, as the discoverers of radium, which led to the development of the atom bomb. Ignoring the content of the film, the film industry and Occupation officials failed to see any irony in presenting this Hollywood film as one of the first American movies to be shown in Japan after World War II. *Madame Curie*, Dir. Mervyn LeRoy, Perfs. Greer Garson, Walter Pidgeon. Metro-Goldwyn-Mayer, 1943.

Figure 9. Doyle, Dane, and Bernbach, "The '51 '52 '53 '54 '55 '56 '57 '58 '59 '60 '61 Volkswagen," 1961. The Creative Revolution in advertising, here represented by an ad from William Bernbach's agency, gave advertising professionals an escape from the conformity of 1950s life. This magazine ad, while spoofing the culture of consumption in which automobile styles changed every year, also reimposed conformity since all Volkswagen beetles looked alike. Used with permission of Volkswagen, North America.

Figure 10. Nilay Patel, "iSASA," poster distributed at Brown University, March 2006. This poster announcing the South Asian Students Association annual culture show at Brown University illustrates how students use such productions to think about their hybrid identities. Used with permission of the artist.

CHAPTER THREE

Reorientation and Entertainment in Occupied Japan

Kissing: Ideology in Both Form and Content

WHAT DO THE following films have in common: *Snow White and the Seven Dwarfs* (1937), a Walt Disney cartoon; *My Friend Flicka* (1943), starring Roddy McDowall; *Meet Me in Saint Louis* (1944), starring Judy Garland and directed by Vincente Minnelli; *Mr. Bug Goes to Town* (1941), a musical comedy cartoon; *Annie Get Your Gun* (1950), starring Betty Hutton; *Northwest Passage* (1940), a Western starring Spencer Tracy and directed by King Vidor; and *All About Eve* (1950), starring Bette Davis and directed by Joseph L. Mankiewicz? The U.S. military chose these films, and several hundred others, to help "reorient" and "democratize" the Japanese people after their defeat in World War II. The seeming randomness of the choices, when added to the mundane and sometimes silly subjects of the films, makes the idea laughable. But if popular culture expresses ideology, why wouldn't such a scheme work?

Of the case studies in this book, the U.S. government's use of Hollywood films to teach democracy to the Japanese seems the most straightforward example of popular culture's being ideological. Through the General Headquarters, Supreme Commander Allied Powers (SCAP), in the person of General Douglas MacArthur, the U.S. government controlled Japan for six and a half years. SCAP's Theater and Motion Picture Division reported that it had reintroduced commercial foreign films as soon as possible, although "approval of selected films was required to insure the choice of imports . . .

would best aid the democratization program, affording the people, long isolated from the rest of the world, additional means for familiarization with the life and thinking of other peoples."[1] The Occupation forces, collaborating with American film studios, intended the Hollywood films to aid in the reorientation of the Japanese people after World War II, but the films did additional ideological work as well.

The films taught Japanese movie audiences to think of popular culture as escapist; at the same time, the Occupation exploited the Hollywood imports as propaganda, and the industry saw the movies as an opening wedge in the exportation of American cultural products. Despite the varying ways they used film, all the players proclaimed the ideological importance of the movies' content without mentioning the economic structure of the film industry. Hollywood, supported by the federal government and the military, moved quickly to secure international film markets in Germany and Japan after World War II. The movie studios sought the economic stability and protected markets needed to reach global audiences, the next step in the move from a popular to a mass culture. With consumer goods like nylon stockings, U.S. business had learned to engineer products and market them to an emerging American mass culture. After World War II, U.S. business and government sought to build an international market without raising charges of cultural imperialism. The global reach of American media, so essential to the growth of mass culture, had important roots in the Occupation experience. The Occupation authorities themselves, however, had more narrow and immediate goals. They saw films as uncomplicated propaganda promoting the American way of life, and yet they failed in their attempts to use movies as simple ideological instruments. But Hollywood's global success, and the international growth of mass culture, proved the success of the ideology of government-supported, commercialized cultural production.

The polysemic nature of popular culture content continually worked against the expression of strong ideologies in individual films. The Americans supervising the film program, and the Japanese watching the films, took a wide range of meanings from the reorientation movies. In addition, the miscellaneous Hollywood movies chosen (*All About Eve* and *Mr. Bug Goes to Town*?) showed both the difficulty of using commercialized popular culture for propaganda purposes and the ideological confusion of any particular piece of popular culture. The American official in charge of the importing Hollywood films admitted that "because of the intangibles involved, it is obvious that there will be differences of opinion as to whether reorientation value is present in many pictures and, if present, the degree to which it is present."[2] The ideological messages embedded in the films' content remained so difficult to read that no one—the American film companies, the importers, SCAP, or the Japanese public—agreed on which films sent what messages.

This means not that the films didn't send messages but that their content was supplemented by a capitalist ideology contained in the films' production and distribution systems. The Japanese learned about American life not only from the stories the films told but even more directly from the ways the films were made and sold. These Hollywood films, and their exportation to Japan during the Occupation, contained ideas about American popular culture, the proper role of the state in relation to the media, and the worldwide role of U.S. cultural exports. While the fight over the films' content happened in the foreground, an even more important ideological move happened in the background as a government-supported, privatized, and commercialized media system grew and spread in mid-century.

In many ways, the Occupation presented a generous and idealistic response to the end of the war. Americans believed that they could, and should, rehabilitate their former enemy, not simply dole out punishment. At the same time, U.S. officials, principally MacArthur, also remained willfully ignorant of Japanese culture and society and assumed that imposing quite particular American ideas and customs was the only way for democracy to flourish. In his brilliant and far-reaching book, *Embracing Defeat: Japan in the Wake of World War II*, historian John Dower calls the Occupation "a remarkable display of arrogant idealism—both self-righteous and genuinely visionary," and noted that "the occupation of Japan was the last immodest exercise in the colonial conceit known as 'the white man's burden.'"[3] Dower's attention to race helps explain how the occupation of Japan differed in many ways from what happened in Germany, and his description of the Occupation as colonialism links the use of popular culture in the postwar period to current discussions of American cultural imperialism.[4] In addition, the racialized nature of the Occupation connects the construction of racial hierarchies to the global expression of U.S. nationalism, in much the same way that amateur minstrelsy showed the connections between racial construction and class formation.

SCAP's ideological crusade, operating on the two fronts of content and form, benefited from Japanese good will and met some Japanese resistance. Before the war, Japanese viewers had seen and loved American films. Charlie Chaplin, "Uncle Charlie" as he was called in Japan, received an enthusiastic reception during a 1932 visit. One magazine, *Eiga no tomo*, celebrated the seventh birthday of "Mikki Kun" (Mickey Mouse), in 1936, by showing him surrounded by his American friends, including Charlie Chaplin, Greta Garbo, Eddie Cantor, Buster Keaton, Wallace Beery, Groucho Marx, and Stan Laurel.[5] Until very late in war preparations, American films continued to be shown in Japan, and, of course, Japanese viewers remembered American films even during the war. Historian Miriam Silverberg recounted that Tokyo film students, voting after Pearl Harbor, chose *Mr. Smith Goes to Washington* as the best foreign film of 1941.[6]

After the war, both Occupation officials and ordinary Japanese filmgoers focused on the films' content. The Japanese found kissing the most important issue. Before the war, no films shown in Japan had kissing scenes. The Japanese government censored international films, cutting all kisses, and no Japanese film included one. The Occupation forces thought that kissing in both American and Japanese films would show the Japanese how open societies with equality between the sexes operated.

Culturally, the Japanese found all the emphasis on kissing confusing, since kissing had been an intensely private act. In his essay, "The Japanese Kiss," Donald Richie explains that "the social role that kissing takes in Japan is narrow. It does not mean affection or reverence or sorrow or consolation or any of the other things it can mean in the West. It means just one thing and that is the reason for the ambivalence which surrounds it."[7] While the Occupation set off a new wave of decadent and sexually explicit literature among the intelligentsia, regular movie fans spent their time debating whether kissing was "Japanese" and lining up for films that included it.[8] Historian John Dower lists *Madame Curie* and Deanna Durbin's *Prelude to Spring* as two American films that owed their success to kissing scenes.[9] SCAP also pushed Japanese filmmakers to include such scenes, and the first Japanese film with a kiss was *Twenty-Year-Old Youth*, released in 1946.[10] Kissing operated in the realms of both form and content. The American film industry understood that Japanese audiences had to accept Western forms of sexuality in order for American films to succeed in the Japanese market.

The Japanese, like others around the world, had reservations about the global spread of American films. The Japanese film industry, very well developed before the war, remained one of the few that resisted American domination successfully. But, as art historian Donald Kirihara noted, the "American film industry was intertwined with the Japanese industry from the importation of the first Vitascope," and, for Japanese film companies, the problem remained of "limiting the commercial success of the American product while cashing in on the Hollywood film's undeniable popularity."[11]

Competing with the American film industry became even more difficult after the war. In her important book on the postwar Japanese film industry, *Mr. Smith Goes to Tokyo*, historian Kyoko Hirano reports that, as the Occupation began, the Japanese film industry operated "at half its capacity." Only 845 theaters were open; 260 had closed, 166 were being used for other purposes, and 530 had been destroyed by bombings. Just three film studios produced feature films, and four made documentaries and newsreels.[12] The Japanese film industry saw foreign films as competitors for moviegoers, because of the lack of money available to Japanese studios to produce any films the lack of Japanese discretionary income and the resulting difficulty of buying movie tickets, and the lavishness of Hollywood productions. The SCAP files included translations of many articles from Japanese movie magazines and newspaper cinema pages complaining that American films were unfair competition for Japanese films.[13]

The Japanese had reason to worry about Hollywood competition. The U.S. film industry worked with Occupation authorities to bring Hollywood films into Japan in order to secure the postwar Japanese market for American exports. The Hollywood studios, in collaboration with the Occupation government, tried to teach the Japanese how, in a capitalist system, government and business might best cooperate to promote trade. The ideology carried by American film confirmed the naturalness of such a commercialized and government-supported system and helped hide the ideological work taking place. Struggles over the hegemony of a commodified culture, and over U.S. control of world cultural markets, remained undeclared.

This chapter shows the complex nature of popular culture's ideological expressions. Everyone involved in the Occupation film program believed in the clarity of the films' messages, yet no one could describe how the content worked ideologically. The ideology of a commercialized mass medium was stronger, and more easily recognized, than the ideas about democracy expressed by individual films, yet no one discussed commercialism as a component of the ideological message. Obscured by the fight over the multiple meanings of films' content, the attempts by American cultural producers to gain footholds in world markets could stay hidden. Popular culture's many confused messages and many uncertain readings, and the constant work done by the expanding mass culture industries to hide the implications of their economic structure, led my students to say "it's all just escape."

To understand why the Japanese chose to "escape" with American films requires an understanding of the international economics of the U.S. film industry; of American beliefs about entertainment as a carrier of cultural values, including ideas about consumption; the importance of international markets to the change from a popular to a mass culture; and the difficulty of reading a particular political meaning into any popular culture content and its form.

A Foreign Affair: Contexts for Occupation Film Policy

The Occupations of Japan and Germany drew on the proudly held, and often stated, belief that popular culture carried American ideology around the world. Emily Rosenberg, in *Spreading the American Dream: American Economic and Cultural Expansion, 1890–1945*, noted that this story began in the nineteenth century, when

> The Wild West Show and mass journalism pointed the way toward the American-dominated, globalized mass culture of the twentieth century. America's mass culture, like its mass-produced exports, was democratic in that it appealed to a broad social spectrum, but oligarchic in that it was carefully contrived and narrowly controlled. Appealing to the masses, it could appear revolutionary, yet by its ritualistic, escapist and standardized nature, it could also prove profoundly conservative.[14]

This opposition, American popular culture as at once liberating and conservative, democratic and oligarchic, became attached to the export of films shortly after the founding of the film industry and has followed American products sent abroad to the present day.

By the 1920s, the film industry and its allies in the Department of Commerce proclaimed that "trade follows the film," and explained how U.S. businesses profited when movie audiences sought to buy the American goods they had seen in Hollywood movies. After World War II, the film industry called itself the "Little State Department" to illustrate how closely it worked with the government and the importance of the propaganda it provided.[15] But resistance to American popular culture—because it threatened local cultures and industries, because it presented modern ideas about gender and family relationships, because it depicted non-Americans in racist and ethnic stereotypes, because it failed to address important issues—arose as soon as movies were introduced.[16]

Some of the arguments against the importation of American films grew from an economic fear that U.S. success would harm other national cinemas. But much of the opposition stemmed from the belief that films carried cultural and political messages that audiences read clearly. International audiences rejected American messages, especially if they drowned out more local values. As read by other countries, the economic and political meanings of the messages intertwined. A 1925 *Saturday Evening Post* article, "Trade Follows the Film," reported on "the pother and commotion among foreigners" about American films. The article explained that it wasn't the films themselves that caused "stirrings of uneasiness abroad," since

> They are not concerned with the art of the pale heroes, the calcimined comics or the lovely heroines with the mascara in their eyelashes. None of these things in the least matters. What does concern is the discovery, made abroad before it was made here, that the pictures have become a factor in international trade. They are making the United States the best-known and most widely advertised country to the very remotest habitations of man on the globe.[17]

The potent combination, of consumerism as a way of life, the picturing of American products, and films as the epitome of the commodification of entertainment, raised worries.

Despite the resistance, Hollywood films, at least in part by crushing their competitors, proved extremely popular outside the United States before World War II. That popularity played a crucial role in the economics of the U.S. film industry and convinced Americans that the resistance was unimportant. Emily Rosenberg reported that "In 1925, American films comprised approximately 95 percent of the total shown in Britain and Canada, 70 percent of those in France, 80 percent in South America."[18] American films, because of the large, rationalized production and distribution networks within the United States, could break even and sometimes generate a profit before being shown outside the country. The U.S. film industry invested huge sums of money in each individual movie and so made films that were more elaborate and appealing on a visual level than those of any other country.

Historian Robert Sklar noted that in the interwar years "American motion pictures, and hence American images, ideals and products, almost completely dominated the world's cinema screens—a near-monopoly unprecedented in American overseas commerce, as well as one of the most remarkable hegemonies in the history of intercultural communications."[19] Despite the great economic advantages afforded by a large country with a vertically organized film industry, most Americans chose to believe (then and now) that foreigners found American films appealing because of their content: the ideas they espoused, and the way of life they portrayed. Faced with contradictory evidence—great popularity of American films abroad yet deep-seated and continuing resistance to the same films—Americans believed only that movies carried political, economic, and cultural messages that non-Americans welcomed, in whole or in part.

In sending Hollywood movies to Japan after World War II, the United States depended on the widespread belief that American culture was popular because it was capitalist and not ideological, as well as on the strong relationship between the federal government and the film industry as exporters of a mass-produced commodity. In the decades before World War II, American films had already taken on their complex ideological roles as explicators of American cultural and political ideas, salesmen for themselves and other products, and harbingers of consumerism. The federal government's seemingly successful use of the film industry as propagandists during World War II provided the final link in this chain and led directly to the similar use of films during the Allied Occupations of Germany and Japan.

Film policy during the Occupations of Japan and Germany grew out of the collaboration between the federal government, particularly the Office of War Information (OWI), and the Hollywood film studios on the home front during World War II. Through suggestions, threats, appeals to patriotism, and friendship, the OWI influenced film content. Thomas Doherty wrote that the "alliance between Washington and Hollywood generated not only new kinds of movies, but a new attitude toward them. Hereafter, popular art and cultural meaning, mass communications, and national politics, would be intimately aligned and commonly acknowledged in American culture."[20] The ideals set forth by the OWI in its wartime dealings with the Hollywood film industry informed the way the Occupation forces thought about and chose American popular entertainment to present to the Germans and the Japanese.[21]

A 1944 State Department memo to "American Diplomatic Officers" summarized American feelings about using film as propaganda in the postwar world. The memo resulted from Hollywood pressure on the State Department to anticipate any difficulties the American film industry might have in moving into postwar markets, but it also laid out the reigning ideas about how film functioned as ideology. The State Department asked for information about what kinds of films would be most helpful and acceptable internationally, as well as about national quotas being contemplated anywhere. Protecting American motion pictures from unfair competition was important, according to the State Department, because film differed from other industrial products.

> The right kind of film can present a picture of this nation, its culture, its institutions, its method of dealing with social problems, and its people, which may be invaluable from the political, cultural and commercial point of view. On the other hand, the wrong kind of picture may have the opposite effect. . . . American motion pictures act as salesmen for American products, salesmen that are readily welcomed by their public.[22]

While describing probable postwar resistance to American movies, the *Wall Street Journal* declared that films had "value in selling merchandise" as well as a "propaganda value in selling a 'culture' or way of life," both of which "will be more important than ever in postwar days."[23] So the State Department and American business believed that films should present the United States to the rest of the world and, simultaneously, protect the U.S. film industry and extend American trade. How to reach these intertwined goals remained unclear as the war ended.

At the beginning of the Allied Occupation of Germany, one person believed that he knew how best to use American film as propaganda. In the summer of 1945, the U.S. government asked film director Billy Wilder, an Austrian by birth, to serve as military government film officer in Berlin, where his expertise would be used to reorganize the German film industry.[24] Wilder's first effort at fulfilling his charge was an August 1945 memorandum, "Propaganda Through Entertainment." In it, Wilder rejected that idea that he could be of help in Germany, arguing that he was unsuited either for the "passive job" of reviewing film scripts or for film production, since he "never very much bothered about anything but the actual making of films." Wilder professed that "my further stay in Bad Homburg would be stealing from the government." Luckily, Wilder had a better idea. Noting that Germans would soon tire of the documentaries currently being shown, Wilder wrote:

> Now, *if* there was an entertainment film with Rita Hayworth or Ingrid Bergman or Gary Cooper in Technicolor if you wish, and with a love story—only with a very special love story, cleverly devised to help us sell a few ideological items—such a film would provide us with a superior piece of propaganda; they would stand in long lines to buy and once they bought it, it would stick. Unfortunately, no such film exists yet. It must be made. I want to make it.

Wilder explained that during his two weeks in Berlin "I found the town mad, depraved, starving, fascinating as a background for a movie. My notebooks are filled with hot research stuff." Comparing the proposed fiction film to the hugely popular *Mrs. Miniver* (which "did a job no documentary, no 50 newsreels could have done"), Wilder, who already had a commitment from Paramount for "top stars, the best staff and a budget of 1½ million to do the film," concluded that he could finish the film quickly, and added that "I am conceited enough to say that you will find this 'entertainment' film the best propaganda yet."[25] The resulting film, *A Foreign Affair*, provided the most direct attempt to use the content of a movie to express ideology in the postwar period.

But Wilder didn't produce the film he promised. Despite beginning with a propaganda blueprint, the messages somehow become more complex. In his memo, Wilder outlined what he hoped to do in his hybrid entertainment/propaganda film, seeking to combine sympathy for the German people, surviving under harsh circumstances, with a love story of an ordinary GI who leaves behind his German girl-friend to return to the United States after both of them had learned lessons about fraternization, homesickness, the black market, and, especially, democracy. The resulting film, released in 1948 and starring Jean Arthur, John Lund, and Marlene Dietrich, bore little resemblance to Wilder's outline. Part spy story, part screwball comedy, part film noir, *A Foreign Affair* showed Wilder's affinity both for those who flaunted convention and for the underdog. Wilder presented Dietrich's sexy nightclub singer sympathetically, for example, despite her Nazi past. On the other hand, American congressmen and -women, Army officers, and enlisted men were shown as greedy, conniving, and ethnocentric, hardly the paragons of democracy Wilder's memo led one to expect. The American hero of the film transferred his affections, reluctantly, from Marlene Dietrich to Jean Arthur (after she has been warmed up by Berlin's free-spirited, post-defeat night life) and captured Dietrich's former Nazi boyfriend, but his first incarnation, as an amoral playboy, remained the more interesting character. One of Dietrich's songs, "Black Market," explained what happened on the black market, an explanation that might have been applied to the trade-offs made by the film itself. Dietrich sang, "mink and microscope for liverwurst and soap. . . . You like my first edition, It's yours—that's how I am—A simple definition: You take art, I take Spam" without ever condemning the bartering as unpatriotic or undemocratic. Wilder exposed the contradictions of each situation, criticized the American government, and presented the story in all its complexity.

Like Wilder, the Allied Occupation of Germany found it hard to use entertainment films for propaganda purposes. As early as 1947, *Hollywood Quarterly* published a matched set of essays asking "Our Film Program in Germany: How Far Was It a Success?" and "How Far Was It a Failure?" Even the writer who took the position that the Occupation authorities had used film well admitted that "the motion picture trade press has been waging a steady campaign of adverse criticism against the War and the State Department's film program for Occupied Areas in Europe."[26] The article that called the program a failure raised larger issues about the film program's effectiveness in exhibiting films that presented a coherent message.

While struggling to find commercial films that expressed American ideals, the U.S. government did succeed in moving the American film industry into a strong economic position in postwar Europe. The German film industry, once one of the strongest in the world, never recovered from the war. By 1957, Germany provided the third largest market and 4.4 percent of the entire world market for American film companies. Thomas Guback concluded that "on the commercial side the American program was eminently successful. . . . [T]he American industry had unhindered access to that market and was able to impose its own conditions on it."[27] The strong connection between the film industry and the government both protected the film industry and helped sell the United States. At the same time, the slipperiness of using specific entertainment films (even one made for the purpose!) to express American values was clear, in retrospect, for the German context.

But just as they tried in Germany, the Occupation authorities were poised to try in Japan. Although the German occupation had begun several months before the Japanese, the military men running each government knew very little of what happened in the other theater. While local conditions did vary, the racist and long-held belief that Europeans and Asians had little in common probably underlay this lack of communication. The Occupation officials in Japan, then, drew on the prewar foreign film trade and domestic film use by the OWI to fuel their belief that individual films could help "reorient" the Japanese by showing them American values while simultaneously protecting the international postwar position of the American film industry.

Fairy Tales for the Radium Age: Movies as Blunt Instruments of Propaganda

The film trailer for *His Butler's Sister* described it as "the delirious story of a maid in a bachelor's home . . . who wants to be its mistress!" and noted of its star, Deanna Durbin, that "she's heading straight for your heart." A viewer might describe the film as a show business story presenting the lavish life style of its Broadway composer hero, a fairy-tale vehicle for a growing child star replete with musical numbers to show off her singing, or a screwball comedy full of misunderstandings, misrepresentations, mistaken identities, and coincidences. However categorized, it remained an unlikely piece of government propaganda. Yet the Occupation government approved *His Butler's Sister*, starring Durbin, and *Madame Curie*, starring Greer Garson, as two of the first American films to be shown in Japan after the war ended. *Madame Curie*, a more serious film, detailed the love affair between two famous scientists as they struggled to discover radium, but the irony of explaining the beginning of the nuclear age to those who had suffered its horrible consequences remains palpable.[28]

Historian Carol Gluck believed that the Allied Occupation of Japan proved the indissoluble connection between power and culture. Speaking at a 1988 seminar on the role of arts and culture during the Occupation, Gluck noted that

> Hearing the remark that the Occupation was a "blatant essay in cultural imperialism," the Occupation participants took unanimous exception. Well they might, since both terms have only lately acquired currency in America. In 1945 Americans felt themselves innocent of imperialism, which was what they knew the Japanese had

> practiced in Asia. And culture of the right kind was the best export commodity America had to offer. We have learned but slowly the post-imperial lesson that culture is as incendiary, as potent, as blunt an instrument as man has devised to dominate and subjugate his fellows. Now that America and culture have both lost their innocence, the judgment falls heavier and with greater irony upon the Occupation.[29]

While any individual Hollywood film that played in Japan during the Occupation might seem a "blunt instrument" of propaganda, U.S. power becomes more recognizable if one looks beyond the film's content. While this was clearly evident in the later years of the Occupation, even the first films sent to Japan make more sense when their ideology is seen as operating in several registers: teaching the American way of life, exemplifying American material prosperity, proselytizing for consumption, and serving as opening wedge in the U.S. film industry's drive for global supremacy.

His Butler's Sister and *Madame Curie* illustrated the ideological complexity of using Hollywood films as propaganda in postwar Japan. In content, both films focused on the lives of women who were workers in addition to being sweethearts, wives, and mothers, an important propaganda point for the Occupation. Showing Deanna Durbin in such a role proved especially potent in Japan, where she was enormously popular. An early postwar visitor to Japan wrote:

> One of the first questions I was asked by Japanese friends when I arrived was whether there was any truth in the rumor that Deanna Durbin had died during the war. When I hastened to reassure them that Miss Durbin was alive and healthy and as popular as ever, they were more than visibly relieved.[30]

Durbin's popularity showed the international reach of the prewar American film industry, markets that Hollywood fought fiercely to maintain in the postwar world. A movie starring Deanna Durbin, then, was uniquely suited to do several kinds of ideological work.

Seeking to build on Hollywood's prewar popularity in Japan and to position the American film industry as a successful rival to its Japanese counterpart, Occupation officials first faced the problem of using film as propaganda in a country that had been inundated with it. The Americans needed to eliminate leftover messages from the Japanese wartime government and, at the same time, faced a public wary of political persuasion in the media. From the beginning of the Occupation, film and radio engaged the imaginations of those who worked for SCAP as important tools for changing the hearts and minds of the Japanese. The Occupation authorities believed that the Tojo and Nazi governments had used media to spread both domestic and international propaganda. The Occupation moved quickly to police films, newspapers, books, magazines, and radio to ensure that the media helped in the effort of remaking Japan into a democratic country.[31] Hollywood films played only a small part in the Occupation's larger efforts at education, efforts that included—to name but a few related programs—textbook, classroom, and language reform; documentary, newsreel, and slide show presentations; American libraries and book translation projects; and broadcasting reorganization. But Hollywood films represented something different—an already existing, commodified, and previously loved American cultural export being reintroduced to Japan during the Occupation.

The Office of War Information did worry that American films showed the United States as violent and uncultured at the end of the war and consulted with the Department of State and the film industry's Hayes Commission about a postwar policy. Films exported from the United States should not insult international audiences or portray Americans in an unfavorable light, according to the OWI.[32] Yet no one seriously considered making films particularly for the Japanese market, and even if they had, Billy Wilder had shown that such films worked no better than other Hollywood offerings. Instead, *His Butler's Sister* and *Madame Curie* became the blunt tools of American propaganda operating on the levels both of content and of the film industry's economic organization.

The different forms of ideological messages presented by Hollywood films became deeply intertwined with each other and difficult to untangle. For example, if Hollywood and the Occupation authorities picked Deanna Durbin for her prewar popularity in Japan and her portrayal of a working woman, the film also supported her continuing success as a commercial actress, just as it did in the United States when it was released in 1943. A fairy tale in form and content, *His Butler's Sister* tells a classic show business legend, designed to allow war-weary Americans to escape their worries. In addition, the story depended on a peculiarly American view of the class system that maintained that the U.S. contained two kinds of people: very wealthy people and lucky hard-working ordinary people who easily, and without any social or economic resistance from the rich, became wealthy. In many ways, *His Butler's Sister* presented a Horatio Alger tale of a plucky Iowa singer who, because of her good character and vocal ability, married a wealthy Broadway composer. Durbin's character magically attracted everyone she met and easily overcame all obstacles to make her dream come true. The movie sold an escapist and materialist democracy where everyone lived happily ever after, as evidenced by the three pianos in the fancy New York City apartment. The printed foreword shown on the screen at the beginning of the American version says:

> The Foods, Drinks, Clothes, Shoes, Rubber, Gas and other articles consumed or used in this picture are purely imaginary and have no relation to any actual Foods, Drinks, Clothes, Shoes, Rubber, Gas and other articles of today, rationed or unrationed. Any resemblance is purely accidental. This is a fable of the day before yesterday.[33]

Occupation officials believed that *His Butler's Sister* presented women in a new light and supported the democratic ideal of individuals achieving through their own effort. In addition, Hollywood sought to begin its postwar efforts to invade the Japanese film market with an established star. The film was chosen to send to Japan to build on Durbin's popularity and because instinct told the film industry that fairy tales worked well for war-weary audiences. But the film even more directly presented the material abundance of the United States, as evidenced both by the commodities pictured in the film and by the lavishness of the Hollywood production.

Madame Curie existed in a similar tangle of ideological messages. The film presented an international story rather than an American one, albeit with an overlay of American values. With a Polish heroine who studied, married, and worked in France, the film represented the winning allies in the recent war. A continuing controversy during the Occupation revolved around non-U.S. films, particularly those from the USSR. Unlike in Germany, where Americans shared Occupation duties with Great Britain, France, and Russia, the United States ran the Japanese Occupation virtually alone.[34] For ideological and economic reasons, Americans sought to keep out films from other countries, while insisting that American films showed the Japanese the rest of the world. *Madame Curie* allowed the U.S. government to hide its attempts to strengthen the postwar international position of Hollywood films behind a film that presented an international story.

No one—not Occupation authorities, Hollywood or Japanese film industries, or Japanese film audiences—thought about or discussed such propaganda points in relation to the two films. Rather, the films were part of a rougher, less self-conscious effort to aid the information activities of the Occupation. Early in the Occupation, the U.S. government and the Hollywood film industry showed their conviction that American films transparently reflected American values. This conviction, coupled with a firm belief in the righteousness of U.S. actions, persuaded the authorities that only minimal controls over the choice of films to be imported would be needed for American films to project essential American goodness.

Americans assumed that government and commercial media would work together to forward the economic goals of the media but would maintain a careful separation when it came to media content. American political beliefs held that commercial media were more responsive to their audiences and less liable to manipulation by an evil government. This ideology ignored government-supported media systems, such as the BBC, in other democracies, as well as U.S. government support of its own national film industry. The separation between the government and the media content and the emphasis on American media paying their own way through box office revenues, book or magazine sales, or the sale of advertising made the form of American commercial media part of the message they presented about the role of the media in a democratic society and, at the same time, made controlling the content of American media difficult for the U.S. government.[35] The simple content and complex ideologies expressed by *His Butler's Sister* and *Madame Curie* give an idea of the quagmire into which the Occupation was wading. Part of the ideology of American film exports was that a film's content was free from government interference, but such a belief faced problems when the government sought to use films to "teach democracy."

When he said, "If you want to send a message, call Western Union," movie mogul Sam Goldwyn understood the messiness of passing on a coherent ideology via commercially produced popular culture. The sweet and unattainable fairy tale starring Deanna Durbin and the serious story of the first nuclear scientist may well have confused Japanese viewers trying to understand the minds and culture of their occupiers and were surely examples of Gluck's "blunt instruments of propaganda." Yet these early films worked better at consolidating the different ideologies than did those exported later. As the Occupation continued, the ideas expressed by the content of films came into conflict with the ideologies of protected international markets and the capitalist infrastructures of the U.S. communications industry.

Sordid Situations and Abnormal People: Measuring Reorientation and Market Value

Until the middle of 1950, the Occupation's goal with regard to American films was to import as many as possible and provide a rough oversight of their content. The lack of hard currency in Japan to pay for film importation and the reluctance of commercial filmmakers to wade into a war zone meant that the U.S. government spent much of its time cajoling studios to send films, including *His Butler's Sister* and *Madame Curie.* As conditions changed and more films became available for importation, the Occupation officials became concerned that each film demonstrate "reorientation" value.[36] Quotas, which had always worked to privilege American imports over those of other countries, now included ratios of "reorientation" to "non-reorientation" films. But assigning a particular ideology to a particular piece of popular culture remained difficult. The Occupation officials had a hard time pinning down what they themselves meant by "reorientation." While they and Hollywood film studios agreed on limiting the number of non-U.S. films coming into Japan to protect future markets, they disagreed on what constituted a "reorientation" film. Yet the linking of quotas on foreign and "non-reorientation" films showed the intertwined nature of ideology as expressed in content and form.

Responsibility for overseeing the importation of films into Japan during the Occupation lay with the Theater and Motion Picture Branch of the Civil Information and Education Section (CIE). Japanese newsreel producer Iwasaki Akira, who dealt with CIE workers daily, reported that they were "not soldiers" but "pleasant young men who made me feel as though I had known them as close friends for years. Back home in America, they had been journalists, students, labor union activists, or industrial designers—all people who had been involved in intellectual professions." He added that the Americans in CIE had no race prejudice and were not hierarchical, calling each other by their first names. According to the Akira, the Motion Picture Branch consisted of "conscientious and progressive New Dealers and Marxist leaning leftists who were eager to do everything within their power to quickly and accurately carry out their mission of rooting out Japan's remaining militarists and democratize Japan."[37] Congruent with its New Deal reformism, the Motion Picture Branch saw itself as educators of the Japanese.

Placing the Motion Picture Branch in the Civil Information and Education Section made sense to Occupation officials. In an important essay on planning for the Occupation, Marlene Mayo explained that wartime planners needed "to link educational reform" with "the control and reform of the media."[38] In mid-1948, the Motion Picture Branch's Progress Report noted that

> It is questionable whether abstractions and general statements about democracy mean much to these people. By the use of films, they can see for themselves the democratic processes at work; because of this visual factor, films can be more directly and immediately effective than any other media of expression. The film overrides the lack of education, for it can be understood by people without much formal education. It interests those people while at the same time it instructs them and makes a lasting impression.[39]

Considering control of the media as an educational endeavor helped the Americans differentiate their efforts from those of Nazi and Japanese propagandists.

In this educational context, Lieutenant Colonel Donald Nugent was appointed head of the Motion Picture Branch. Nugent had served in Marine Corps intelligence in the Pacific, studied at Stanford, and even taught in Japan before the war.[40] Explaining the link between education and the media, Nugent noted that most Japanese were currently not in school, so "the books, magazine articles, motion pictures, and related materials available to the Japanese people assume far more importance than they would in a mature, balanced society."[41] In less formal terms, Nugent wrote to a California librarian that "our program is designed to familiarize the Japanese people with the history, accomplishments, and ideals of the United States and other Western democracies."[42] The idea that motion pictures were educational not only helped CIE differentiate its work from propaganda but aided in reconciling the two sides of its mission—to promote U.S. ideals and to censor.

The tension between the positive and the negative, between censorship and education, remained throughout the Occupation, but for Americans it was somewhat ameliorated by the delegation of detailed censorship to a separate department, the Civil Censorship Detachment (CCD), leaving CIE to emphasize education. The CCD, controlled by military intelligence, reviewed all films (imported and Japanese) as well as radio and play scripts, books, magazines, and newspapers.[43] As the Occupation continued, the CCD focused particularly on censoring any mention of the Occupation itself and any ideas that seemed to promote Communism. Because CIE also reviewed all films to be screened in Japan, each movie went through two reviews. The CCD explained that "magazines, books, and motion pictures will be required to submit to a dual screening; one to further the occupation objectives and the other to determine if they are detrimental to the occupation."[44] In practice, this vague distinction seemed to mean that the CCD worked negatively, requiring film producers to cut particular scenes and lines, while CIE practiced a form of positive censorship, worrying about the inclusion of ideas that promoted democracy and American ideals. But both operations often poached in each other's territory, and there was squabbling between them, much to the confusion of both Japanese and American film studios.[45] Even with these confusions, the tension between forms of censorship proved easier to resolve than that between education and entertainment, which would plague the Motion Picture Branch throughout its existence.

The Motion Picture Branch had a big job to do. Apart from the work of the Theater Branch, with which they were administratively joined, the Motion Picture staff oversaw a wide range of activities: reconstruction of the Japanese film industry as well as oversight of newsreels (both those produced in Japan and those from the U.S.), documentaries (both Japanese and American and some produced by the War Department itself for use in Japan), educational slides and filmstrips, and finally, imported international feature films. Each of the other projects alone took more attention than did the importation of entertainment films made outside Japan.

The CIE found the content of documentaries and newsreels easier to control and understand than the slippery ideology presented by commercial films. The final report of the Theater and Motion Picture Branch noted that "documentaries and newsreels were more effective than feature motion pictures as direct aids in the program of public education."[46] But documentaries faced two big problems: good documentaries were hard to find and difficult to place in theaters. Japanese theaters wouldn't willingly show documentaries, and if they did, no one came to watch. CIE tried for a while to force each theater showing a Hollywood film to also show a documentary but soon gave it up because the theaters lost money.[47] In addition, CIE noted a "basic objection" to "forcing War Department and commercial documentaries on Japanese commercial concerns" because "principles of democracy" championed "freedom of all information media."[48] Ignoring the issue of government's controlling media content, Nugent wrote that the "paucity" of enough good documentaries was a "cause of great anxiety." Nugent had definite ideas about which ideas might best be included in documentaries and which ones commercial feature films could express better. About a proposed documentary entitled *American Women*, Nugent wrote that "much of the informational job which it would do already is being done . . . especially by such commercial features as *The Farmer's Daughter*, *The Egg and I*, *The Woman of the Year*, *Enchanted Cottage*, and *Sister Kenny*.[49] He could have added *Madame Curie* and *His Butler's Sister* to this list.

The CIE provided direction before, during, and after production over what should be included in Japanese films and, in fact, exercised complete control over the Japanese commercial film industry. Hirano, in *Mr. Smith Goes to Tokyo*, detailed the reconstruction of the Japanese film industry by the Motion Picture Branch. In a memo of 19 November 1945, CIE laid out "themes" prohibited in new Japanese films. Forbidden were films deemed to be "infused with militarism; showing revenge as a legitimate motive; nationalistic; chauvinistic and anti-foreign; distorting historical facts; favoring racial or religious discrimination; portraying feudal loyalty or contempt of life as desirable and honorable; approving suicide either directly or indirectly; dealing with or approving the subjugation or degradation of women; depicting brutality, violence or evil as triumphant; anti-democratic; condoning the exploitation of children or at variance with the spirit or letter of the Potsdam Declaration or any SCAP declaration."[50] Hirano noted that this list represented "all the contradictions inherent in the occupation," since, despite the Allied wish to bring democracy to Japan, "in order to disseminate and inculcate democratic ideas, they had to suppress some of the ideas that might have inhibited the growth of the new ideology."[51] The Motion Picture Branch paid attention to every detail of the Japanese film industry, including labor relations. But the content of the films and how that content related to CIE's reorientation and educational objectives took up much of their time. In slightly different ways, CIE supervised the content of the American films imported by the Hollywood studios into Japan, but to ease the interactions with the U.S. film industry, CIE set up and promoted an organization that operated as Hollywood's representative in Tokyo.

The Motion Picture Exchange Association (MPEA) embodied the close relationship between the Occupation authorities (the agents of the U.S. government) and the American motion picture industry. The MPEA, a trade industry group representing the large Hollywood studios, was formed in 1945 to overcome the problems of exporting films into Germany and soon expanded to serve other international markets, principally Japan under the Occupation. A 1949 "Operation Report" of the Motion Picture Branch in Germany noted that it cooperated with MPEA in order to "maintain a high standard of American imported films," so that the films "serve our reorientation objectives in Germany as well as maintain American picture making prestige in the post war world."[52] Meeting these two objectives—to import good films and to reopen markets for American movies—deeply involved Occupation authorities in both Japan and Germany in the movie business.

Illustrating the close relationship between the government and the film industry, the first head of the MPEA in Japan worked for CIE and was paid by the State Department.[53] The MPEA began in Japan at "the express invitation" of Occupation authorities in 1946, and Nugent recalled that "for more than a year . . . the Association operated directly under the CIE Section." Nugent described how the Occupation later licensed MPEA with an independent administrative structure but noted the "close cooperation" between SCAP and MPEA "in the selection of films to be exhibited."[54] Charles Mayer, the second MPEA director, who headed the organization until its dissolution in 1951, perfectly blended government service and industry experience. Mayer worked as Twentieth Century Fox Far Eastern Manager between 1924 and 1942 and served during the war as officer in charge of film entertainment under the Far East Command in New Guinea and Manila. Familiar both with the American film industry's Asian activities and with the military, Mayer proved a useful insider in both worlds.[55]

In Japan, MPEA negotiated with CIE over which films and how many were admitted into Japan, schemed to make a profit on showing films in Japan, worked with Japanese film distributors and movie houses to get Hollywood films shown, lobbied for and publicized American films in Japan, protected and extended the market for American films, and helped distribute newsreels and documentaries that accompanied the feature films.[56] Large and small matters occupied the time of the MPEA. Charles Mayer complained to Occupation authorities that a Japanese film plagiarized the Warner Brothers' feature *Dark Victory*; argued with Japanese film reviewers over their "anti-American" comments and threatened to cancel previews for critics of American films; protested the film quota system to General MacArthur; tracked comments about American films in Japanese newspapers; and maintained a voluminous correspondence with CIE about individual films.[57]

The MPEA's first job was to counter the refusal of individual Hollywood studios to send movies to occupied areas because of regulations forbidding the export of local currency or its exchange into dollars. In Japan, CIE noted the "reluctance" of film companies "to continue what they consider poor business practice by releasing films in Japan for blocked yen—when the same films could be released at a later date (even 5–10 years hence) for a dollar return."[58] As the situation in Japan became more stable and monetary problems became less pressing, CIE and the MPEA turned from enticing film studios to send movies to Japan to the idea that particular American feature films should serve as "reorientation" for the Japanese public. While this had always been one of the stated aims of the Occupation, the growth in the number of films coming into the country, the better organization of the MPEA, and the reorganization of the Japanese film industry made it necessary for the CIE to pay more attention to "reorientation" films. In this activity, the Motion Picture Branch confronted the problem of assigning a single meaning to a piece of commercial popular entertainment and became involved in trying to control the content of films. The definition of "reorientation films" and the content necessary to influence the hearts and minds of the Japanese proved difficult for the CIE to articulate. In addition, reorientation value became confused with "quality," and the CIE often labeled reorientation films as "superior" or "meritorious." Most importantly, these activities clashed with the need of the MPEA to protect and expand the market for Hollywood films.

In order to decide which films had "reorientation value," the CIE compared "reorientation" films to "entertainment" films. The CIE wanted to admit more reorientation films but agreed with the MPEA that the most popular American films lacked reorientation content. Most importantly, the importation of entertaining films would keep the MPEA profitable and the Japanese going to the movies. As one memo noted, "CIE recognized the necessity for enough films of high entertainment value to permit MPEA to attract and hold exhibitors and the public."[59] But if there were too many entertaining movies, the "reorientation" message would not be heard. Nugent wrote, "CIE is anxious to maintain such a ratio between motion pictures . . . of positive usefulness and those which are merely harmless that the latter will not swamp the former."[60] Pressure from the constituent film companies who wanted to bring in a greater number of more profitable films brought conflict between the MPEA and the Motion Picture Branch on the number of reorientation films to be admitted.[61] In early 1949, the MPEA threatened dissolution. In trying to dissuade the member companies from leaving the MPEA, the CIE wrote that such an action "would affect seriously the reorientation objectives of the Occupation" and allow other nations to "capture the Japanese market." The CIE felt that it had allowed the MPEA a good proportion of pure entertainment or "escape" pictures compared to reorientation films, but the MPEA disagreed.[62]

The disagreements, and the MPEA's lack of cooperation, pushed the CIE to become more rigid about ensuring that admitted films had "reorientation value" although discussions continued to be vague on exactly what was meant by that phrase. In an attempt to appease the movie studios, a new ruling in July 1950 (the so-called Circular 8) mandated that if half of the films brought in under the country's quota had "manifest reorientation value, as distinguished from purely entertainment value," then the country could bring in additional films provided that all the additional films were "recognized by this headquarters as having reorientation value."[63] Instead of settling the issue, the new ruling made the disagreements between the Motion Picture Branch and the MPEA even worse. Seemingly to help shed light on the situation, the CIE changed the wording of its form letter to the MPEA to include a definition of "reorientation" value. Nugent, head of the Motion Picture Branch, wrote to Mayer, director of the MPEA, that certain films had reorientation value "because of what they say, because of the attention they attract to admirable aspects of American life, or because they are recognized generally as superior examples of mature and intelligent American motion picture entertainment."[64] This statement remained one of the few to actually outline what the Motion Picture Branch meant by reorientation value. Yet confusion still reigned over what reorientation value was and how to find it in a film.

The CIE maintained a consistent ideological line on only two issues presented in the films it reviewed: either violence or unequal relationships among different races could bring outright banning, and neither could ever appear in a "reorientation" film. The concern about violence carried over from the CIE supervision of the Japanese film industry and the continuing censorship of historical swordplay and other violence in Japanese films made during the Occupation. A regional Occupation official noted, "the spirit of the Potsdam Declaration and of the entire occupation is to eliminate the admiration for violence and disorder which has characterized so much of

Japanese history and literature" and asked "that gangster films and murder mysteries be eliminated from the selections offered to the Japanese."[65] Outside the CIE, the feeling was that violent films (in this case, *The Oklahoma Kid* starring James Cagney) showed Americans as "hypocrites in our preaching of democratic law and order."[66] Even as the New York Field Office bragged, "You will notice that pictures of crime and violence have been completely eliminated and that every effort has been made to concentrate upon a positive, healthful approach towards life in America," the CIE itself had some difficulty applying the antiviolence idea to actual films.[67] The MPEA questioned the concern over *Johnny Belinda* because "no misinterpretation by the Japanese is anticipated of a shooting by a mother to protect her child from a man who raped her" while *Dallas* was at first rejected because "with three men killed without punishment of any kind for the killer, it would be difficult to give clearance for this picture" but finally received clearance.[68]

Eliminating violence also helped in the presentation of racial harmony. Explaining that Westerns weren't necessarily forbidden, Nugent wrote:

> Westerns vary in content and effect just as much as pictures in other categories. When they are "souped up" with such elements as murder, brutality, torture and arson; when they present in a favorable or sympathetic light men who flaunt the law, kick other people around, and use treachery and violence; when Indians and Mexicans are mistreated by dominant Whites, and when the triumph of virtue over evil is dragged in during the final three minutes, then we have film which we ought to hesitate to approve for showing to the Japanese people.[69]

SCAP personnel remained extremely conscious of the racial dimensions of their work. As one memo noted, about the film *Hurricane*, "the clash in it between the white man and people of a different culture makes it somewhat less than ideal for release in Japan at the present time."[70] But applying even these apparently coherent criteria to particular films proved very difficult.

The difficulties increased when the CIE reviewed general releases that displayed neither violence nor racial problems. Classifying a film as either reorientation or entertainment became an important, and increasingly difficult, part of the CIE's duties. The MPEA sought to have as many films as possible classified as reorientation films because it could import almost unlimited numbers of those, but the categories became so murky that sometimes, prior to a CIE decision, importers couldn't tell if a particular film would be classified as "reorientation" or "entertainment" or banned altogether.[71] Struggling with this problem, Nugent wrote to the MPEA, "that they are based on novels of Theodore Dreiser in itself does not qualify 'Place in the Sun' and 'Carrie' for designation" as reorientation films.[72] Yet a film with literary or historical credentials often seemed to find it easier to gain the valuable "reorientation" label.

The murkiness of the criteria, and their seemingly random application to specific films, frustrated the U.S. film studios. In memos to the Motion Picture Branch, individual film studios and the MPEA presented films as "historical" or "famous" to sway the reviewers in their favor."[73] Charles Mayer accused the Motion Picture Branch of favoring more expensive films for designation as reorientation films, raising again the question of whether CIE confused quality with ideology. Nugent conceded that

> Though admittedly high expenditure does not always yield superior films of reorientation value, the conscientious producer who has elected to concentrate on quality rather than quantity is likely to have an advantage over quantity producers when reorientation films are selected.[74]

But the arguments over particular films showed most clearly the impossibility of the task the CIE had set for itself: conveying a specific ideology through a particular commercial product.

In August 1951, the vice president and general manager of the MPEA, Irving Maas, who worked out of Los Angeles, complained about one CIE reviewer and his decisions. Maas compared a range of films approved as "reorientation" films by Donald Brown of CIE with those judged to be only "entertaining." Maas wrote:

> If "Annie Get Your Gun," "Showboat," "Look for the Silver Lining," "Meet Me in St. Louis," rate for reorientation category, I must insist that "Phantom of the Opera" rates equally. The music in "Phantom" is outstanding. In all of these musicals a vehicle was used to mount music and why there should be a distinction between the four I mention and "Phantom of the Opera" is something that apparently only Don Brown can comprehend. It makes no sense to me. . . . "Ali Baba" is a fantasy. So too is "King Solomon's Mines,"

> "Connecticut Yankee" and "Mr. Bug Goes to Town." True they are not identical in the presentation of fantasy but surely "Ali Baba" based on one of the most widely read classics handed down through the centuries can lay claim to a more solid and important literary background than the other pictures mentioned. . . . Possibly the thinking of Brown which confuses me most of all is his approval of certain types of pictures which deal with sordid situations and abnormal people as you so often have pointed out to him. For example: "Harvey," "Glass Menagerie," "All About Eve," and "The Heiress."[75]

The memo included other comparisons of films classified "reorientation" with similar ones not so favored. In passing along Maas's memo, Charles Mayer reassured Nugent that "in no way are we asking that inferior pictures be designated as superior, nor that you lower your criteria" but asked for reconsideration of twenty-five titles that had "counterparts in pictures already designated reorientation or superior either for ourselves or for others."[76] Confessing to the problem, Nugent replied:

> The opinions of Mr. Maas . . . have been pondered with no little soul searching. The conclusion which has been reached is that error was probably made, out of desire to be generous, in attaching reorientation value to such pictures as "Northwest Passage," "Mr. Bug Goes to Town" and "Annie Get Your Gun" rather that to such pictures as "Northwest Mounted Police." "Blood and Sand" and "Phantom of the Opera" possess qualities entitling them to designation as pictures of merit.[77]

Maas, in a letter to MacArthur, explained that the MPEA's complaint was not with CIE control but with the "quantitative quota" because the MPEA and the CIE disagreed about particular films and the MPEA believed "that a film is either suitable for release or it is not and that it is impractical to attempt to allocate a quota on the basis of degree of suitability."[78] The quotas, of course, merely tried to clarify an unworkable situation. When only a few films were allowed into Japan and there was little profit to be made, the CIE and the film industry could agree on which films would be shown. As the number of imported films increased, new distributors entered the market, and the stakes became higher, the lack of straightforward criteria for judging the ideology presented by a particular film became a greater problem.

Arguments over the meanings of particular films were only one aspect of the growing complexity of the Japanese film market. MPEA members sought to set up individual distribution deals while American film companies, which were not members, sought to enter the Japanese market. By the end of 1951, the MPEA dissolved, individual companies took over responsibility for importing and distributing their films in Japan (often in collaboration with Japanese studios), and the CIE handed control over the import process to the Japanese government.[79]

When the CIE tried to use Hollywood films to "send a message," it began a fight that brought it into conflict with the MPEA, in part because of the American ideal of government noninterference in content; in part because, as Billy Wilder and Sam Goldwyn knew, controlling the polysemic nature of Hollywood films in the name of propaganda was difficult; and in part because a film's content wasn't the only, or even the most important, expression of ideology. One way to consider the dual nature of ideology – as both form and content – is to examine America's competitors in the Japanese film market. From this vantage point, the arguments over reorientation value become simply another way for the United States to mask its attempt to control the Japanese film market.

The same ruling in 1950 that mandated certain numbers of reorientation films reaffirmed national quotas on film importation because at the same time as the CIE juggled the ideological implications of particular American films, it also struggled with significant external rivals to Hollywood movies. The first competition came from Japanese films, made and distributed in a different kind of film system and maintaining a hold on Japanese moviegoers. Japanese movies provided economic competition, both for tickets and for ideas about how a film industry should be organized. Films from other countries, both World War II allies and enemies, competed in similar ways as other national film industries sought access to Japanese markets. Additionally, as the Cold War took shape, Russian films posed a particular ideological threat, on the intertwined basis of content and economics.

Japanese critics and the CIE often blamed the Japanese film industry for its lack of competitiveness. Most Japanese commentators found the problem to be a combination of the industry's lack of funds and the popularity of American films. A former Japanese film studio executive noted that "people are . . . attracted to foreign films . . . to learn foreign ways and customs" and concluded that "it is not unreasonable for Japanese movie-goers to prefer foreign movies."[80] In remarks prepared for the tenth anniversary of the Daikei Motion Picture Company, Nugent blamed the Japanese film industry for its own problems and laid out the case for unfettered American access to the Japanese film audience. He called on Daikei to make "superior motion pictures which transcend the local and special and touch the hearts and minds of men everywhere." Nugent informed his Japanese audience that "if the domestic industry is not producing pictures able to compete effectively with foreign pictures in appealing to the public, the remedy is to make better pictures."[81] Both the CIE and the MPEA worked hard to extend the reach of American films into everyday Japanese life. Supporting long-held U.S. government and film industry beliefs that an open market favored lavish Hollywood productions, the CIE and the MPEA used the Occupation's power to protect the Japanese market for American films. Their view of open markets as the proper way to conduct a competitive business like the film industry, when added to the belief that American movies would always triumph over all competitors, provided a coherent economic ideology from which to operate.

Like most businesses, the U.S. film industry wanted markets open to it and closed to all others. U.S. allies in World War II complained about lack of access to Japanese audiences. The quotas applied to films made in other countries illustrated the extent to which the United States sought control over the Japanese film market. The CIE explained that it set quotas for the importation of films into Japan, based on the number of films a country had imported into Japan before the war, to protect the Japanese film industry "from the competition of foreign films." The resulting quotas maintained "the relative positions which the motion picture industries of the various countries had achieved in the Japan market in the years when imports were free of control." Under Occupation rulings, each country could import "as many films as it had sent to Japan in any one year before the war, or 299 for the United States, 24 for France, 14 for the United Kingdom, 7 for the Soviet Union, and 5 for Italy, with 3 allowed for any other country."[82] Such control made "possible the inclusion of commercial motion pictures among the media brought in from abroad to help the reorientation of the Japanese people."[83] The CIE also applied reorientation/entertainment quotas to non-U.S. films. Such rulings caused even more confusion when applied, for one example, to French films (often seen as "immoral") than it had with American films.[84]

The British government argued against content censorship on the economic grounds that such controls distorted the free market Americans said they were protecting. The British Liaison Mission in Japan noted that, by 1951, imported books and periodicals had been placed on a "normal commercial basis" while films "remained subject to restrictions not imposed solely by economic conditions." The British saw the content restrictions as a pretense, with the Americans using quotas to protect their primacy in film importation. Such restrictions "discriminate quite sharply against the British film industry now that commercial conditions have returned to more normal levels," said the British officials, who sought to give their films a "chance of being bought on their own merits."[85] The CIE response to this memo showed that the CIE saw its job as to provide protection for American companies, using any means and explanations available. Considering an answer to British complaints, an internal CIE memo noted that

> the American motion picture industry, which in the pre-war years of unrestricted motion picture imports had dominated the Japan market, was not likely to acquiesce quietly in any limitation system which reduced that dominance, especially under an American occupation.[86]

The British were right. Occupation film policy used both numerical and content quotas to promulgate a specific American economic ideology of government support of U.S. businesses to protect them from free-market forces.

The Occupation's relation to Soviet films presented the best example of the contradictory uses of "free-market" rhetoric and the use of content restrictions to control market access. The formal quotas and rules, laying out regulations regarding film importation into Japan under the Occupation authorities, existed, at least in part, to cover up one main goal of Occupation policy—to keep Soviet films out of Japan and respond to constant USSR complaints and inquiries about the rules and to arguments over their enforcement. From the beginning of the Occupation, the CIE designed the quotas on the importation of foreign films into Japan "to keep to a minimum the number of Soviet commercial films to be brought into Japan."[87]

In describing the forms taken by Soviet propaganda in film, the CIE presented a detailed description of how it hoped American films might work. On the one hand, direct descriptions of the joys of communism and the horrors of individualist capitalism were "spotted easily." But the CIE considered "subjective propaganda elements" even more important. Examples included *Far Away from Moscow*, which "seeks to convince the people that the communist spirit can overcome any obstacle and that work in Siberia is both noble and stimulating," and *Mussorgsky*, which "tries to strengthen Russian nationalism by distorting facts and disparaging what is good in other cultures." Finally, the CIE reported that promotion by Japanese communists and the Soviet Union, as well as word of mouth, multiplied the impact of a Soviet film on the Japanese.[88]

The USSR Liaison Mission and SCAP continued fighting throughout the Occupation, and the many memos between the Russians and the Americans, and among various Occupation offices over how to handle the Russians, attested to the constant friction.[89] In internal memos, the CIE admitted that the Russians had grounds for complaint. The CIE explained its policy with regard to Soviet films as "one of obstructing their release in Japan" but noted that Soviet "complaints will do less harm than would the showing of the films."[90] Furthermore, Nugent wrote "Because of their propaganda content and intent and/or the propaganda purpose to which they are put by Japanese communists, CIE has endeavored for the past three years to obstruct the release and showing of Soviet films in Japan."[91]The quota systems, defended on various economic grounds, existed primarily to keep Soviet propaganda out of Japan. The ideological bases of economics and content joined as two different economic systems fought.

Long before World War II, and especially during the Occupations of both Germany and Japan, the U.S. government joined the Hollywood film industry to provide propaganda for the American way of life, much as the Soviets did for their system. American propaganda depended on direct content (as in Billy Wilder's attempt to make the perfect propaganda film for German audiences), exploiting the "subjective" impact of American consumer capitalism displayed in Hollywood movies, and working to promote American films through the MPEA in Japan and other trade groups in other areas of the world. Thus, the CIE description fit their own efforts as well as those of the Soviet Union. By joining content to such economic measures as quotas on importation of other countries' films and imposition of an American model of filmmaking (privatized but dependent on government support), the U.S. government ensured that American films presented a strong ideological message while seeming to be random entertainment. Examining any individual film raised issues about how well it expressed an "American" ideology but set within an economic structure and joined with a range of other films, the ideology expressed by *His Butler's Sister* and *Madame Curie* became powerful. Occupation authorities worked diligently to hide their activities, much as the U.S. government and American popular culture worked hard to present films as "just" entertainment or escape. Yet the power of the state, when joined to the power of the, seemingly, privatized Hollywood film studios, allowed American films to dominate foreign markets and present a rosy picture of American life.

Without examination, it might be easy to believe that the Occupation's film program presented a strong ideology. After all, the U.S. government seemed to be using popular American films to "teach democracy" to the Japanese. However, when one looks at the films chosen, and the difficulty of pinning down the meaning of any particular film, the certainty that the Occupation film program expressed a coherent ideology disappears. The films need to be considered in economic and political contexts, as part of a government-industry collaborative effort that began before World War II, before the complex ideology that they expressed becomes clear again.

It is not surprising that the ideological work of the Occupation film program proves difficult to untangle. The Hollywood films shown during the Occupation of Japan illustrated one of the most important attributes of the ideology of capitalist mass culture. Observers and participants at the time agreed that ideologies could be simply read in the media content, its presentation, and its interpretation. That popular culture was open to multiple interpretations – in fact, that's what made it popular – helped critics believe that they had focused on the main site of struggle. The ideological work done by the economic structure, although often deeply intertwined with and embedded in the content, remained hidden. Critiques by intellectuals and ordinary viewers alike often ignored the forms of persuasion represented by the structure of the culture industry in favor of arguing over the content of the films. Because the content provided a site where audiences and producers contested meaning, most observers overlooked any other ideological work. A final example shows how such cultural misdirection of attention worked.

One important American intellectual saw American films in Japan as losing a Cold War competition for Japanese allegiance because they represented a degraded form of "mass culture." The Japanese public believed that American films symbolized a more open sexuality, part of a modern sensibility, which competed against Japanese traditions. Norman Cousins, editor of the *Saturday Review of Literature*, used the films sent from the United States to Japan after World War II as the occasion for an extended critique of mass culture. Cousins's Cold War fears illustrated how one influential group of cultural critics viewed the ideological implications of American film internationally.

Cousins, adopting the mass culture critique soon to be extended by the New York Intellectuals and the advertising novelists discussed in the next chapter, worried about "the effect on people abroad of the Hollywood movie" and focused particularly on Japan. In three short editorials published in early 1950 ("The Free Ride, Parts I, II, III"), Cousins drew on his world travels to consider the work American films did abroad. He told of watching "several thousand people in a line three-deep that ran completely around a large city block" in Osaka waiting, during a typhoon, to see an American film. But Cousins worried about what the Japanese learned from the "'kiss-kiss-bang-bang' standard formula of the Grade-B movie." His interpreter was pleased by the imitation of American life by Japanese kids and enthused, "Isn't it wonderful the way we Japanese are being democratized?" but Cousins wrote, "It was wonderful all right – so long as you didn't try to look too closely for the somewhat deeper proof of true democracy: ideological content, for example."[92]

Cousins saw what happened in Japan as part of a bigger problem. Hollywood made films for the lowest common denominator, underestimating the American public, and so provided a false idea of life in the United States for those abroad. In the last editorial, Cousins contended "that an impression was being created of America as a nation consisting largely of quick killers and quick kissers, with a collective intelligence at ceiling zero and practically no contact with civilized values." If the "American movie is the main source of information about Americans for most of the peoples of the world," then, Cousins believed, "the United States finds itself on an absurd treadmill: it is spending millions of dollars abroad to counteract Soviet propaganda against us, but much of the damage is being spun off our own movie reels." Combining Cold War fears with a critique of mass culture, Cousins concluded, "Hollywood may come to realize that no art can exist or justify itself without a basic respect for the integrity and intelligence of human beings. Once it develops this respect, the American motion picture will find that the great audience, in Whitman's phrase, is ready."[93]

Cousins combined a critique of mass culture within the United States with Cold War fears about how such a degraded culture might prove a puny weapon abroad and thus tied the Occupation of Japan, seen as the end of World War II, to what came next internationally and domestically, but his focus remained on the content of the films. Scholars have increasingly noted the importance of America's image abroad to Cold Warriors and how the tensions of that conflict shaped both culture and politics.[94] Just as minstrel shows disappeared when the United States found that it needed to present African American culture abroad as more than stereotypes, much of the Occupation of Japan occurred within, and must be explained by, its Cold War context.[95] The response of the CIE to Soviet films remained one small example of this phenomenon. The mass culture critique, coming out of World War II and responding to the Cold War, increasingly turned its attention to the culture of consumption, as will be seen in the next chapter.

The American use of popular culture during its Occupation of Japan turned into an important moment, a crucial site, where the fact that ideology existed in both the form and content of popular culture became clear.

I am not arguing that content doesn't matter, that popular culture isn't open to many interpretations, or that audience members don't make meaning out of what they watch. Rather, I contend that the content is only one component of a complex set of ideologies presented by any popular culture form. Often the economic, political, and global structure gets taken for granted as observers focus on arguments over the meaning of an individual film. Such misdirection helps obscure the importance of the capitalist form to the content, as well as the complex ways in which the form operates. Moments when and sites where American mass media existed in a different culture help foreground the intertwined nature of form and content. Placing the American system of commodified and government-supported culture, with government so deeply implicated that it has no need to censor content, alongside other systems makes the structural ideologies easier to discern.

Popular culture most often acts like the wizard in the film version of *The Wizard of Oz* (1939), manipulating levers and buttons to create a show while saying, "Pay no attention to that man behind the curtain." In the transnational setting of the U.S. Occupation of Japan, the seams showed. SCAP didn't conspire with the movie studios to hide what they were doing; rather, the ideology presented by the structure of the culture industries was so strong that everyone saw it as natural and reproduced it unthinkingly. The arguments over content and how it was read by different audiences distracted attention from "the man behind the curtain." The U.S. film industry and the government acted together to protect the market for American commercial films while also focusing on finding movies that "taught democracy." No one challenged the idea that a commercialized medium best represented democracy as government, and industry spent time figuring out which films could be classified as "entertainment" and which as "reorientation."

In Occupied Japan, the American film industry learned how to direct attention away from an expanding commodified realm, one in which worldwide audiences shared cultural products without control over their production. I see the use of American films during the Japanese Occupation as one of the moments that helped disguise the ideological work of American popular culture as "just escape." The misdirection of attention onto the messages contained in the scripts and plots of Hollywood films, much like blaming women consumers for nylon shortages and the product's shortcomings, made mass culture easier to sell abroad. At the end of the Occupation, American popular culture, with government support, had taken important steps to cement its dominant global position.

The spread of U.S. culture around the world contributed greatly to popular culture's becoming "mass," more homogeneous, with less chance for differing interpretations. Using popular culture to teach a particular point of view also contributed to the growth of the mass market. After World War II, writers worried about the change from popular to mass culture and constructed a critique of consumer culture, much like the one Norman Cousins made of the American films sent to Japan. The next chapter outlines their postwar critiques.

CHAPTER FOUR

Advertising Novels as Cultural Critique: Dry Martinis, Rare Steaks, and Willing Women

Best-Selling Criticism

BETWEEN 1946 AND 1960, advertising industry insiders wrote and published at least twenty-three novels set in advertising agencies and eight others that took up allied institutions like television stations and public relations firms.[1] These novels presented a sustained critique of mass culture written by the forward scouts of the culture of consumption, those who worked in advertising, broadcasting, marketing, and public relations. *Time* magazine conflated the conformist ad agency employees, and their seeming opposites, when it headlined one review "The Drumbeatniks."[2] Like their beatnik brethren, the advertising men who wrote and starred in these novels criticized a culture that promised salvation through consumption and individuality through conformity. The novels, and the films made from them, influenced society's acceptance of advertising and consumption and how individuals thought about their mass cultural lives.

As "apostles of modernity," in Roland Marchand's wonderful description of advertising professionals, the novelists felt keenly what Daniel Horowitz has named the "anxiety of affluence."[3] They had seen a fully commodified future and disliked it intensely. Working to expand the realm of consumption, advertising professionals saw, before most people, the drawbacks to a consumer culture. Their novels outlined the dishonesty of the advertising business and the meaninglessness of advertising as a profession; bemoaned the conformity of commodified life; and decried the emptiness of consumption. Repeatedly, the novelists questioned the place of the individual in a mass culture, referring to their lives as intellectuals, advertising professionals, and consumers. Their firsthand experience made the admen's descriptions of the dangers ahead more harrowing than that of any scholarly screed.

The advertising novels presented a deeply ambivalent and politically unstable middle-class critique of mass culture. These fictions prove that mass culture had arrived by the 1950s and that even quite skilled cultural producers found opportunities for resistance limited. As managers of the culture of consumption, the ad novelists lived the life constructed by amateur minstrel shows, nylon stocking advertisements, and the government-supported Hollywood film industry. After World II, middle-class Americans recognized an increasingly ubiquitous mass culture, worried about its implications, and began to accept a quite restricted role in its production, becoming primarily consumers.

No one remembers men in gray flannel suits (using the title of one of the most famous novels) as intellectuals. The serious authors of the time, including the members of the Frankfurt School, the New York Intellectuals, social scientists like David Riesman, David Potter, and Vance Packard, as well as the Beat writers, mounted sustained attacks on mass culture, and their work proved important to later critics. Lacking the theoretical and analytical background, particularly in Marxism, of some of the critics whose ideas they shared, the ad novelists worked in a popular fiction form. At least six of the novels appeared on the *New York Times* best-seller list; several became Book-of-the-Month Club selections; Frederic Wakeman's *The Hucksters* was the 1946 number four best-selling novel with total sales of 712,434; Sloan Wilson's *The Man in the Gray Flannel Suit* was the fifth best-selling novel of 1955 and sold just under 100,000 copies.[4] The popularity and genre of the books may have caused their critique to be overlooked, but the novels explored the impact of mass culture on individuals in personal and moving terms, presenting the same ideas as nonfiction writers to larger audiences.

Neither the well-known social critics nor these lesser-known novelists found either individual or societal solutions to the problems posed by mass culture. All the postwar mass culture critiques remain unsatisfying for their lack of prescriptive answers to the questions they raise. Each of the genres, fiction and nonfiction, had drawbacks as political and economic theories. A comparison of the two helps pinpoint the analytical obstacles each faced as the authors grappled with the new mass culture. Considering the novels as serious critiques, despite their formulaic aspects, also pinpoints one way popular culture expressed an oppositional ideology. The ideologies previously described upheld the status quo—racial, gender, and national identities constructed through commodified and capitalist goods and entertainment—but the advertising novelists questioned, within limits, the world in which they found themselves and the world they could see coming.

Postwar America, with its increased emphasis on domesticity, a consumption frenzy spurred by the gratification delayed during the Depression and World War II, hypernationalism, and the introduction of new forms of advertising, particularly television, became the incubator of the critique presented by the advertising novelists. The novels themselves proceeded via a number of set pieces with few unusual plot twists or characters. The *Time* review noted in 1958:

> The salient feature of this season's supply of advertising and public-relations fiction, all written more or less from the inside, is that people, plots, and other parts are virtually interchangeable. If ad fiction can become plentiful and anesthetic enough, it may yet rival science fiction; the bug-eyed monsters will be replaced by tyrannical clients, the clean-cut spacemen by bright eyed space-buyers, and the half-dressed blondes by half-dressed blondes.[5]

The novels featured a wide range of fictional genres including melodrama, science fiction, mystery, humorous satire, and paperback original thrillers. Yet each fabricated its plot and characters from a few basic building blocks common to all. Their intertextuality seemingly resulted from authorial awareness of advertising conventions, familiarity with the other novels, and their common critique.

The popular novelistic form brought with it a series of problems for social critics. Novels traditionally focused on the tribulations or journey of an individual and so seemed well suited to take up the important postwar issue of the role of the individual in a mass culture. But, beginning before World War II, novelists who examined the problems of consumption and advertising proposed individual solutions to social problems. The novels' heroes founded their own firms to do advertising "right," moved to smaller cities to open agencies away from the corruption of Madison Avenue, or left advertising altogether for the love of a good woman and the appeal of running a Western ranch or a private school. If the novel's hero changed, the authors had satisfied the fictional form and had no incentive to propose additional social reform. Although employing the conventions of realism and a repeated set of plots and characters, the advertising novelists complicated their own formula. They addressed issues around individuality by referencing the traditional doubled consciousness of advertising men, who sold to both consumers and clients, and their own double positions as novelists and subjects. Yet citing their realism and the formulaic nature of the novels, book reviewers, as well many within the advertising industry, refused to read these fictions as social critiques and dismissed them as literature.

In addition to the intellectual ferment of the time, Thomas Frank has shown how the corporate community's dissatisfaction with business life and practice in the 1950s contributed to the counterculture of the 1960s.[6] Restlessness on the part of corporate employees, when added to the new rigidity in advertising practice brought on by a reliance on statistical research, paved the way for the so-called Creative Revolution in advertising. These novels also documented the professional unrest of the 1950s and clearly pointed to the ways advertising agencies changed in the 1960s. In fact, the Creative Revolution marked the end of advertising novels. There were virtually none published in the 1960s, and they returned in the 1970s and later primarily in order to have women and people of color take up the roles of the previously white male heroes. Presumably, the Creative Revolution's expansion of the possibilities for how advertising men could behave and work, as well as a growing cultural acceptance of the very mass culture they critiqued, made the novels' form and content less relevant.

None of the critics of mass culture, whether nonfiction writer or novelist, outlined solutions that seemed possible in the 1950s. Despite their lack of a systematic program for change, the social critics had influence. Daniel Horowitz wrote of the nonfiction authors that "popular books spoke to audiences in ways that established the terms of the debates, generated social momentum, and helped define oppositional identities," and the novels performed all those tasks, and reached more people.[7]

A new group of social scientists actually measured the influence of one of the advertising novels. The Rockefeller Foundation funded the Bureau of Applied Social Research (BASR, begun as the Office of Radio Research), headed by Austrian immigrant sociologist Paul Lazarsfeld, to conduct media surveys in the 1940s and 1950s. BASR, with close ties to the Frankfurt intellectuals, served as a base for communications studies scholars whom Kathy Newman has named "audience intellectuals."[8] Lazarsfeld included Frederic

Wakeman's novel *The Hucksters* (1946), as well as the 1947 movie made of the book, in one of his first surveys.[9] Lazarsfeld examined how the novel, which offered a sustained criticism of broadcasting, affected "attitudes toward radio, and especially toward radio advertising."[10] The survey, itself part of the new reliance on numbers in the advertising business, consisted of 3,529 personal interviews with a cross section of the U.S. adult population, and was accurate "within 2 per cent of true opinion." Lazarsfeld found that "those who were exposed to Wakeman's satire on radio advertising are considerably more critical of commercials, even when education is held constant" explaining that "this relationship undoubtedly comes about in a variety of ways: Some people were made more critical by seeing or reading *The Hucksters*; others exposed themselves just because they were more critical." Lazarsfeld concluded that

> The critic who reads *The Hucksters* does not become a critic as a result of this experience, but he most probably becomes more critical. He finds new arguments to bolster his position; he finds new criticism which he had not thought of before; and so on. In other words, his criticism is strengthened and reinforced by his exposure.[11]

Lazarsfeld believed that Wakeman functioned as an intellectual working, within a commodified framework, to reinforce the critique of advertising shared by radio listeners. Lazarsfeld sought the same position for himself, of course, desperately hoping that his work in explaining audience psychology to advertisers had a social purpose beyond expediting the growth of capitalism. The novelists who set their stories in advertising agencies in order to criticize the growing culture of consumption faced the same contradictions as other anticapitalist intellectuals while having at least some influence on the thought of a large number of readers.

Written in a comic tone, Herman Wouk's first novel, completed while he was still in the navy, *Aurora Dawn* (1947), mounted the same critique as Wakeman's *The Hucksters*. Wouk noted in his Preface, "the recent publication of more than one novel intended to expose the inner workings of the advertising industry, which this story may be said to resemble in setting and certain points of detail, though not, surely, in matter or manner."[12] *Aurora Dawn*, a satire in the style of a Fielding romp, featured an advertising agency called Leach and Grovill and a multipage "Oration Against Advertising" delivered by an artist. The plot of *Aurora Dawn* contained points that became familiar in later advertising novels: the sincere young advertising man, the beautiful model with whom he falls in love, the capricious and cruel client (here the manufacturer of Aurora Dawn soap), and the honest man chosen to help sell the soap who proves incorruptible. The novel excoriated advertising and broadcasting as attempts to commercialize all life, enforce consumption conformity, and sell products curing every problem, real and imagined. The happy ending has everyone paired off in couples, far from Madison Avenue.

In many ways, Wakeman's *The Hucksters* and Wouk's *Aurora Dawn* set the stage for the novels that followed in genre, tone, content, plot, and the role of the author as a cultural critic. But these novels, written just after the war, had roots in earlier fiction that explored the relationship between commerce and personal identity.

Precursors

Many of the attributes of the advertising novels published after World War II can be seen in earlier popular fiction. Five novels published between 1914 and 1941 took up advertising, publicity, and publishing and treated these subjects in ways that would become more familiar in the late 1940s and 1950s. Written in a range of genres, these books portrayed the advertising business as a creative lifestyle in contrast to a staid business world inhabited by wealthy conformists. Relying on the early history of advertising, particularly as part of the newspaper business, the novels framed a critique that mirrored that of Progressive muckrakers. The authors, all of whom had experience in advertising or publishing, created a formula that both allowed and contained cultural criticism of the important and newly emerging social, cultural, and economic forces of advertising and consumption.

Early novels presented careers in advertising as a creative lifestyle, often in contrast to the staid life of the businessmen who surrounded the admen. John P. Marquand's *H. M. Pulham, Esquire* (1941) told the story of a wealthy New England man who prepped at a boarding school, went to Harvard, entered a bond firm, and married a woman he had known since childhood. Taking his place in a rigid social routine, Harry's dull life, revealed as an interior monologue, had only three breaks in routine: his friendship with Bill King, a creative guy from outside his social circle at Harvard; his service in World War I; and his one year at an advertising agency as an assistant to

King. For the rest of his life he measured everything that happened against the liberating year he spent in New York City with the sometimes silly, but never boring, advertising professionals. In *H. M. Pulham, Esquire*, Marquand examined wealthy Boston society and its effect on individuals, but also began to consider the role of advertising as a profession and as a social force.[13]

The creativity of the advertising profession, its freedom from routine, and its colorful language and characters made it a perfect setting for fiction in several genres. Dorothy Sayers, the British scholar, advertising copywriter, and mystery writer, set one of her Lord Peter Wimsey novels in an advertising agency. In *Murder Must Advertise* (1933) Wimsey went undercover as a copywriter, a job that allowed him even more latitude for mischievous and creative behavior than his usual Jekyll and Hyde roles as lord of the manor and detective. Sayers used Wimsey's detective work to comment on the shallow dullness of British society life, and pushed the idea farther in using the advertising agency, in which she had once worked, as the setting for this novel. The last twist of the mystery has Wimsey disguised as a harlequin in Sayers's final comment on the role of advertising in society.[14]

Like Marquand and Sayers, Edwin Lefevre, in his 1915 novel *H. R.*, skewered upper-class manners and morals, while satirizing a new form of advertising—the sandwich board—in a highly stylized story of a clerk who organized the sandwich board men into a union. Lefevre's description of sandwich boards as a new medium put the novel into the category of "alternative present" science fiction as well as satire. The "perambulating publicity" of the sandwich boards as well as the attempts at mobilizing and manipulating public desires eerily presaged the introduction of radio broadcasting. The marriage between the hero and the daughter of the leading opponent of advertising proved an early example of how the novels suggested personal solutions to the problems posed by advertising.[15]

Daniel Pope, in *The Making of Modern Advertising*, noted that early advertising smelled of printer's ink.[16] Like the 1950s authors who would tell the story of the Creative Revolution in the advertising industry, several early writers contextualized their fiction in advertising history by writing of the uneasy alliance between advertising and newspaper publishing. In the process they, like those who followed, used their novels to extend current political critiques into popular fiction. Nathaniel C. Fowler, Jr.'s *Gumption: The Progressions of Newson New* (1905) featured a young newspaper publisher's attempts to run an honest paper and reform his community. In the end, aided by his childhood sweetheart, he settles in his Midwestern birthplace to work out the central question of the novel: "Was it right for me to allow the *Lamp* to shed subsidized rays, to take pay for saying good things of those who were willing to pay for printed praise?" by finding both the perfect community and the perfect wife.[17]

In *The Clarion* (1914), Samuel Hopkins Adams, a muckraking newspaper reporter, explored the importance of patent medicines as one of the first advertised products and of newspapers as one of the first media to depend on advertising revenues).[18] The novel's hero, the idealistic son of a patent medicine mogul, returns from Europe to run the local newspaper. The crusading young editor unmasks the hypocrisy of the town business leaders in his paper and then faces their refusal to advertise. Confronting the fact that his father's advertising lied about products, the editor asks: Was newspaper advertising honest or dishonest? The hero decides, "this is a question fraught with financial portent of the honorable journalist."[19] The climax, featuring a typhus epidemic and a worker attack on the newspaper, finds the father switching from selling tonics and "relief" pills that promise abortions to selling health food. The hero solves the problem of advertising by making sure no one influences the newspaper's content and ensuring that the advertised products are good for people. His engagement to the town's beautiful heiress. who tore down her tenement house, scuttled an expensive libel suit against her fiancé, and persuaded the town's leading citizens to advertise in the newspaper at an even higher rate than before, provides a personal solution to his problems and a happy ending. One reviewer wrote of *The Clarion* that there was "nothing distressing about the book," since Adams, "makes us . . . realize that after all it is more a matter of conscience that will set things right and he is explicit in his faith that it is human nature's desire to be honest."[20] Built on newspapers as the first advertising medium and with the critique of advertising solved through a series of personal and professional decisions that left the institution standing, these books presaged later advertising fictions.[21]

The novels highlighted the power of advertising to deceive, but the honest hero never (in the end) profited from the deception. In this way, the novels drew on the structure of the advertising industry itself. Advertising men worked for the good of clients but never profited directly from their efforts—bigger sales brought greater profits for manufacturers, not for the copywriters, who simply went on to sell the next product. In other ways, the lack of individual profitability helped the novels propose individual solutions to larger problems. Once the honest adman (or publisher or public relations specialist) realized that he, personally, was untainted and thus could change, all was right with the world.

One of the best examples of an advertising executive's inability to profit from his efforts came in an early novel that had an advertising copywriter at its center. The satirical novel *The Virgin Queene* (1928), written by former adman Harford Powel, revealed the advertising man's classic dream—to quit the business and write literature.[22] Once freed of advertising, the hero, Barnum Dunn (referring to both P. T. Barnum and Bruce Barton) writes a play that everyone believes is a lost classic by Shakespeare. Because he can't explain that he wrote the play without exposing himself as a trickster, Dunn never profits from his literary masterpiece. The novel posited advertising men as creative and talented—they wrote as well as Shakespeare—and, while Dunn made no money from his play, he suffered no consequences for the hoax. Beating even the advertising industry insiders of the 1950s who quit to write the great American novel, and whose characters do the same, Powel's hero wrote the great Elizabethan drama.

In her insightful reading of *The Virgin Queene* (and other advertising fictions of the 1920s), in *Living Up to the Ads*, Simone Weil Davis noted that Powel's hero, Barnum Dunn, although believing that advertising was full of lies, accepted it in the end as "the finest hoax in the world." Davis wrote that, despite never profiting from their efforts, admen underwent a continuing "crisis of faith."[23] Personal solutions didn't solve the problems with consumption and advertising in the 1920s and, after World War II, novelists took up these issues again.

Advertising Fictions, Advertising Lives

The novel's hero, newly returned from the war, wisecracks about advertising as he undertakes an exciting job in a top agency (or public relations firm or broadcasting network). The hero shows his underlying but genuine sincerity (symbolized by his war service) only to readers and possible lovers. His picaresque journey connects him with a range of sniveling agency executives, sexy secretaries, hack copywriters, insanely demanding clients, and a single honest man. At first he betrays his true nature by deceiving the honest man in the interests of his client, sleeping with a woman not his wife or intended wife, and/or thinking he must practice advertising in a boring or soul-destroying way. Eventually the hero sees the light and is converted to honesty and sincerity by the love of a good woman and the faith of colleagues. The conversion brings with it new domestic and professional beginnings.

These familiar characters and formulaic plot recurred often in postwar advertising novels. The Wouk and Wakeman novels—in their plots, characters, and settings—began the cycle that the novels that followed repeated. Introduced by Wouk (as comedy) and Wakeman (as tragedy), these formulaic elements of plot, character, and realism proved more than coincidence or simply a clever writer's ploy to sell books. In part, the authors shared ideas on how to achieve huge book sales. They sought popularity both reflexively, as former copywriters who tried to reach the largest audience, and democratically, as writers who entered advertising to communicate with ordinary people. In addition, their writing styles, derived from their work in advertising, resembled each other, and their careful reviewing of other advertising novels contributed to the similarity of plots and characters. The similarities among the advertising novels also arose from the authors' overriding interest in the same issue—the role of the individual in a mass society. The distillation of the critique into the story of a particular individual kept the critique itself easily contained while the realism and other formulaic elements made the novels easy to dismiss.

In *The Social Construction of American Realism*, Amy Kaplan brilliantly outlined how critics, from the turn of the century to the present, denigrated realist writers. Much of what Kaplan wrote about the earlier novels also applied to the advertising novels of the 1950s. The two eras, both periods of great social change, shared concerns about mass culture and middle-class status. Kaplan described realism as a dialectical process of reporting and constructing American social life. William Dean Howells, Edith Wharton, and Theodore Dreiser moved beyond passively recording "the world outside" to creating and criticizing "the meanings, representations, and ideologies of their own changing culture."[24] Kaplan noted that this earlier realism represented "not a seamless package of triumphant bourgeois mythology but an anxious and contradictory mode" that articulated and fought against "the growing sense of unreality at the heart of middle class life."[25] The unreality resulted from the developing mass culture, and Kaplan wrote that realistic novels argued with "emergent forms of mass media" from which they gained their power and against which they asserted themselves. In many ways, Kaplan concluded, realism became "a strategy for defining the social position of the author" in a changing world.[26]

Kaplan ended her book with a useful exploration of the unsatisfying conclusions to realist novels. Kaplan wrote that readers see the endings of the novels as retreats into "nostalgia and sentimental or genteel rhetoric which undermine their realistic premises." She concluded her book, "realistic novels have trouble ending because they pose problems they cannot solve, problems that stem from their attempts to imagine and contain social change."[27] The earlier novels and the advertising novels have much in common. Both respond to middle-class status anxieties over the rise of mass culture. The novelists worked to shape reality and used the novels to define their own social positions. And both sets of novels have unsatisfying endings as the authors outlined the necessity for social change without fully understanding how to achieve it.

The conventions of realism became part of the advertising novels' formula for the reasons Kaplan outlined. The novelists counted on their position as insiders for their authority to write about advertising, and their insider status reinforced their right to criticize mass culture. But realism brought a number of problems. By portraying themselves as authentic reporters of what happened in advertising agencies, the authors painted themselves into narrative corners and left themselves open to criticism. An unsophisticated view of realism brought easy dismissal of their social concerns when critics pointed out that the fiction did not faithfully represent the experiences of all those who worked in advertising.[28] Despite the criticisms of inaccuracy from within advertising, many of those working in the industry came to think of themselves, either positively or negatively, in reference to the language, plot, and characters of the novels. And they weren't the only ones so influenced. Just as had the novels of Howells, Wharton, and Dreiser in an earlier moment, the advertising novels changed the way the culture thought about advertising and consumption.

The authors of the advertising novels moved well beyond the simplistic realism of which their critics accused them. The cultural critiques presented by the novels drew complexity from the doubled subject positions held by the authors and their characters. Advertising professionals had always sold to both clients and consumers. In addition, the writers were at once author and object of their own fiction, both intellectuals and cultural workers, the most individualized of artists and cogs in the mass culture industry. The novelists also led double lives with their own stories matching those of their protagonists. A *Saturday Review* discussion of six of the novels noted: "since many of these books are first novels—there is often an almost embarrassing parallel between the authors' careers and those of their protagonists."[29] The novels told the story of an advertising guy who quit to write the great American novel, and they were written by men who had done just that. The contradictions raised by such doubled consciousness remained the subject of their fiction, as they considered their own "social positions."

In *Living Up to the Ads*, Simone Weil Davis described 1920s novels about advertising noting the doubleness of the author's position "marketing themselves and their work to a predominantly middle-class consumer culture, addressing and simultaneously participating in it," and describing how the novels she read set out new "metaphors for personhood" in a consumer culture. Davis wrote of the realism used by the novelists as "an engagement with the mode of the advertisement," because the novelists "use the metaphoric figures of advertisement, display, and consumption to develop the personae and plots they are creating."[30] Kaplan described how the earlier realistic novelists participated in the process whereby "commodification makes all forms of the quotidian perform in what Guy Debord has called the 'society of the spectacle.'" Kaplan wrote that "realism is similarly related to the culture of surveillance, in which the realist participates in the panoptic forces which both control and produce the real world by seeing it without being seen in turn."[31] In the advertising novels of the 1950s, doubleness, surveillance, and spectacle operate as intertwined modes of realism.

The novelists often recreated their own double consciousness, and their feelings of being watched, by pairing the characters of a wavering hero and an honest man of whom the mass culture made a spectacle. Prewar novels presented the advertising (or newspaper) man hero as the honest keeper of the truth. After the war, authors heightened the plots' tension by dividing this character into an uncertain hero and an honest man who resisted advertising's blandishments. The honest man showed the individual's importance in the face of mass culture and, in so doing, influenced the hero to change his life. Wouk's *Aurora Dawn* provided the first conversion narrative of this type when broadcasting moguls dispatched Andrew Reale, the young radio advertising executive (with a name that represented his true nature), to convince a country evangelist to star on a sponsored radio program. The preacher served as the perfect foil for the demanding (and insane) client and joined a painter as the novel's only truthful characters. In the end, the preacher broadcast a sermon against advertising and, inspired by his honesty, Andrew married his true love and moved to New Mexico.

One comic novel and one tragic novel, written in the mid-1950s, took up the same story of the advertising executive changed by contact with a single honest man. Robert Alan Aurthur, in *The Glorification of Al Toolum* (1953), and Gerald Green, in *The Last Angry Man* (1956), used this device as the centerpiece of their novels. In addition, four novels set in the world of public relations—Charles Yale Harrison, *Nobody's Fool* (1948), Jeremy Kirk, *The Build Up Boys* (1951), Al Morgan, *The Great Man* (1955), and Middleton Kieffer, *Pax* (1958)—told variants of the tale, while several others turned the plot upside down by featuring evil heroes. In the simplest version of the story, the mass culture juggernaut met the average man and lost—the honest man didn't change in any way. Advertising, which claimed to affect consumer decisions, was shown as ineffective in altering a particular consumer's behavior. The only change was in the advertising man's personal life.

In *The Glorification of Al Toolum*, an advertising agency chooses a working-class husband and father as the most average man in the country. The young advertising executive offers Al Toolum publicity and new products in exchange for his endorsements.[32] In every possible way Al Toolum would be under constant surveillance as a spectacle. One adman explains:

> You'll be known throughout the whole country as a result of this campaign. . . . Once you're known, once you've been built as a figure of trust, you'll be—I won't say the word used, but rather employed—employed as a combination guinea pig for new products and endorser of old. . . . You see, the manufacturer in this country depends mainly on the average man—the mass market. . . . You as the *most* average man will carry a lot of weight. People will believe you.[33]

The novel proved most compelling when describing the particularity of the Toolum family. The young adman in charge of the campaign becomes disillusioned with the advertising business as he observes Al Toolum's interesting family and Toolum's stubborn refusal to change, despite national attention.

In *The Last Angry Man*, Gerald Green's portrait of a Jewish doctor practicing in a poor New York City neighborhood overwhelms the story of the advertising and broadcasting business. In the novel, a cynical advertising executive, facing a plot against him within the agency and in order to please a difficult client, designs a television show spotlighting a "real" person. He becomes involved with a septuagenarian Jewish doctor, slated to be the subject of the first program, who teaches him the meaning of life.[34] The doctor's lessons are difficult to understand, but the comparison of a "real" life to one led in, and through, the mass media is palpable as the doctor explains:

> Every year I live it seems to me there are less and less useful things to do in the world. Everything seems to be getting pallid, conformed, stereotyped, people as alike each other as one epithelial cell to another. Medicine is one of the few places where nothing you do is ever a waste, a drain, a bore.[35]

Green presented a detailed picture of the an advertising career with its instability, sterile suburban life, bored suburban wife, career girl mistress, shallow businessmen, and the dress, manners, mores, and homes of advertising professionals. Yet the doctor, as a complex and finally inexplicable character, takes over most of the book. The author described the novel as an "autobiographical but not photographic" portrait of his own father. Himself a journalist and television producer, Green struggled to make a statement about mass communications and its relation to individual lives.[36] He wrote that "the most overwhelming fact of the twentieth century is the assault on the public ear and eye, the incessant, relentless avalanche of useless information."[37] The doctor dies before being broadcast "live" from his home. The novel ends with the advertising executive going back to his wife and his suburban life with the belief that creative work, done well, honors the doctor's memory.

The plot of an honest man allowed authors to explore advertising's basic dishonesty, while also considering how to maintain an unobserved individuality in the face of mass culture. The *New York Times* review of *The Glorification of Al Toolum* wrote of its honest man that "the real average American would, indeed must, fight to save himself from the mold into which the machines and the mathematics seek alternately to cozen and to force him," while the *Saturday Review* noted that the honest man "was not a statistic, not a page out of the 'World Almanac,' but a man."[38] The idea of manliness as expressed through individuality, of manliness as the opposite of conformity, became one of the most important of the novels' critiques of mass culture.

Unmanly conformity came to stand for all the other problems with mass culture and the culture of consumption. The novelists often used the intertwined issues of individuality and masculinity as shorthand for the crisis presented by mass culture. The selfishness of an atomistic world with its lack of communal or family life, where everyone is out for him- or herself, remained a big issue, in part because selfishness brought loneliness. In pondering a business decision, one of the heroes muses:

> But the whole idea somehow made him feel a little cheap, and uneasy. He did not understand this, nor why he felt so suddenly alone. And now, for just an instant, he wondered whether it really was worth it, any of it, all of it—down through the years from the very beginning. He wondered this because he had never before felt such acute aloneness.[39]

Life outside the observation of the media, as part of the mass, brings loneliness.

Another hero calls the postwar the "chameleon years," describing his actions as, "Find what they're drinking and drink it. Find what they're thinking and think it. Find what they're wanting and want it."[40] The white male advertising heroes of these novels hate the conformity of always having to agree with their clients and their bosses, agreements that wear on a "real" man. The novels are filled with "yes-men" who agree with their clients and bosses despite their better judgment and to the disgust of the heroes. Wolcott Gibbs noted in his review of *The Hucksters* that "the yes-man motif" had "been established far beyond the strict necessities of satire, if not up to the limit of reader endurance."[41] With the war over, how could men make satisfying lives for themselves and prove their worth?

One book's title came to symbolize postwar worries about conformity and mass culture. Sloan Wilson's *The Man in the Gray Flannel Suit* (1955) represented public fears over the loss of individuality and masculinity. Despite the fact that the hero worked in public relations, the public remembered him as an advertising executive. In an introduction, written twenty-eight years after the novel's publication, Wilson wrote that mistaking his hero for an advertising man was not the only misreading of his first novel. The hero, "attacked as a proponent of materialism, bad thinking or no thinking at all, a guy who would never go on the road with Jack Kerouac or rock around the clock with anybody," really had a different problem. Wilson felt that "the main problem which concerned Tom Rath, the usually forgotten name of the man in gray flannel, was that he felt the world was driving him to become a workaholic in order to succeed at business enough to support his family well."[42] Despite Wilson's protestations, Tom Rath also had to understand how to please his boss, the head of a broadcasting company, who sought favorable publicity. Rath thought of himself as a "yes man":

> I should quit if I don't like what he does, but I want to eat, and so, like a half million other guys in gray flannel suits, I'll always pretend to agree, until I get big enough to be honest without being hurt. That's not being crooked, it's just being smart. . . . How smoothly one becomes, not a cheat, exactly, not really a liar, just a man who'll say anything for pay.[43]

One reviewer noted that the author of *The Man in the Gray Flannel Suit* "probably imagined that there was a deal of moral fiber in this story of the faceless man who, as it turns out, is faceless, not because he is Everyman, but because he is no man at all."[44] Mass culture brought frightening anonymity, a kind of conformity in itself. At the end of the novel, Tom Rath tells his boss the truth about his reservations, gets a less demanding job so he can spend more time with his family, and begins a construction company where he can be his own boss. He becomes more of a man than when he worked for someone else.

For the novelists and the critics, individuality remained intimately tied to the issue of masculinity. The honest characters exuded not only individuality but maleness. One character explains of Al Toolum, Aurthur's "average man," that "he's a man, a real man with all the complexities of a man. When you come in contact with him, he surprises you by showing that the so-called average standards are a minor part of his make-up."[45] The novels often featured emasculating women who sought to make men either conform to boring business or domestic strictures or serve their evil ends. The presence of a number of evil heroines among the advertising novels also highlighted the identification of individuality and honesty with masculinity.[46]

The novels asked how a man can retain his individuality in an age of mass consumption. These novelists believed the advertising presented an instructive and important case study that would help answer that question. In *The Hot Half Hour* (1958), Robert L. Foreman wrote that Madison Avenue was "a lot of different people who come from all sorts of different places and make widely different salaries and drink very different brands of liquor. But often in their lives—many times a day in fact—they all act exactly alike" because "they're beset by the same worries and fears and maybes, all of which are set in motion by the same thing—the Ad Game."[47] The authors compulsively replayed the same situations, tinkering with details, to find a way out of the conundrum that they, as advertising professionals, had been first to observe. Mass culture, along with its benefits, brought fearful consequences.

Despite, or perhaps because of, the important questions raised, the advertising industry as well as literary critics dismissed this critique by focusing on a simplistic view of realism and by ignoring the doubleness built into the novels' structures and context. The criticism of the novels when they were published dismissed any possibility that the authors presented a coherent critique of mass culture and instead focused on the novels' sameness and therefore lack of imagination, and whether they accurately portrayed or were unfair to the advertising industry. To discredit the authors' concerns, critics explained that "real" advertising men were not like those in the novels but were, in fact, nice, ordinary guys doing an honest job. Writings by and about advertising professionals, as well as book reviews, focused on the veracity of the details or the novels' tendency to exaggerate, rather than the overall truth of the portrait, as the mass culture industry worked to protect itself from criticism. One of the authors, Al Morgan, who penned *The Great Man* (1955), wrote in a review of James Kelly's *The Insider* (1958):

> Along with Abraham Lincoln's boyhood, infantry life in the South Pacific, and the last days of Pompeii, the expense-account, charcoal-gray world of Madison Avenue has been completely documented by a long succession of good, bad, and indifferent writers. It's been open season on the admen, "sincere" has become a dirty word, and working for an advertising agency is a close second to playing piano in a bawdy house.[48]

Morgan criticized the repetitive and formulaic quality of the novels, made fun of their lack of realism, and attacked their negative view of advertising but he never took up the novels' ideas about mass culture or the problems with advertising.

Despite rejecting the ad novels' view, many in the industry came to think of themselves in terms, characters, and dialogue from the novels. With advertising newly entrenched as the "language" of capitalism in the postwar period, and the advertising industry as the teacher of consumption and mass culture, career guides suggested that bright young men, and a few women, found advertising an interesting and creative profession.[49] One of the textbooks my mother used in her advertising courses at Pennsylvania State University between 1949 and 1952 explained that

> Although motion pictures, short stories, and books often portray the modern advertising agency or department as something of a glamorous madhouse, where sudden inspiration is all that is needed to evolve a million-dollar idea and where a day's work is likely to be no more laborious than dashing off a piece of copy or passing judgment on some artwork, actual investigation seldom reveals such dramatic elements. Advertising is a business, just as any other trade or profession is a business.[50]

In describing itself to job seekers, the industry presented advertising in novelistic and filmic terms and also rejected that view. Life in advertising agencies in the postwar period showed an intensification of the uncertainty and bustle of the 1920s agencies Marquand described, and presaged the anxiety of those advertising executives whom sociologist Michael Schudson visited in the 1970s.[51] The novels reflected the tensions involved in advertising as a profession and, in turn, supplied a way to think about the cultural service advertising workers undertook.

The job application essays and internal publications of the J. Walter Thompson agency (JWT), a large shop headquartered in New York City, illustrate the insecurity of a creative person's job with many firings (and subsequent hirings to refill positions). The personnel files show that those who went to work in the creative side of advertising had an interest in people, a love of New York City, and a yearning to be writers.[52] Internal publications reinforced the stereotypes the novelists drew on: advertising men sailed, renovated their houses, and smoked cigarettes. Research and sales departments remained important, to the despair of the "creatives," and television loomed as an important new player adding complexity to already difficult lives. And many of the copywriters included novel writing among their pastimes, in both their application essays and their interviews with the company newsletter.[53]

The J. Walter Thompson newsletters both captured and directly refuted the advertising novels' portrait of advertising agencies and their employees. Despite the clear similarities between the lives reported in the company newsletter and those depicted in the novels, one short bio noted:

> If the world of advertising bore a passing resemblance to that gilded jungle smoked up by current novels and columns, Storrs Haynes would shortly find himself on the Rules Committee's blood-stained carpet. The charges would be devastating: "Not a cliché all week, Haynes!" . . . "Where's your gold Dunhill lighter?" . . . "You never shout!" . . . Where's that attaché case?" . . . "Haynes, *turn in your gray flannel suit*!" . . . Storrs manages . . . without the celebrated techniques of fictional advertising men.[54]

The newsletter, and other commentators, most often took on the cliché that all thwarted advertising copywriters worked on novels in their spare time. The *New York Herald Tribune* described one JWT copywriter as different: "You know the popular conception: He's writing about Frabjous Krispies for his pocketbook but here are tears in his beard. His heart, you see, is with that novel in his desk drawer—or in his den in that fifteen-room modern Colonial in Westport." This copywriter, the article told readers, found that writing advertising "gives him the overwhelming satisfaction that came to Thomas Wolfe when he filled an orange crate with part of one of his novels," and that he described his slogans "with the reverence of a poet who has just been advised that his works will be included in the 'Oxford Book of English Verse.' "[55] So the article proclaimed that advertising men weren't novelists, but then described the rewards of an advertising career in terms used by fiction writers.

Critics often compared copywriters to characters in the advertising novels or to the novelists themselves. While the comparisons began negatively—the characters were very different from "real" admen—they often ended by pointing out that the advertising men behaved exactly as the novelists depicted them. Perhaps the best example of denying the stereotype while simultaneously applying it appeared in 1948, when the newsletter called one executive "a shining refutation of 'The Hucksters' " who "occupies his leisure time writing novels."[56]

Critics found Wakeman's title, *The Hucksters*, the most troubling aspect of the novel, and the least realistic. A 1958 *Advertising Age* article, "Novels of Past Decade Paint Lurid Ad World," noted the similarity of characters and plots across the novels and that "however admirable the adman hero was or became, from this book on, admen have been known as hucksters, a label with dubious connotations."[57] A later article in *Advertising Age*, "Is It True What They Say About Admen?" claimed the problems started with Wakeman because his novel "set the tone for the advertising novel." The problem was that "Mr. Wakeman, an ex-adman, not only coined a word that has stuck to the industry," but a "flock of advertising novels written and published in the last 10 years" followed Wakeman in portraying advertising as "cut-throat, high-pressure, amoral."[58] The article continued that "while there may be likeable admen in novels, there is never any question about the advertising business itself being anything but a debasing and basically dishonest way to make a living," and noted that "advertising industry leaders who are dismayed at this representation of their trade" should realize that the novels were written, not by "by outsiders with an axe to grind" but by "former tillers of the Madison Avenue soil—or even by current members of the industry."[59]

In 1956, James Kelly, later author of *The Insider* (1958), a novel that presented one of the most evil of the advertising antiheroes, defended his business (he was a vice president of Compton Advertising) in an article in the *New York Times*. Kelly wrote that many critics indicted advertising as "America's pagan religion," but noted that "advertising is not a hungry predator on the prowl nor is it a fey branch of show business; it is an integral part of society and should be judged as such."[60] At once, Kelly showed his belief in the basic goodness of advertising and illustrated the industry's growing concern about criticism from outside, particularly from the social scientists who wrote in the popular press. The novelists worried about the advertising industry while attempting to set the terms for how they saw themselves. But the advertising industry believed that a simplistic attack on the realism and repetition of the novels could contain the critique expressed by the novelists. When eminent social scientists and other intellectuals took up the same critiques, the industry became more anxious.

Novelists as Intellectuals

Why were so many novels set in advertising agencies published between 1946 and 1960? The reinvigorated culture of consumption and the growth of mass media, both brought by postwar prosperity, surely served as the main impetus. These novelists joined a range of commentators who reconsidered the impact of mass culture on American life after the war. The authors participated in at least four often related intellectual streams that flowed through the 1950s. A radical critique of mass culture came from an increasingly splintered Left, principally the Frankfurt School and a loosely tied group of followers who came to be called the New York Intellectuals. Another allied group of best-selling social scientists, whose work has been best explored by Daniel Horowitz in *The Anxieties of Affluence*, denounced an increased emphasis on consumption. The Beats mounted a cultural critique of conformity through art, literature, and lifestyle. Finally, businessmen (according to Thomas Frank in *The Conquest of Cool*) criticized the stifling atmosphere of American corporations as antithetical to the creativity needed to revitalize the economy. The authors of popular advertising novels combined the concerns expressed in the other critiques with their own firsthand knowledge of the advertising industry to produce accessible fictional appraisals of culture and society.

On the surface, the novelists shared the least with the New York Intellectuals. Neil Jumonville, in his excellent analysis of the group, *Critical Crossings: The New York Intellectuals in Postwar America*, described them as "the mid-century's most prominent group of generalist cultural critics" noting that they advocated a "highbrow socialism divorced from the common people, a radicalism for intellectuals" and concluded that "the group's constant hostility to populist politics and mass culture is hardly unusual: by nature, most intellectuals are antipopulists, especially in the realm of culture."[61] Appearing in a popular, mass-cultural form—several of the advertising novels were best-sellers and even more were Book-of-the-Month Club selections—at first glance, the advertising novels seemed a likely target of the New York Intellectuals, not companion critiques. Yet, while no one at the time thought of them as "intellectuals," advertising novelists took up two of the New York Intellectuals' main concerns, the totalizing and negative effect of mass culture and the contested definition of an intellectual, and presented them in a popular form.

Dwight MacDonald, the writer of the time who most directly addressed mass culture, saw it, as historian Alan Wald wrote, as "a one way, monolithic medium of indoctrination."[62] MacDonald's most important statement of his thinking appeared in an essay, "A Theory of Mass Culture," published in the 1957 anthology *Mass Culture: The Popular Arts in America*,. For this essay, MacDonald reworked a 1944 article in *Politics* and changed the title (from Popular Culture to Mass Culture). According to his biographer, the changes reflected a changed political message as well. Michael Wreszin noted that MacDonald began reworking the essay in 1952, "removing its explicit and provocative radical message and making it into a piece of cultural criticism with decidedly conservative implications."[63]

Agreeing with the intellectuals of the Frankfurt School, MacDonald wrote that "Mass Culture is imposed from above. It is fabricated by technicians hired by businessmen; its audiences are passive consumers, their participation limited to the choice between buying and not buying."[64] Using the example of *Life* magazine, with its jumble of articles and advertising on a range of subjects from serious to silly, MacDonald concluded that mass culture, "mixes and scrambles everything together, producing what might be called homogenized culture. . . . Mass Culture is very, very democratic: it absolutely refuses to discriminate against, or between, anything or anybody. All is grist to its mill, and all comes out finely ground indeed."[65] MacDonald found mass culture a "manufactured commodity," which "tends always downward, toward cheapness—and so standardization—of production."[66] The essay presented mass culture as all-encompassing, routinized, tied to consumption, and manipulative, with MacDonald's critique located politically somewhere between his 1940s radicalism and the neoconservatism of his later views. In almost every particular, the novels set in advertising agencies had the same perspective.[67]

Because they made the most exaggerated claims, comic science fiction novels best presented advertising, and consumption, as totalizing tools of control. Fiction with more literary pretensions may have made these points more subtly, but the work of Frederik Pohl and C. M. Kornbluth simultaneously depicted and satirized the idea of advertising and consumption as all-encompassing, thus showing Pohl and Kornbluth as complex thinkers about the current moment. The *Herald Tribune* reviewer of Pohl and Kornbluth's science fiction novel *The Space Merchants* wrote that "Whether you want entertainment or sharp social criticism, don't miss this!"[68] Pohl and Kornbluth's *The Space Merchants* (1952) and Pohl's *The Merchants' War* (1984) illustrated worlds in which advertising became a religion, a way of seeing the world. Through overdrawn plots and situations, the authors ridiculed the concerns of other intellectuals as they explored them. In the end, Pohl and Kornbluth presented the only radical alternative to advertising that appeared in the 1950s.

Part of the same radical political groups and activities as the New York Intellectuals, Pohl and Kornbluth (beginning writers working at the edges of publishing) retained a Left-leaning political critique that made the ending of their novel unlike any of the others. They collaborated on *The Space Merchants*, the story of a "copysmith, star class" assigned to the Venus account. Because of his interest in the "conscies" (radical resistors, "Conservationists" who objected to the hegemony of the advertising agencies), the hero gets busted to lowly consumer status. Pohl and Kornbluth made advertised products physically addictive to underline the impossibility of escaping advertising's thrall and to satirize those, like MacDonald, who felt ordinary consumers had no choices. They explained that each product sample contained a habit-forming chemical so that "after ten weeks the customer is hooked for life." The costliness of the cure for the addiction made it easier for the consumer to drink the coffee substitute, "three cups with every meal and a pot beside his bed at night, just as it says on the jar," than be cured of his addiction to it.[69] The copywriter hero, forced to take his turn as a consumer, thinks:

> I was becoming the kind of consumer we used to love. Think about smoking, think about Starrs, light a Starr. Light a Starr, think about Popsie, get a squirt. Get a squirt, think about Crunchies, buy a box. Buy a box, think about smoking, light a Starr. And at every step roll out the words of praise that had been dinned into you through your eyes and ears and pores.[70]

In the future, advertising agencies controlled not only individual consumers but entire economies. When taking over Venus, the agency "hoped to repeat on an enormously magnified scale" their success organizing "all of India into a single giant cartel, with every last woven basket and iridium ingot and caddy of opium it produced sold through Fowler Schocken advertising."[71] Yet Pohl and Kornbluth presented the only political solution to the problems of mass consumption among the intellectuals of the 1950s or the advertising novelists. Their novel ends with the hero on his way to Venus to help lead the Conscie Revolution. In the 1984 sequel, *The Merchants' War*, another copywriter hero falls in love with a Venutian revolutionary and helps bring the revolution back to earth, using advertising techniques for good rather than evil.[72]

What's an intellectual to do? Is an intellectual critique possible in a totalizing culture of consumption? Historians have noted that the New York Intellectuals found the role of the intellectual in society one of the most pressing they addressed.[73] The novelists shared an interest in the role of the culture broker, the intellectual, from inside mass culture. If the New York Intellectuals took an "outsider" position, the advertising professionals found themselves "insiders" with each position holding its own contradictions. The New York Intellectuals concluded that only outsiders could be intellectuals, at least in part because they never could break into the mass culture industry they critiqued. But the roads that brought both intellectuals and novelists to an interest in the roles they played were very similar.[74]

Reviewing three books about the New York Intellectuals, Michael Denning focused on the idea of how those working during the 1950s, and the historians who wrote about them, defined intellectual work. Denning found both definitions too narrow. Referring to Alan Wald's *The New York Intellectuals* (1987), Denning wrote that to follow Wald in redeeming "the promise of socialist intellectuals first augured in the writings of Marx and Engels," what was needed was not only "to reconstruct the political legacy of the anti-Stalinist left intellectuals, but to map the political terrain of that vast culture industry in which they, and we, find ourselves."[75] Denning urged, in advance of his own book, *The Culture Front* (1997), a move from intellectual history to cultural history, for the inclusion of workers in the mass culture industry as taking part in the radical critiques offered by more conventional, leftist "intellectuals."[76] The self-reflectivity of the advertising novels, where the main task of heroes and authors becomes to understand their intellectual place, is mirrored in the work of the more traditional intellectuals of the time and those who wrote about them later.

Like Michael Denning, historian Daniel Horowitz, in *The Anxieties of Affluence: Critiques of American Consumer Culture, 1939–1979*, sought to expand the ways historians thought about the postwar intellectual sphere. For example, in his analysis of postwar intellectual history, Horowitz included popular nonfiction writers, many taking up the same issues as the advertising novelists and New York Intellectuals. Horowitz wrote that David Riesman's *The Lonely Crowd* (1950), David Potter's *People of Plenty* (1954), Vance Packard's *The Hidden Persuaders* (1957), John Kenneth Galbraith's *Affluent Society* (1958), and Betty Friedan's *The Feminine Mystique* (1963) identified "problems that connected affluence with a series of larger issues" including "the spread of mass culture" and "the implications for politics of a world that seemed increasingly privatized and controlled."[77] The limitations of the critique outlined in these popular books also interested Horowitz. He wrote that, while talking about affluence, the authors ignored or downplayed poverty, in part because they focused on the middle class and in part because they ignored race. The advertising novelists shared the concerns and blind spots of these "critiques from within" as Horowitz termed them.

The ad novelists displayed a generalized anxiety over the affluence of postwar America in a subset of novels featuring evil antiheroes. Less successful as fiction than the novels with likeable heroes—who served as sympathetic reader-surrogates thrust into the belly of the consumption beast—these anti-heroes represented fears about the effects of advertising and consumption on individual lives. Many of the novels contrasted the self-sacrifice of World War II culture with the selfishness of postwar consumption. The evil heroes directly rejected the wartime experience rather than, as the sympathetic heroes did, remembering it nostalgically.

Two of the earliest novels in this sample featured nasty main characters and also emphasized the importance of the war to both plot and ideology. Both published in 1946, Arkady Leokum's *Please Send Me, Absolutely Free* and Fielden Farrington's *The Big Noise* used characters' negative reactions to the war as markers of their insincerity.[78] Leokum's novel, set during the war, ends with an advertising executive refusing an ad campaign that is too hard on the Germans, Italians, and Japanese because they were future clients. The hero's disgust with this cold-blooded approach shows his conversion to sincerity. Despite his late in the novel reconsideration, Leokum's vain, self-centered hero may have been, according to the *New Yorker*, "much more of a heel than the author apparently suspects."[79] The *Saturday Review* noted the book's "basically negative quality" and concluded, "it is difficult for a reader to like a subject or a set of characters when the author obviously has contempt for them."[80] In contrast, the evil hero of *The Big Noise* begins by regarding the war as no more than a radio play and ends with that conceit being broadcast. The author presented the hero as irredeemably loathsome from his introduction as someone who rejoiced in his 4F designation as psychologically unfit to serve.[81] The comparison between the sacrifice of war and the self-indulgence of consumption, exemplified by the radio and advertising businesses, could not be clearer. One character accosted the radio director:

> I've come to the conclusion that you're the most complete heel I've ever seen and I've spent my life in a racket that breeds heels. There isn't really anything a man can call you. A son of a bitch? Hell, I've heard reasonably decent people called that. I don't like to put you in their class. It's a sad commentary on the state of the world that, with all the shooting and killing that goes on today, it's still illegal to take a shot at a guy like you.[82]

Like Leokum, Farrington, a radio writer, used the nastiness of the people involved in advertising and their selfishness in wartime to comment on the industry. One of Leokum's characters sums up the attitude of both novels by saying, "The trouble with working in advertising . . . is that it keeps body and soul apart."[83]

A later novel, *A Twist of Lemon* (1958) by Edward Stephens, presents an unsympathetic hero who turns out to be a nice guy misled by the glitter of Madison Avenue and the lure of competition and consumption. The novel painstakingly details an education in advertising and the various dirty tricks on what the dust jacket called a "young man's desperate scramble up the cold and treacherous plate-glass cliffs of Madison Avenue." The surprise ending shows the top-level advertising executives as having been caring and interested mentors, long ignored by the hero. One of them explains: "I think I am helping our clients, which is what I am getting paid for, and I think I am helping the people whom I help to persuade to use our clients' products."[84] Saved by the boss and his secretary/lover, the hero decides that "advertising was his life" because "he loved the thought of finding a good product and advertising it properly and conscientiously to people who had never before heard of it or who had never before heard of it properly, so they felt they should buy it." The problem was "the trapped, imprisoned, unnatural feeling of living out his life seventeen stories above Madison Avenue."[85] Willoughby, his lover, and their child born without his knowledge leave the city to go to Phoenix where he will work in a smaller agency.[86] In an ending reminiscent of the prewar advertising novels, *A Twist of Lemon* implied that advertising, like its hero, is basically good-hearted but often led astray by the bright lights of the big city. The problems faced by the advertising men, the forces that made them evil, could be fought by appealing to their innate morality, and even the nastiest hero, representing the affluence and conformity of mass culture, could be redeemed.

Among the best-selling nonfiction authors, Vance Packard most directly addressed advertising as dishonest and manipulative in his *The Hidden Persuaders* (1957). Packard raised concerns about new forms of psychological insight into consumer desires—so-called motivational research—as an unfair weapon taken up by the powerful advertising industry. He concluded that "the most serious offense many of the depth manipulators commit . . . is that they try to invade the privacy of our minds."[87] But Packard showed a grudging respect for his advertising adversaries, writing "the persuaders themselves, in their soul-searching, are at times exceptionally articulate in expressing their apprehensions and in admitting some of their practices are a 'little cold-blooded.' "[88]

In many ways, Packard's ideas resembled those of the New York Intellectuals, with advertising and consumption totalizing and inescapable evils. In a similar way, science fiction presented the best counterpart to Packard's work, just as *The Space Merchants* expressed many of Dwight MacDonald's ideas. Shepherd Mead's *The Big Ball of Wax* clearly shared Packard's worries about the insidious new motivational research, which borrowed its methodology from psychology. Mead depicted advertising as maintaining societal control, with the help of techniques borrowed from religion, while the small resistance was nutty, and the future was more of the same. An advertising executive and recent best-selling author of *How to Succeed in Business Without Really Trying* (1952), Mead's novel told the story of the ultimate advertising technique, discovered by a religious group, that gave consumers virtual experiences through neurological links. Churchgoers plugged into headsets that provided them with a pleasurable, and addicting, experience. The advertising executive hero wrestles the technique from the church and brings it to his advertising agency to create "the best of all possible worlds," where "we never have to worry about *selling* anything any more."[89] Mead recapitulated the history of advertising, as Packard explained it in *The Hidden Persuaders*. In *The Big Ball of Wax*, marketing began by giving consumers what they wanted, as determined by extensive surveying:

> Haven't we got guys walkin' around with surveys . . . all over the whole country, seven days a week? What flavor pudding do they want? What color washing powder? What kinda television programs, what kinda commercials? Is there a single thing we don't check with 'em?[90]

And moved to creating demand for particular products through brainwashing consumers.

Mead's satire put the ideas about the problems of such hidden persuasion in the mouths of "dangerous crackpots" who challenged advertising's power over all aspects of life in this future world. The radicals worried that "notch by notch . . . thinking was decreasing, self-expression dying out. Year by year we've become more passive . . . the individual is dying, the mass is rising. And freedom of thought is going."[91] In his science fiction novel, Mead presented advertising as destined to get worse with no possibility of escape, using words and ideas similar to those of both Dwight MacDonald and Vance Packard.

Like their nonfiction counterparts, the novelists thought warnings about the excesses of consumers and advertisers could lead to what Horowitz named a "new moralism" that could save the nation from the dangers of consumption and mass culture. David Potter, in *People of Plenty: Economic Abundance and the American Character* (1954), found abundance a defining characteristic of the "American character" and at once a blessing and a curse. The novelists shared Potter's almost moralistic aversion to advertising and consumption and portrayed advertising as out of control and threatening to individuality, at the same time as they appreciated affluence after wartime hardships.[92]

Potter tied advertising and consumption together. He remained interested in how a citizen was "educated to perform his role as a consumer, especially as a consumer of goods for which he feels no impulse or need," and believed that advertising became the institution "for instilling new needs, for training people to act as consumers, for altering men's values, and thus for hastening their adjustment to potential abundance" so that advertising was "distinctively the institution of abundance."[93] Advertising enabled the culture "to exalt the materialistic virtues of consumption."[94] He dismissed the advertising novels themselves as a form of criticism, writing:

> The excesses of advertising and of advertising men have been a favorite theme for a full quorum of modern satirists, cynics, and Jeremiahs. From the patent-medicine exposes in the early years of the century to the latest version of *The Hucksters*, advertising men have incurred fairly constant attack—their unscrupulous natures and their stomach ulcers being equally celebrated.[95]

Potter maintained that an examination of "advertising as an institution" comparable to school and church, rather than attacks on advertising men themselves, had been ignored by social scientists, historians, and other critics. But several of the advertising novels took up Potter's interest in the connection between abundance and advertising.

Despite his dismissal of them as critiques, the advertising novels went farther than Potter in condemning consumption as ultimately empty. Eric Hodgins, who had a career at Time-Life, notably as the publisher of *Fortune* magazine, wrote two satirical novels that critiqued the middle-class obsession with consumption. *Mr. Blandings Builds His Dream House* (1946) and *Blandings' Way* (1950) describe an advertising executive who builds a house in Connecticut and leaves advertising for a more meaningful life in the country but, in the end, gives up and moves back to the city.

The novels detail the domestic life of an advertising man, one who is preternaturally attuned to the status implications of consumption. In one long passage from the beginning of *Mr. Blandings Builds His Dream House*, Hodgins details the meaning of a suburban home to an advertising executive.

> When Mr. Blandings, fresh out of Yale, landed his first job with an advertising agency . . . he had taken a little one-room-and-bath apartment for himself in the East Thirties. When, after a few years of menial writing . . . he had permitted himself to expand to two rooms, and moved to the East Forties. He had married not long after that; as newlyweds, Mr. and Mrs. Blandings took up quarters in the East Fifties. When their first baby arrived, they skipped fifteen blocks in one bold leap and moved to the East Seventies. There they stayed.

Mr. Blandings succeeds in advertising, being "lucky enough to hit upon a three-word slogan for a laxative account" and "the happy agency" rewards him "with several handsome bonuses," and raises "since the three portentous words had first occurred to him." Mr. Blandings "loathed his calling with a deep, passionate intensity, but . . . if a business of his own did not tempt him, something that he and his friends called "the good life" did." As Hodgins notes, "Mr. and Mrs. Blandings realized that not only could they now afford to expand their modest horizons, but that, in the eyes of their professional colleagues, they could not afford not to."[96]

The rest of the novel outlines exactly how Mr. Blandings bought a tumbledown farmhouse and precisely how much he spends in renovations. The humor in the novel comes from the minute descriptions of products and services he purchases and in his inability ever to succeed in his plans. Mr. Blandings, like the advertising men on whom he is based, desperately seeks to understand living with what Potter called "abundance" and how to make that abundance meaningful. The review in *Atlantic Monthly* noted that the novel was "funny and you laugh and laugh, but all the while your pocketbook bleeds in sympathy with theirs. It is most horribly true."[97] In fact, many of the advertising men whose lives are detailed in the J. Walter Thompson Archives remodeled old houses. In 1950, in the company newsletter, one copywriter said he "ran Mr. Blandings a close second," while another, in 1957, wrote that he lived in a "'it-keeps-me-doing-it-myself' Westport ranch house."[98]

In *Blandings' Way*, Hodgins "turned serious" and explored his hero's attempt to find meaning in his life.[99] Blandings seeks "something to do in my personal life that's going to help me compensate for what I have to do in my professional life" and so left advertising to run a country newspaper. Blandings's boss notes:

> the terrible restlessness that was likely to strike a writer of advertising copy in his late thirties or early forties; a restlessness that made him yearn to snap the gold cords of salaries and bonuses and profit-sharings and stock dividends and find, by some means, in some obscure place or bizarre fashion, something he thought would be simpler and more rewarding.[100]

One reviewer noted that the novel "puts a crucial personal (and social) question out where some people may trip over it, and think about it, and probably despair over it in a business-like way, as does Mr. Blandings."[101] But most reviews ridiculed Blandings's attempt to find a more meaningful life, perhaps because the humor of the novel overwhelms its attempt to explore what had become the familiar effort of the advertising novel hero to escape advertising and a life based on consumption. The *New Yorker* wrote that the novel ended with Blandings's "resignation to becoming middle-aged and making lots more money."[102]

The New York Intellectuals, nonfiction popular writers, and advertising novelists agreed that conformity was one of the main dangers of mass culture.[103] The advertising industry became known as a stronghold of conformity, and even more as home to the "other-directed" personalities described by David Riesman in *The Lonely Crowd.* As the ultimate salesmen, advertising men had to please not only difficult clients and demanding bosses, but also finicky consumers. Consumers had similar problems. Blandings, as well as the brainwashed consumers depicted in *The Space Merchants* and *The Big Ball of Wax*, couldn't express themselves as individuals in a world defined by artificial and identical products. Advertising created consumers who eagerly bought the same products, who embraced conformity as an identity. One other group also critiqued conformity. Historian Lizabeth Cohen identified the Beat writers as making a cultural critique of consumption, as serving as "cultural rebels" in the 1950s.[104] The Beats believed that mass consumption, as aided by advertising, threatened individuality.

While Riesman scientifically outlined a personality type that conformed, the Beat writers laid out an emotional and cultural critique of conformity. Advocating a spontaneous and improvised individualism, the Beats rebelled against a "conformist, bourgeois society."[105] In his provocative *Countering the Counterculture: Rereading Postwar American Dissent from Jack Kerouac to Tomás Rivera*, Manuel Luis Martínez showed that the kind of individualism advocated by the Beats became "reactionary" by the 1960s and identified the fear of conformity as related to white masculine fears of the incipient feminist and civil rights movements.[106]

The advertising novels also presented white masculine hysteria about difference as a foundation of the advertising world. The idea that advertising and public relations men wore gray flannel suits highlighted a particular form of conformity called for by advertising. Bosses and clients wanted to work with those who looked and thought like them. Historians have traced this industry attitude back to at least the 1920s.[107] George Panetta's 1957 comic novel *Viva Madison Avenue!* illustrated the clash between WASPs and the few Italian Americans then working in advertising. Panetta, himself an advertising executive, wrote this tongue-in-cheek account of two Italian American advertising men as if his heroes embodied all the stereotypes Anglo-Saxons (as the Italian Americans called them in the novel) had of them. In return, the heroes skewer the conformity—in ideas, dress, lives, and backgrounds—of the advertising industry. The ethnicities represented also have class inflections since the heroes' humor comes from maintaining working-class sensibilities in a determinedly upper-middle-class milieu. The heroes describe themselves:

> Me and Joe worked in a big advertising agency, and after we worked there a couple of years, they find out we were worse than Italians: we were Italians who were never going to move to Westchester or Connecticut no matter what happened and from that time on it was us against the Anglo-Saxons. . . . We were small and dark, and even though we changed our socks and underwear every day (a concession to our wives, not the Anglo-Saxons) . . . at Lowell & Lynch everybody noticed us, looking like we looked and being what we were, and it annoyed them because they couldn't believe what they saw.[108]

Viva Madison Avenue! had no plot, but proceeded through a series of episodes based on the contrast between the heroes and everyone else who worked at the agency. At the end of the book, Panetta returned to the issue of masculinity with a final comparison:

> The Anglo-Saxons have very little blood, and when they don't go to bed with their wives, they make up for it by going to musical comedies, or, if there's snow in Vermont, by going skiing. But not me and Joe. When we don't go to bed with our wives (for one reason or another: sometimes by accident Joe goes to sleep under the bed, sometimes his wife is scared; sometimes my wife is reading *Good Housekeeping*, sometimes I'm scared), we go all over town looking at girls and hoping that one of them will look back at us and do with us what our wives didn't do.[109]

One review noted that a "would-be reader" might expect "another expose of the Grey Flannel Suited, Exurbanite Great Man who has become almost as universal a target today as, say, the Nazi of the 1940s. Nothing could be farther from the truth."[110] Another review compared *Viva Madison Avenue!* with other advertising novels: "From deep in the heart of Advertising-land comes this tale of liquor and lubricity which, intertwined, have become the insigne of the advertising novel. But this time there is a kicker."[111] Panetta's critique of the advertising industry and the conformity of business culture became more pointed through the use of humor.

The critique of conformity came not only from outside but from within the business community. In *The Conquest of Cool: Business Culture, Counterculture, and the Rise of Hip Consumerism*, Thomas Frank described the movement within the advertising industry that came to be called the Creative Revolution. Frank contended that creativity and the hip attitude adopted by advertising in the 1960s was not a reaction to or cooptation of the counterculture, but was a preceding, overlapping, and continuing criticism from within advertising and business of 1950s conformity and consumption. The advertising novelists proved Frank's point that, by the late 1950s, advertising and business leaders criticized their own industries for "creative dullness," a critique "that had much in common with the critique of mass society which gave rise to the counterculture." Frank noted that, by the 1960s, the counterculture and the corporate world both "deplored conformity, distrusted routine, and encouraged resistance to established power."[112]

In his second novel about advertising, *The Admen* (1958), Shepherd Mead detailed the conformist form of advertising to which Frank alluded and the creative possibilities that lay ahead as part of the Creative Revolution. The young hero wanders through the world of advertising, testing his ideas against those of other characters. In an interior monologue, the hero muses that his boss "stood for all the things he hoped advertising had outgrown, the old-line hard sell, the big block-letter headlines, the heavy hand." He thinks his own approach is "crisp and frank," using "good and striking art, to delight and intrigue as far as possible, to establish a position for a product by the quality of its advertising" noting finally that "this was as far from [the boss's] approach as you could get."[113]

The Admen also showed that the advertising industry sought its own solutions to this crisis of conformity. As Mead put it, everyone in advertising had "an escape plan," including those who "had bought islands, studied farming, learned about fish liver oil, started direct-mail advertising companies, begun novels, plays and children's books, learned metal working and gone to postgraduate night school for teaching degrees." The narrator noted that "not one in fifty would escape; most didn't really want to, but they had to believe that the door was real. A room with a door was always better than a room without one, even if you never used it."[114] The advertising men, as canaries in the mineshaft, had seen the stultifying nature of the conformist business culture and wanted out. Some of the ad novels showed advertising executives escaping by running away, but others became creative and fought the old-fashioned guardians of boring advertising to do interesting and fulfilling ads.

Many historians have traced the beginnings of the so-called Creative Revolution to William Bernbach, whom Frank called "at once a hard-headed adman and one of postwar consumerism's most trenchant critics, Madison Avenue's answer to Vance Packard."[115] A Jewish immigrant, whose father was a designer of women's clothes, as well as a graduate of public school and New York University, Bernbach was the ultimate Madison Avenue outsider. Bernbach's advertisements—created within the agency he founded in 1949 (Doyle, Dane, Bernbach; DDB)—featured flashes of brilliance, simplicity, and photographs, with the most famous being the Volkswagen campaign begun in 1959.[116] The creative revolution affected not only the advertising itself but also the agency's relationship with clients. In an interview, Bernbach asserted that "we don't permit any client to give us ground rules. We think it's bad for the client," and went on to say:

> I can tell you that a very, very big prospect once said to me, "What would you say, Bill, if you were told exactly where to put the logo

> and what size it would be." I had over $10,000,000 riding on my answer, and I said, "I would say we are the wrong agency for you." Now, in the long run I think this makes for a very healthy agency because we preserve our point of view. It lets us do the kind of creative work we really believe in and not prostitute that talent for that 15%.[117]

So, when advertising novelists looked for a way out for their heroes, they had the model of a creative agency, like DDB, where the advertising men ruled the clients and did interesting work.

Frank carefully outlined the limitations of the critique offered by the Creative Revolution and, by extension, that by the advertising novels. Frank pointed out that "for the new Madison Avenue, the solution to the problems of consumer society was—more consuming."[118] Indeed, just as Frank might have predicted, the endings of the advertising novels remained unsatisfying as critiques. Despite their misgivings, the advertising guys often chose to do advertising "the right way," so the solution to their problems was more advertising. With the exception of *The Space Merchants*, no novel offered a criticism of the larger system of which advertising was a part.

In the novels, the heroes must find a way to be creative within the boundaries offered by advertising.[119] Harold Livingston, in *The Detroiters* (1958), set a familiar advertising novel scenario in the automobile industry. A returned veteran takes a job with a Detroit agency tyrannized by its biggest client, the head of Coronado Motors Corporation. In a telling passage, the client expresses his inflexibility, "We in the advertising business . . . must be extremely cautious. Each word of Coronado copy must be chiseled in stone. It must convey the meaning *we* wish, no other."[120]

The hero, David Manning, a cynical heel at the beginning of the book, by the end finds redemption in creative advertising. Manning works, throughout, within the demands of the automobile industry, where "success was not measured by whimsical sales graphs, or vague figures of factory production. Automobile sales could be seen, heard, touched," and where ad agencies needed to remember that "we're trying to sell cars, not originality. This is an advertising agency, not a creative arts course."[121] The novel made fun of advertising writers who wrote novels, with one copywriter wisecracking that he is writing a novel titled "*Son of the Hucksters*" and the hero noting:

> I know too many dedicated souls, talented people who've broken themselves fighting the system. Spent their whole lives searching for

> causes and social battlegrounds. They believe their only purpose for existence is to influence the course of events. Writers, for instance. Good writers who look down their noses at advertising. They'd rather starve. So what does it get them? Self-respect? Integrity? Try paying your bills with integrity.[122]

Along the way, the hero receives a lot of advice and the novel privileges two advisors, a grizzled copywriter and a younger protégé, representing the voices of creativity before and after the conformist 1950s. The copywriter emphasized that "because you're a huckster, you don't have to be a whore. This business can be worthwhile, and gratifying. Even selling automobiles. But only if you maintain your creative integrity"; the protégé explains, "I believe the business can be creative, and a man can be independent, and you can have all that and still make good money."[123]

The novel concludes with a discussion of how the story could end, an exchange between the hero and his unhappy wife, who constantly worries that advertising is changing her husband. The hero begins, "But as sure as I'm sitting here, I know there's a cleaner way of operating. More honorable." His wife agrees and presents a way out, 'You chuck the dirty old advertising business, and walk off into the sunset—on your way to Tahiti to write a novel exposing the dirty old advertising business." But the hero decides leaving advertising would show he is "beaten," and instead asks his copywriter friend to form a new agency, "a creative agency. An advertising agency, not a convalescent home for no-talent slobs."[124]

A 1981 novel, *Women's Work* by Anne Tolstoi Wallach, uses much the same story about the automobile industry and a young advertising woman trying to do good work and make her way to the top in what *Newsweek* called "a new pop-fiction genre, the co-ed corporate cliffhanger." While the author, an advertising veteran, received the biggest author's advance ever given up to that time, *Newsweek* noted "as fiction, it's good journalism" and other reviews agreed. The ending mimicks that of *The Detroiters* with the heroine and her boyfriend (her former competitor in the advertising business) starting their own agency where they can be more creative and open to women and African Americans.[125] The author, Wallach, taking the other route, makes money selling her novel. In many ways, the advertising novels published after 1960 retold the same stories with new main characters; the authors had the same relationship to the advertising industry as their predecessors had in the 1950s.

The advertising novelists joined others who critiqued the mass consumption culture after World War II. They brought a deep understanding of consumption to their analysis of mass culture that allowed them to see, perhaps even more clearly than the nonfiction and scholarly writers, the ways in which mass consumption, as both sold and expressed by advertising, threatened individuality and creativity while reinforcing conformity. But their position as insiders hobbled their ability to frame a radical or even useful critique. Like the nonfiction writers Horowitz described, their work, lives, and writing focused on white, middle-class consumers with money—those to whom they directed their advertising.

Furthermore, facing the issues of consumption and operating in an advertising model, the advertising novelists couldn't see collective solutions. They took an individual approach, just as did advertising. Advertising addressed consumers individually, as someone who made individual decisions despite, or to mask, the fact that advertising urged consumers to join large groups, all of whom made the same decisions. The novels' heroes also came to individualized solutions, but they came to them together, with novel after novel ending the same way. As novelists, working in a form from its beginning based on the journey of a single person, these writers were the ultimate individualists. But the advertising novelists weren't alone in this blind spot. They joined a diverse group of thinkers from Dwight MacDonald to Vance Packard to Jack Kerouac who also came up with individual solutions. The business critique of the conformity of mass culture provided the only alternative to an individual reaction. This response became the Creative Revolution in advertising and several of the novels ended with the heroes becoming more "creative."

Both critiques of advertising and mass culture—the one that resulted in a different kind of advertising and the one that ended in individual solutions—showed how mass culture operated after World War II. Advertising interpellates critiques. In many ways, advertising has always used critiques of itself to validate its goals and approaches. The acceptance of critiques by advertising, and mass culture, institutionally and in content, made their existence less sinister. So the Truth in Advertising campaign of the Progressive movement allowed advertisers to contend that their advertisements were "true" without further questioning an institution that lied regularly. By defining "truth" narrowly, the industry escaped further scrutiny. When advertising declared itself "creative" and the heroes of novels found redemption in this new kind of advertising, no one needed to worry about the excesses of consumption promoted by advertising. When individual advertisements, like Bernbach's for the Volkswagen Beetle, joked about conformity, how big a problem could it be?

In 1972, a Doyle Dane Bernbach vice president published an advertising novel that showed a greater acceptance of advertising and mass culture than novels published immediately after the war, such as *Aurora Dawn* and *The Hucksters*. Jack Dillon's *The Advertising Man* takes place in a creative advertising agency where the president has just died and been replaced by a more conventional packaged goods man. The novel follows ten days in the life of the chief copywriter, at the end of which he is fired and divorced with no resolution to any of his problems. Unlike Wouk or Wakeman, Dillon doesn't worry about the nature of advertising or mass culture, but cares only about the creativity of the advertising agency at which his hero works. An older and revered copywriter tells clients:

> I think advertising's had it. I don't think people believe it any more. I think it's a waste of money. I'm not even sure it's moral. Anyway, we don't have any formulas here. There's no book we go by. I don't even know what to tell you. Half the time, I don't even know what I'm doing.[126]

Interesting advertising professionals embrace that uncertainty, and the creativity it represents. The hero's estranged wife finds his life "phony," but he rejects that viewpoint and her—in earlier novels, she would have persuaded him to quit and leave town. In Wouk's and Wakeman's novels, the women represented the "real" life chosen by the heroes. Dillon's hero walks away from his wife and the possibility of a more meaningful life. In the book's last sentence, the hero muses, "Well, that's life, right? No skyrockets. No parades. You just wind up drunk on somebody's lawn."[127] Martin Levin wrote in the *New York Times* that the novel was "entirely believable" and "minus the hokum writers have confected since Frederic Wakeman laid the facts of Ad Alley life on the line, back in 1946."[128] The general critiques that had been possible in earlier novels now seemed unrealistic. Jack Dillon wrote that creative advertising connected Madison Avenue with the "people." Creative advertising was fun, democratic, and nothing to worry about.[129]

Again, the critiques mounted by the advertising novels mirrored the critiques of the New York Intellectuals, nonfiction writers, and Beats. Because of their multiple subjectivity, as salesmen, advertisers, cultural workers, and consumers, the advertising novelists, working in a popular form, explored the role of the individual in mass culture with an intensity and practicality that other critics lacked. By bringing a wavering heroic everyman into contact with the one person who had held out against the blandishments of a consumer culture, for example, the novels showed how ordinary people might individually resolve the contradictions they faced in the commodified, and newly entrenched, mass culture.

Neither the nonfiction nor the fiction writers thought the situation hopeless. They proposed solutions, including strong individuality, to resist mass culture. In addition, like earlier American reformers, both sets of authors believed that bringing the problem to light would help solve it. While it is tempting to dismiss the advertising novelists as neither radical nor intellectual because they failed to present a coherent or successful alternative to mass culture, other critiques written at the same time demonstrated the same problem. The novels proved that a wide readership knew of the mass culture critiques beyond those who read nonfiction and small magazines. The critique presented in the novels also influenced advertising's form and the culture in which it operated, as evidenced by how the advertising industry and society took up the novels' phrases and formulas to talk about advertising. The ways advertising and the culture of consumption contained the critiques of the advertising novels illustrate the mechanisms by which capitalism worked to maintain itself at a particular cultural and micro- level. Mass culture proved particularly resistant to all forms of critique, in part because it was able to incorporate all the criticisms into new and improved cultural forms.

With other intellectuals of the time, the postwar advertising novelists worried about mass culture. By 1972, advertising had changed and mass culture had become familiar and accepted, in just the way the novels had predicted. All was advertising: some types better than other types, and the only protest had Jack Dillon's hero on a drunken bender. The critiques presented by the novelists had most often been dismissed because they occurred in popular novels, or because they weren't realistic enough, or because they were formulaic. When compared with a novel published twenty-five years later, Herman Wouk's and Frederic Wakeman's novels stand as trenchant social protests of an individual's place in mass culture.

Appendix: Novels Examined in This Chapter

Advertising

Samuel Hopkins Adams, *The Clarion* (New York: Houghton Mifflin, 1914).

Harford Powel, Jr., *The Virgin Queene* (Boston: Little, Brown, 1928).

John P. Marquand, *H. M. Pulham, Esquire* (Boston: Little, Brown, 1941).

Fielden Farrington, *The Big Noise* (New York: Crown, 1946).

Eric Hodgins, *Mr. Blandings Builds His Dream House* (New York: Simon and Schuster, 1946).

Arkady Leokum, *Please Send Me Absolutely Free* (New York: Harper, 1946).

Frederic Wakeman, *The Hucksters* (New York: Rinehart, 1946).

Herman Wouk, *Aurora Dawn* (New York: Doubleday, 1947).

Eric Hodgins, *Blandings' Way* (New York: Simon and Schuster, 1950).

Jeremy Kirk, *The Build-Up Boys* (New York: Charles Scribner's Sons, 1951).

Frederik Pohl and C. M. Kornbluth, *The Space Merchants* (New York: Ballantine, 1952).

Robert Alan Aurthur, *The Glorification of Al Toolum* (New York: Rinehart, 1953).

Howard Browne, *Thin Air* (New York: Simon and Schuster, 1954).

Robert Bruce, *Tina: The Story of a Hellcat* (New York: Lion Book, 1954).

Alfred Eichler, *Death of an Ad Man* (New York: Abelard-Shuman, , 1954).

Ian Gordon, *The Whip Hand* (New York: Crown, 1954).

Matthew Peters, *The Joys She Chose* (New York: Dell, 1954).

Samm Sinclair Baker, *One Touch of Blood* (Hasbrouck Heights, N.J.: Graphic Publishing Company, 1955).

Gerald Green, *The Last Angry Man* (New York: Charles Scribner's Sons, 1956).

Samm Sinclair Baker, *Murder—Most Dry* (New York: Graphic Publishing Company, , 1956).

George Panetta, *Viva Madison Avenue!* (New York: Harcourt, Brace, 1957).

Robert L. Foreman, *The Hot Half Hour* (New York: Criterion, 1958).

James Kelly, *The Insider* (New York: Henry Holt, 1958).

Harold Livingston, *The Detroiters* (Boston: Houghton Mifflin, 1958).

Shepherd Mead, *The Admen* (New York: Simon and Schuster, 1958).
Edward Stephens, *A Twist of Lemon* (Garden City, N.Y.: Doubleday, 1958).
Edward Hannibal, *Chocolate Days, Popsicle Weeks* (Boston: Houghton Mifflin, 1970).
Jack Dillon, *The Advertising Man* (New York: Harper's Magazine Press, 1972).
Jane Trahey, *Thursdays 'til 9* (New York: Harcourt Brace Jovanovich, 1980).
Anne Tolstoi Wallach, *Women's Work* (New York: New American Library, 1981).

Public Relations/ Marketing/ Broadcasting Novels
Shepherd Mead, *The Big Ball of Wax: A Story of Tomorrow's Happy World* (New York: Avon Book Division, Hearst Corporation, 1954).
Al Morgan, *The Great Man* (New York: E.P. Dutton, 1955).
Sloan Wilson, *The Man in the Gray Flannel Suit* (New York: Arbor House, 1955).
Robin Moore, *Pitchman* (New York: Coward-McCann, 1956).
J. Harvey Howells, *The Big Company Look* (New York: J. Harvey Howells, 1958).
Middleton Kiefer, *Pax* (New York: Random House, 1958).
Sterling Quinlan, *The Merger* (New York: Doubleday, 1958).
Robert Van Riper, *A Really Sincere Guy* (New York: David McKay, 1958).

CONCLUSION

Stories of *Otaku* and *Desis*

PERHAPS COLLEGE STUDENTS see popular culture as without political expression, as escape, because mass culture has won—or, at least, because they have ceded large swathes of ground to it. My students, and now my former students since I've been doing this for so long, still make their own popular culture, and it's there that they recognize political statements—while enjoying anime, performing in South Asian cultural productions on college campuses, and working for local cultural institutions like San Francisco's Killing My Lobster performance troupe and Providence's AS220 unjuried art space. My students see politics not in reality shows but in their satires of reality shows on Brown TV; not in Britney Spears but in reggaeton and bhangra; not in video games but on their own websites and blogs. They recognize forms existing on the margins as political but don't see the same possibilities for the culture that exists in the middle. Mass culture's enormous growth, as well as its continuing and successful efforts to hide any ideological purposes, brought them to this partial vision.

In this book, I've sought moments when popular culture expressed an ideology (or set of ideologies) in order to examine how ideas got expressed and understood in amateur theatricals, consumer products, advertisements, Hollywood and its films, and popular fiction. Because I looked at the middle of the twentieth century, I found something more. While reading the popular culture forms (and sometimes the producers' conscious and unconscious intentions and sometimes the audiences' multiple interpretations), I found that these cultural forms also illustrated how popular culture changed over this time period. The interactive minstrel shows, constructing the racialized class positions of their middle-class performers, began the process with how-to books that promised to provide their readers with a standardized "system" to make the show easy and successful. Nylon, as a product of the beginnings of corporate science, contained gender ideas both in its molecular structure and its advertising, ideas put there by the national company that had invented it. Other companies had pioneered new products and marketed and advertised in new ways, but the scale on which DuPont operated, and the way in which it both appealed to and dominated women consumers, differed from what had come before. The involvement of the federal government in the exportation of American films to Japan after World War II and the idea that those films contained ideologies showed the ways in which American culture both defined and outgrew the American nation so that mass culture could be global. The case studies described here illustrated the expanding corporate takeover and commodification of popular culture, and the advertising novelists found that a frightening prospect. The enormous postwar growth of mass culture, and its subsequent sterility and oppressiveness, justified their fear. Unlike the worried 1950s writers, my students ignore mass culture and look for alternative spaces in which to express and think about ideologies.

Two Brown seniors recently wrote honors theses in the Department of American Civilization exploring, through ethnography, how students use contemporary popular and mass culture. Moye Ishimoto began her 2003 project, "Anime in America and the American *Otaku*," convinced that young American men who watched Japanese animated films were racist and sexist pigs, orientalizing and exploiting Asian women. An online survey of about one hundred members of twelve college anime clubs, attendance at several conventions, and a lot of viewing later, she had a different analysis. Male and female anime lovers explained that they found mainstream American culture boring and superficial. Films and television series made in the United States failed to address important questions or take up the issues of an individual's place in society, at least in the more substantive way Japanese animation did. One student wrote, "American culture and entertainment seems so shallow and flat, dry and unimaginative in comparison."[1] Furthermore, a significant number of fans identified as Asian American, and they used anime, which often drew on tropes familiar from their childhoods, to fashion a pan-Asian racial identity in the United States. Finally, the white students regularly explained how their attraction to anime led them to a deeper interest in Japan, often to language study, travel, or even career choices that they might not have made without exposure to a different culture.[2]

These *otaku*, the Japanese term for committed fans, looked outside the globalized mass culture exported by the United States, to find cultural productions more serious, more useful in crafting an identity, and more inclusive than anything they found on U.S. screens. Yet, when Ishimoto and I introduced anime to the students in the pop culture lecture class, they explained patiently that anime didn't count as popular culture because not enough people watched it. Students understood her thesis that the *otaku* found ideological content in anime, but that only confirmed their view that anime was a specialized form, not part of mass culture. In part because of the commitment of its fans, in part because of how the fans thought about anime's content, my students saw anime as outside mass culture. Defining out any political or oppositional forms meant that mass culture could still be described as escapist. Anime importers and repackagers do operate on the fringes of the American film industry.[3] Yet many members of college anime clubs developed their tastes through Japanese imports on American children's television, including *Pokemon*, *Yu-Gi-Oh! Sailor Moon*, and the *Mighty Morphin Power Rangers*. And Hollywood film studios have worked hard to integrate anime, with Disney signing a deal to distribute the movies of Japanese master animator Hayao Miyazaki in the United States.[4] I wonder how long it will be before students dismiss anime as escapist mass culture.

Anime as participatory, with *otaku* joining clubs and attending conventions dressed as their favorite characters, takes us back to the issues raised by amateur minstrel shows. The relationship of white fans to the Asian characters they portray tells us about the construction of class, gender, national, and racial categories. Amita Manghnani's 2006 senior thesis exhibit, "Rhythm Nation: South Asian America Performs Race on Stage," connects to the amateur minstrels even more directly. Presented as a multimedia exhibit, her thesis addressed

> the ways South Asian American students on college campuses use culture shows to define themselves and their communities. These colorful and incredibly energizing performances function as an arena for the negotiation of racial and ethnic identity for South Asian American youth. The exhibit raises questions of how self-representation is both empowering and problematic. In performing, South Asian Americans put themselves on display, recreating an orientalist gaze, but also attempt to counter racist stereotypes by redefining what it means to be South Asian American.[5]

Through an online survey sent to seventeen campuses (with fifty replies), a series of interviews, and visits to four campus cultural shows in different parts of the country, Manghnani learned how students performed their race, ethnicity, gender, nationality, and class in these immensely popular amateur productions.

The mostly second- and third-generation Indian Americans (*Desis*, in their own terms) who participated in the campus cultural shows disagree on what happens when they perform, for their peers, a mixture of Indian classical dance, Bollywood production numbers, and "fusion" pieces blending hip-hop and bhangra music. Some learn about Indian and Indian American culture for the first time; some cement ties to India or particular Indian regions; some feel empowered by "coming out" as culturally Indian to the larger college community. In many ways, the cultural shows operate for South Asian, middle-class college students just as minstrel shows did for white middle-class Americans from the 1910s to the 1950s. By performing a racial masquerade, the college students can be South Asian on stage and Americans when they leave it. They dress in elaborate costumes, turbans, and fake beards to signify that they are not the people they portray. The participants reinscribe and reinforce their membership in the middle class and the nation by becoming, on stage, those who belong to neither. In a post-Civil Rights era, a marginalized group masquerades, and that remains a large difference between the operations of the cultural shows and the amateur minstrels.

Amita Manghnani carefully uncovers other contradictions in the performances: the omission of, and prejudice against, Indian Muslims or other South Asian groups; the exploitation of female sexuality as a way to sell tickets; the students' search for "authentic" or "essential" Indianness; and the lack of interest by South Asian American college students in any politics other than the narrow cultural politics enabled by the shows. Despite these very important issues, she and her classmates who staged the shows (she was a participant-observer, having worked on the Brown cultural show for four years) used the performances to make sense of their lives and their identities, employing popular culture in familiar ways.[6]

The shows include a range of mass cultural materials, from Bollywood and U.S. sources, which students both accept and manipulate. And the moment must be close when traveling consultants will provide students with costumes and expertise in putting on cultural shows, selling them a system of materials to make productions easier to stage, pushing the shows and the performers into a more rigid format. Mass culture's appetite for new content is so voracious that I predict that most forms, including anime and campus cultural shows, will lose any battle to stay marginal.

Some scholars take to extremes the idea that popular culture is made by the audience. When mass culture has become so commodified, so corporate, and so unchangeable, audience modification becomes less likely, and scholars and students alike need to take notice. On the other hand, I think that most of us don't want to think about the ways in which we are oppressed by mass culture. Students won't see the ideologies expressed; they want to believe that they have some control over what they think and how they act. Some question the seriousness of the oppression imposed by an amateur theater production, an advertisement, a movie, or a novel.

Looking back, the case studies in this book can be seen as the soft side of ideological formation, although each had a harsher, and sometimes violent, accompaniment. Lynching, which can rather coldly be described as a form of performative violence, occurred at the same time and probably in front of the same people as the minstrel shows. Domestic violence and its constant threat showed women their normative roles at the same time as they saw advertisements for the new nylon stockings. The United States conducted the Occupation of Japan through memos, as seen in the notes to Chapter 3, but also through the presence of an American army on Japanese soil. New forms of structural poverty accompanied postwar prosperity as did U.S. armed aggression around the world and the Hollywood blacklist, and all these happened as the novelists made their critique of mass culture and consumption. Perhaps remembering its more deadly accompaniments makes the ways in which mass culture works to control its audiences easier to see.

Like Susan Douglas, Michael Denning, and George Lipsitz, the Brown students, Moye Ishimoto and Amita Manghnani, successfully juggled the oppressive and liberating aspects of commodified culture, explaining how current college students both use and are used by anime and cultural shows. Ishimoto and Manghnani maintained a lively interest in the relationship between politics and commodified popular culture in a way that helped illustrate student thought.

The students in my class saw mass culture as escape because they couldn't imagine how to use it to affect social change. My friends and I had exploited the cracks in 1960s and '70s popular culture to express our own identities in ways no longer open to young audiences. Popular culture didn't seem all that different from what we could make ourselves; the extreme commodification of all performative forms had not yet taken hold; and we could conceive of our own voices being taken up in popular culture without the cynicism that our students have as a result of seeing the cooptation that followed our efforts. In part because of technological changes, in part because of the growing rigidity and power of mass culture, in part because of the changes brought by identity politics, students have turned to local, specialized, and niche cultures to express and understand their lives. My students believe mass-produced culture, with the possible exception of hip-hop, serves as escape while marginalized forms can be expressions of political ideas and engagements. But even if mass culture isn't politically engaging, that doesn't mean that it's merely escapist. Students seeking to avoid thinking about its oppressive power may call popular culture escapist, but that naming doesn't make it unimportant or nonideological.

But there might be another way of thinking about this issue. Perhaps the students are right. With the growth of an educated and consumption-oriented middle class, a growth that popular culture helped facilitate, mass culture's ideological work has become, precisely, to provide escape. By this I mean two things. First, mass culture tries increasingly to convince the audience that it contains no ideology; it does so by misdirecting attention from the ways in which products, including amusements, and their distribution systems support particular and interlocking constructions of class, race, gender, and nation. Second, over the century, middle-class consumers understood more about mass culture's contradictions, so cultural producers had to work harder to persuade audiences that nothing was happening. As such a process continued into the present, escapism became the ideological work of mass culture, especially if one defines escapist entertainments as those that direct audiences to ignore ideology.

After consideration, my argument with the students was different than I had first thought. I needed to understand what they meant by "escape." When I did, I decided that while mass culture might be an escape, I still found it worth studying. I believed more strongly than ever that the ideological power created and expressed by mass culture made it a critical site for anyone interested in social change. In this book, I looked for and found evidence of the power exerted through popular culture forms and content and saw too how the expressions of that power changed over time, including changes that increasingly presented cultural productions as "escape." We need to examine, think about, worry over, and act against the structural oppression mass culture brings, find ways to enjoy its content, and consider how to use its power for social change. I hope that examining the moments,

NOTES

INTRODUCTION. ESCAPING POPULAR CULTURE

1. Roland Marchand, *Advertising the American Dream: Making Way for Modernity, 1920–1940* (Berkeley: University of California Press, 1985).

2. Michael Kammen, *American Culture, American Tastes: Social Change and the Twentieth Century* (New York: Knopf, 1999), particularly chap. 1; George Lipsitz, *Time Passages: Collective Memory and American Popular Culture* (Minneapolis: University of Minnesota Press, 1990), 12–20.

3. Paul Buhle, "Introduction," in *Popular Culture in America*, ed. Buhle (Minneapolis: University of Minnesota Press, 1987), x and passim.

4. For the ideas explored at the CCCS at Birmingham see Graeme Turner, *British Cultural Studies: An Introduction* (New York: Routledge, 1996) and Stuart Hall, "Cultural Studies and the Centre: Some Problematics and Problems," in *Culture, Media, Language: Working Papers in Cultural Studies, 1972–79*, ed. Stuart Hall, Dorothy Hobson, Andrew Lowe, and Paul Willis (London: Hutchinson, 1980), 15–47.

5. Stuart Hall, "Notes on Deconstructing 'The Popular'," in *People's History and Socialist Theory*, ed. Ralph Samuel (London: Routledge, 1981), 227–40.

6. Robert C. Toll, *Blacking Up: The Minstrel Show in Nineteenth Century America* (New York: Oxford University Press, 1974).

7. For some of the positives and negatives of the Birmingham school approach to media audiences, see Andrea Press, *Women Watching Television: Gender, Class, and Generation in the American Television Experience* (Philadelphia: University of Pennsylvania Press, 1991), 15–26.

8. Sociologist Richard Butsch has written a wonderful history of audiences, *The Making of American Audiences: From Stage to Television, 1750–1990* (New York: Cambridge University Press, 2000), which may settle the issue for a while.

9. Michael Denning, "The End of Mass Culture," *International Labor and Working Class History* 37 (Spring 1990): 8.

10. Janice Radway, "Maps and Constructions of Boundaries," *International Labor and Working Class History* 37 (Spring 1990): 20.

11. Kammen, *American Culture, American Tastes*, 18, 22 (italics in original).

12. James W. Carey, *Communication as Culture: Essays on Media and Society* (Boston: Unwin Hyman, 1988), 97.

13. James Cook, "On the Return of the 'Culture Industry' Concept," paper delivered at The State of Cultural History Conference in honor of Lawrence Levine, George Mason University, September 2005.

14. Susan Douglas, *Where the Girls Are: Growing Up Female with the Mass Media* (New York: Times Books, 1994), 20 and passim.

15. Michael Denning, *The Cultural Front: The Laboring of American Culture in the Twentieth Century* (New York: Verso, 1997), xvi (boldface in original).

16. Denning, *The Cultural Front*, 42, 446, and passim.

17. George Lipsitz, *Dangerous Crossroads: Popular Music, Postmodernism, and the Poetics of Place* (London: Verso, 1994), 153.

18. Thanks to Teresa Murphy for helping me confront this idea.

19. Terry Eagleton, *Ideology: An Introduction* (New York: Verso, 1991), 106–7.

20. Lawrence Levine, *Highbrow/Lowbrow: The Emergence of Cultural Hierarchy in America* (Cambridge, Mass.: Harvard University Press, 1988). While Levine never describes the split between highbrow and lowbrow cultures in class terms, his evidence certainly supports such a description.

21. Eagleton, *Ideology*, 43.

22. Eagleton, *Ideology*, 113 (boldface in original).

23. John B. Thompson, *Ideology and Modern Culture: Critical Social Theory in the Era of Mass Communication* (Stanford, Calif.: Stanford University Press, 1990), 3.

24. I am indebted for this insight to Michael Schudson's review of Thompson's work: Michael Schudson, "Review of Ideology and Modern Culture: Critical Social Theory in the Era of Mass Communication," *Contemporary Sociology* 21 (January 1992): 106–8. Schudson believes that one flaw in Thompson's work is the failure to take nationalism into account when discussing ideology and mass communication, a lack I hope to partially rectify in Chapter 3.

25. Johann Visagie, "The Games Theorists Play: Ideology Between Discourse and Domination," *Society in Transition* 29 (December 1998): 130–41.

26. Thompson, *Ideology and Modern Culture*, 8.

27. Thompson, *Ideology and Modern Culture*, 25.

28. Stuart Hall, "The Problem of Ideology: Marxism Without Guarantees," in *Marx: A Hundred Years On*, ed. Betty Matthews (London: Lawrence and Wishart, 1983), 59.

CHAPTER 1. MINSTREL LAUGHS: POPULAR CULTURE, RACE, AND THE MIDDLE CLASS

1. Fred Hillebrand, *Burnt Cork and Melody* (New York: Marks Music, 1953), 2.

2. Arthur LeRoy Kaser, *Kaser's Complete Minstrel Guide* (Chicago: Dramatic Publishing, 1934), 8.

3. LeRoy Stahl, *The High School Minstrel Book* (Minneapolis: Northwestern Press, 1938).

4. For a book that has a detailed description of the first part but leaves amateurs on their own for the olio, see Harold Rossiter, *How to Put On a Minstrel Show* (Chicago: Max Stein, 1921).

5. Rossiter, *How to Put On a Minstrel Show*, 11.

6. I have based my estimates on the Harris Collection of American Poetry and Plays at the John Hay Library, Brown University, which has collected minstrel materials for many years. The Harris Collection lists seven plays with "minstrel" in the subject heading published between 1900 and 1909; six between 1910 and 1919; forty-five between 1920 and 1929; forty-four between 1930 and 1939; and four between 1940 and 1949. Research in other collections and examination of publishing catalogs convinces me that these proportions are approximately right. Thanks to Rosemary Cullen, Curator of the Harris Collection, John Hay Library, Brown University, for her help in collecting these numbers, and for sharing her deep knowledge of minstrelsy. In addition, an amazing undergraduate researcher, Tara Rodgers, did the first summer's work on the instruction books that helped me understand their importance.

7. For detailed instructions see Carrie B. Adams, *Old Cabin Home Minstrels: A Minstrel Entertainment in Three Acts* (Dayton, Oh.: Lorenz Publishing, 1921), Federal Theatre Project Collection, George Mason University; for a simple first-part, see Vance Clifford (Arthur LeRoy Kaser), *Minstrel Laughs* (Chicago: T.S. Denison, 1927), whose back cover included an advertisement for "Ready-Made Minstrel First-Parts."

8. With thanks to Alan Stauffacher, Chair, Social Studies Department, Monroe High School, Monroe, Wisconsin.

9. Merrill Denison, "Do You Know Aaron Slick? A Note on the Real American Theater," *Harper's Monthly* 176 (March 1938): 386–93.

10. William Courtright, *The Complete Minstrel Guide* (Chicago: Dramatic Publishing, 1901), 7.

11. Le Roy Stahl, *The Five Star Minstrel Book* (Minneapolis: Northwestern Press, 1938), 12. Some books advocated red grease paint for the lips; see Rossiter, *How to Put On a Minstrel Show*, 20. Others agreed with Stahl that the lips were best left natural; see Arthur LeRoy Kaser, *Baker's Minstrel Budget* (Boston: Walter H. Baker, 1928), 9.

12. Sophie Huth Perkins, *Mirandy's Minstrels: A Minstrel Entertainment for Women* (Chicago: T.S. Denison, 1901), 6; Frederick G. Johnson, *The Minstrelettes: A Ready Made First-Part for Ladies' Minstrels* (New York: Fitzgerald, 1927), 4; Arthur LeRoy Kaser, *The Parody Ladies Minstrel: A Minstrel First Part for Ladies* (Boston: Walter H. Baker, 1929), 4.

13. Kaser, *Baker's Minstrel Budget*, 10; Kaser, *The Parody Ladies Minstrel*; Stahl, *The Five Star Minstrel*, 12.

14. Arthur LeRoy Kaser, *The Sunbeam Minstrelettes* (Chicago: Dramatic Publishing, 1930), 3; Arland Jenkins, *Station Jazz: Blackface Minstrel Show* (Portland, Me.: Debaters Information Bureau, 1933), 2. Also see Stahl, *The Five Star Minstrel Book*, 9; Adams, *Old Cabin Home Minstrels*; Effa E. Preston, *Bandanna Junior Minstrel First-Part* (Chicago: T.S. Denison, 1933).

15. See, for example, Perkins, *Mirandy's Minstrels*; Arthur LeRoy Kaser, *The Burnt Cork Entertainer: Blackface Sketches and Monologues for the Amateur or Professional Stage* (Boston: Walter H. Baker, 1925); and Arthur L. Kaser, *Jolly Pickaninnies Minstrels: A Complete Minstrel Program for the Grades* (Dayton, Oh.: Paine Publishing, 1937).

16. Melvin Patrick Ely, *The Adventures of Amos 'n' Andy: A Social History of an American Phenomenon* (New York: Free Press, 1991), 46, 38.

17. John Lawrence, *Ladies' Minstrel First-Part* (Chicago: T.S. Denison, 1929), 29.

18. On the role of minstrel shows in nineteenth-century class formation, see Alexander Saxton, *The Rise and Fall of the White Republic: Class Politics and Mass Culture in Nineteenth-Century America* (New York: Verso, 1990); David R. Roediger, *The Wages of Whiteness: Race and the Making of the American Working Class* (New York: Verso, 1991); Eric Lott, *Love and Theft: Blackface Minstrelsy and the American Working Class* (New York: Oxford University Press, 1993).

19. Robert C. Toll, *Blacking Up: The Minstrel Show in Nineteenth Century America* (New York: Oxford University Press, 1974).

20. An older book, with many flaws, has one of the best descriptions of the end of professional minstrelsy. See Carl Wittke, *Tambo and Bones: A History of the American Minstrel Stage* (Raleigh, N.C.: Duke University Press, 1930), 122–25.

21. For the black musical theater, see Thomas L. Riis, *Just Before Jazz: Black Musical Theater in New York, 1890–1915* (Washington, D.C.: Smithsonian Institution Press, 1989); Allan Woll, *Black Musical Theatre: From Coontown to Dreamgirls* (Baton Rouge: Louisiana State University Press, 1989); Thomas L. Riis, *More Than Just Minstrel Shows: The Rise of Black Musical Theatre at the Turn of the Century*, Institute for Studies in American Music Monographs 33 (Brooklyn, N.Y.: Conservatory of Music, Brooklyn College of the City University of New York, 1992); Joseph Boskin, *Sambo: The Rise and Demise of an American Jester* (New York: Oxford University Press, 1986); on the traveling blues shows see Ben Bailey, "The Minstrel Show in Mississippi," *Journal of Mississippi History* 57 (Summer 1995): 139–52; Henry Lewis Gates, "The Chitlin Circuit," *New Yorker* 72 (3 February 1997): 44–50+.

22. For a great description of minstrelsy on radio, see Michele Hilmes, *Radio Voices: American Broadcasting, 1922–1952* (Minneapolis: University of Minnesota Press, 1997), 75–81.

23. On the Mystic performance, see "The Minstrel Tour: A Short But Successful Trip," *Brown Daily Herald* 2 (4 April 1893): 1; on other tours, "The Brown Minstrels in the West: Tour of 'The Brunonian Club' During Spring Recess," *Brunonian* 12, 16 (12 April 1890): 220; "The Brown Minstrels Greeted at Home by Great Audiences," *Brunonian* 23, 15 (29 March 1890): 234.

24. *Providence Opera House Program, 1890–1891 Season 4*, Rhode Island Historical Society, Providence.

25. Eric Lott, "Love and Theft: The Racial Unconscious of Blackface Minstrelsy," *Representations* 39 (Summer 1992): 38.

26. Brander Matthews, "The Rise and Fall of Negro-Minstrelsy," *Scribner's Magazine* 57 (June 1915): 754–59.

27. Gene Arnold, *Gene Arnold, Complete Modern Minstrels*, Book 1, *A Complete Minstrel Routine for Clubs, Schools, Churches, and Fraternal Organizations, with Suggestions and Directions for Staging* (New York: M. Witmark, 1933), 3.

28. Billy S. Garvie, "Minstrel Songs of Other Days: Famous Ballads, Songs and Ditties Sung by the Minstrel Boys of '68–'73," *Americana* 7 (October 1912): 945; "Passing of the Minstrels," *Literary Digest* 62 (16 August 1919): 28–29; see also "The Minstrel Joke," *New York Times* (26 July 1919): 8.

29. Kaser, *The Parody Ladies Minstrel*, 5.

30. Daniel Czitrom, *Media and the American Mind: From Morse to McLuhan* (Chapel Hill: University of North Carolina Press, 1982).

31. Robert C. Toll, *The Entertainment Machine: American Show Business in the Twentieth Century* (New York: Oxford University Press, 1982).

32. Robert Allen, *Horrible Prettiness: Burlesque and American Culture* (Chapel Hill: University of North Carolina Press, 1991).

33. Lawrence Levine, *Highbrow/Lowbrow: The Emergence of Cultural Hierarchy in America* (Cambridge, Mass.: Harvard University Press, 1988); on the Astor Place Riot, see Peter Buckley, "To the Opera House: Culture and Society in New York City, 1820–1860," Ph.D. dissertation, State University of New York, Stony Brook, 1984.

34. For radio's use of vaudeville as a step toward national audiences, see Susan Smulyan, *Selling Radio: The Commercialization of American Broadcasting, 1920–1934* (Washington, D.C.: Smithsonian Institution Press, 1992); for radio as a nationalizing force, see Hilmes, *Radio Voices*.

35. Evelyn Gill Klahr, "Interesting People: He Has Trained Thousands of Amateur Actors," *American Magazine* 98 (August 1924): 62–63.

36. Denison, "Do You Know Aaron Slick?" 392.

37. Arthur LeRoy Kaser, *The Old Maids' Minstrel Show* (New York: Fitzgerald, 1933), inside front cover; for another puff piece on an author, see Jack Mahoney, *Mahoney's Modern Minstrels: A New and Original Complete Minstrel Show* (New York: Central Music Publishers, 1945).

38. Kaser's first published minstrel material seems to have been Arthur LeRoy Kaser, *Alabama Minstrel First-Part: A Complete Routine for the Circle* (Chicago: T.S. Denison, 1922).

39. "Arthur Leroy Kaser," *Books at Brown* 18, 3 (1958).

40. Perkins, *Mirandy's Minstrels*, 6.

41. Arnold, *Gene Arnold, Complete Modern Minstrels*, inside back cover; see also Will Rossiter, *Echoes of the Past* (Chicago: Will Rossiter, 1904), inside back cover; Clifford (Kaser), *Minstrel Laughs*, inside back cover; Kaser, *Alabama Minstrel First-Part*; and Lawrence, *Ladies' Minstrel First-Part*.

42. Arthur LeRoy Kaser, *Baker's Minstrel Joke Book* (Boston: Walter H. Baker, 1928), 3.

43. Rossiter, *How to Put On a Minstrel Show*; see also Courtright, *The Complete Minstrel Guide*; Stahl, *The Five Star Minstrel Book*.

44. Arthur LeRoy Kaser, *Staging the Amateur Minstrel Show* (Boston: Walter H. Baker, 1930), 14.

45. Clifford (Kaser), *Minstrel Laughs.*

46. On historical pageants, forerunners of the amateur theatrical movement, and professional pageant masters, see David Glassberg, *American Historical Pageantry: The Uses of Tradition in the Early Twentieth Century* (Chapel Hill: University of North Carolina Press, 1990) and Naima Prevots, *American Pageantry: A Movement for Art and Democracy* (Ann Arbor, Mich.: UMI Research Press, 1991).

47. Klahr, "Interesting People," 62–63; William Corbin, "Everybody Wants to Be an Actor," *American Magazine* 118 (November 1934): 51, 119–21; Webb Waldron, "Nothing Amateur But the Cast," *Reader's Digest* 35 (July 1939): 74–76; David Dempsey and Dan Herr, "Everybody Gets in the Act," *Saturday Evening Post* 221 (27 November 1948): 34–35, 47–48, 55; Paul F. Healy, "Big Hit on Main Street," *Saturday Evening Post* 232 (2 April 1960): 36–37; E. M. D. Watson, "Amateur Theatricals Are Big Business," *Cosmopolitan* 149 (November 1960): 62–65; for the story of one director and the company she worked for, see Lorelei F. Eckey, Maxine Allen Schoyer, and William T. Schoyer, *1,001 Broadways: Hometown Talent on Stage* (Ames: Iowa State University Press, 1982).

48. "King of the Minstrel Circuit," *American Magazine* 152 (July 1951): 59.

49. Ely, *The Adventures of Amos 'n' Andy*; for an example of an actual radio minstrel show see Kolin Hager, *Darktown Ebony Revue: A Forty-Five Minute Minstrel Show Adapted for Radio or Stage Production* (Boston: Walter H. Baker, 1927) and the descriptions in Hilmes, *Radio Voices*, 79–80.

50. Melvin Patrick Ely has done a wonderful job of recreating the activities of the Bren coaches from Correll's scrapbooks; see Ely, *The Adventures of Amos 'n' Andy*, 35–46.

51. Michael Rogin, *Blackface, White Noise: Jewish Immigrants in the Hollywood Melting Pot* (Berkeley: University of California Press, 1996), 14.

52. Saxton, *The Rise and Fall of the White Republic*; Roediger, *The Wages of Whiteness*; Lott, *Love and Theft.*

53. Advertisement in Kaser, *Baker's Minstrel Budget.*

54. Walter Ben Hare, *Frills and Frolics* (Boston: Walter H. Baker, 1921), 83; Preston, *Bandanna Junior Minstrel First-Part*; Arthur LeRoy Kaser, *Kiddie-Kutups Minstrels* (Chicago: Dramatic Publishing, 1934); Kaser, *Jolly Pickaninnies Minstrels*; Stahl, *The High School Minstrel Book.*

55. Loren Baritz, *The Good Life: The Meaning of Success for the American Middle Class* (New York: Knopf, 1988), xi.

56. Stuart Blumin, *The Emergence of the Middle Class: Social Experience in the American City, 1760–1900* (New York: Cambridge University Press, 1989), 3.

57. Blumin, *The Emergence of the Middle Class*, 9–10.

58. Denison, "Do You Know Aaron Slick?" 392.

59. Kaser, *Staging the Amateur Minstrel Show*, 14.

60. Joan Shelley Rubin, *The Making of Middlebrow Culture* (Chapel Hill: University of North Carolina Press, 1992).

61. Rubin, *Making of Middlebrow Culture*, 3.

62. Corinne Robert Redgrave, "What Every Amateur Actress Ought to Know," *Ladies Home Journal* 30 (October 1913): 108.

63. James Barnes, "Amateur Theatricals," *Century* (March 1911): 673.

64. Charles Belmont Davis, "The Thespians: The Story of a Chorus Girl's Experience with an Amateur Dramatic Company," *Colliers* 47 (8 April 1911): 23 (boldface in original).

65. See, for one example, Kaser, *Kiddie-Kutups Minstrels*.

66. Kaser, *Staging the Amateur Minstrel Show*.

67. For male minstrels making fun of women, see Kaser, *Alabama Minstrel First-Part* and Hillebrand, *Burnt Cork and Melody*. For minstrel shows for women that contained jokes about gender, see Perkins, *Mirandy's Minstrels*; Lawrence, *Ladies' Minstrel First-Part*; and Arthur Kaser, *Parody Ladies Minstrel*.

68. Rogin, *Blackface, White Noise*, 12.

69. Jean Provence, *Cotton Blossom Minstrel First-Part: A Complete Routine for the Circle* (Minneapolis: T.S. Denison, 1950).

70. Hillebrand, *Burnt Cork and Melody*.

71. Albert Julian, *56 Minstrels* (New York: WPA, National Service Bureau, Federal Theater Project, 1938) and "Production Bulletin," *All-American Minstrels*, Variety Theatre, New York, November 1936, both in Box 971, Federal Theater Project Collection, George Mason University, Fairfax, Virginia; "WPA Minstrel Show Wins Applause At Majestic Theatre," *Brooklyn Times Union* (16 June 1936).

72. "The Theatre and the Armed Forces," *Theatre Arts* 27 (March 1943): 172.

73. Jean Provence, *We're-in-the-Army Minstrel First-Part* (Chicago: T.S. Denison, 1942); Arthur Kaser, *Uncle Sam Minstrel First Part* (Chicago: T.S. Denison, 1945).

74. See Provence, *Cotton Blossom Minstrel First-Part*; Charles George, *Minstrel Jubilee: A Merry Minstrel Cruise* (Minneapolis: T.S. Denison, 1951); Hillebrand, *Burnt Cork and Melody*; Wilbur Braun (Reed Driscoll), *The Whiz Bang Minstrel Show* (Boston: Walter H. Baker, 1954).

75. Penny Von Eschen, *Satchmo Blows Up the World: Jazz Ambassadors Play the Cold War* (Cambridge, Mass.: Harvard University Press, 2004); see also Mary L. Dudziak, *Cold War Civil Rights: Race and the Image of American Democracy* (Princeton, N.J.: Princeton University Press, 2000).

76. Melvin Patrick Ely carefully outlined these fissures in the African American debate over "Amos 'n' Andy" throughout the program's long history but noted as well the sustained campaign by the *Pittsburgh Courier* against the show in the 1930s. See Ely, *The Adventures of Amos 'n' Andy*, 160–93.

77. "Editorial: Is the Negro Clown Sick," *Color* (July 1950): 3; Edwin C. Berry, "Is It Fair?" *National Education Association Journal* 39 (October 1950): 485; for the reactions of individuals to minstrel shows, see Frank J. Corbett, *Racial Implications in the Black Face Minstrel Show* (Bridgeport, Conn.: Bridgeport Inter-Group Council, 1959), Schomburg Center for Research in Black Culture, New York Public Library, New York.

78. "The Minstrel Show Must Go!" *Interracial Review* (May 1950): 68.

79. "Blackface Minstrels: 10 Reasons Why They're Not So Funny," *Catholic Interracialist* (April 1952): 1–2.

80. "What the Branches Are Doing: Suggested Changes in Minstrels," *The Crisis: A Record of the Darker Races* 60 (June/July 1953): 368–71.

81. "Minstrel Show Barred as 'Objectionable' in New York," *Afro-American* (22 March 1958): 7; "Legion to Do Minstrel Show; Asks NAACP Membership Lists," *New York Amsterdam News* (22 March 1958): 3; Russell P. Crawford, "You and the NAACP," *New York Amsterdam News* (29 March 1958): 10. For other local protests see "Jersey Town Bans Show Until It Drops 'Minstrel,'" *Afro-American* (21 May 1955): 7; "Won't Permit Minstrel Show," *Pittsburgh Courier* (28 May 1955): 15; "NAACP Asks End to Blackface School Shows," *Jet* (17 January 1957): 26; "New Rochelle NAACP Fights KC Minstrel," *New York Amsterdam News* (10 May 1958): 13.

82. For a series of shows and protests in the early 1960s, see "Annual Minstrel Show of Whitehall [Michigan] High School Canceled After Negroes Protest," *Jet* 19 (15 December 1960): 9; "Negroes' Protest Cancels Reno Church Minstrel," *Jet* 19 (10 March 1960): 21; "NAACP Protests Minstrel Show Turns 'White'," *Jet* 21 (21 December 1961): 62; "Connecticut NAACP Protests VFW 'Blackface' Show," *Jet* 21 (14 December 1961): 58.

83. One can find examples in the archives of almost any university, but for examples that made the national press, see Peter Baker, "Judge Lifts Penalty for GMU Fraternity," *Washington Post* (28 August 1991): B1–2, and "U. of Alabama Students Protest Skit with Whites in Black Face," *Jet* 81 (11 November 1991): 24; for an overview ten years later see Thomas Bartlett, "An Ugly Tradition Persists at Southern Fraternity Parties," *Chronicle of Higher Education* 30 November 2001).

84. Kaser, *Kaser's Complete Minstrel Guide*, 9.

85. Allen, *Horrible Prettiness*, 185.

86. Kenneth Ames, *Death in the Dining Room and Other Tales of Victorian Culture* (Philadelphia: Temple University Press, 1992); Blumin, *The Emergence of the Middle Class*.

CHAPTER 2. THE MAGIC OF NYLON: THE STRUGGLE OVER GENDER AND CONSUMPTION

1. For some good examples, see Carolyn Marvin, *When Old Technologies Were New: Thinking About Electric Communication in the Late Nineteenth Century* (New York: Oxford University Press, 1988) and Lisa Gitelman, *Scripts, Grooves, and Writing Machines: Representing Technology in the Edison Era* (Stanford, Calif.: Stanford University Press, 1999).

2. Jeffrey Meikle, *American Plastic: A Cultural History* (New Brunswick, N.J.: Rutgers University Press, 1995); David Hounshell and John Kenly Smith, *Science and Corporate Strategy: DuPont R&D, 1902–1980* (New York: Cambridge University Press, 1988); Yasu Furukawa, *Inventing Polymer Science: Staudinger, Carothers, and the Emergence of Macromolecular Chemistry* (Philadelphia: University of Pennsylvania Press, 1998).

3. Stuart Hall, "Notes on Deconstructing 'The Popular'," in *People's History and Socialist Theory*, ed. Ralph Samuel (London: Routledge, 1981), 227–40.

4. Furukawa, *Inventing Polymer Science*, 136.

5. Furukawa, *Inventing Polymer Science*, 137.

6. Patent application, W. H. Carothers, "Linear Condensation Polymers," 3 July 1931, dated 16 February 1937, 20710250; Wallace A. Carothers and Julian W. Hill, abstract of paper to be given at the Buffalo meeting of the American Chemical Society, 1 September 1931, "Artificial Fibers from Synthetic Linear Condensation Superpolymers," Accession 500, DuPont Company Records, Series II Part 2, Rutledge Scrapbook for Nylon, 1930–1941, Hagley Museum and Library (hereafter cited as HML).

7. "Silk Is Done," *American Textile Reporter* 51 (8 July 1937): 1, 37; "New du Pont Fibre May Threaten Market for Silk," *Wall Street Journal* (26 August 1938): 1; "New Silk Made on Chemical Base Rivals Quality of Natural Product," *New York Times* (22 September 1938): 25. For an even earlier account, after Carothers gave the first scientific paper on his discovery, see "Chemists Produce Synthetic 'Silk'," *New York Times* (2 September 1931): 23, Accession 500, Series II Part 2, Rutledge Papers 1930–1941, HML.

8. "Stocking Panic," *Business Week* (9 August 1941): 25.

9. On rivalry see "Fiber Made from Coal Called 'Rival' of Silk," *Indianapolis Times* (28 October 1938); "Silk Threatened by New Fibers," *Buffalo News* (31 October 1938); "Coal and Castor Oil Challenge Silkworm," *Washington News* (22 September 1938); "New Silk Made on Chemical Base Rivals Quality of Natural Product," *New York Times* (22 September 1938): 25; "New du Pont Fibre May Threaten Market for Silk," *Wall Street Journal* (26 August 1938): 1, all in Accession 500, Series II Part 2, Rutledge Papers 1930–1941, HML.

10. "$10,000,000 Plant to Make Synthetic Yarn: Major Blow to Japan's Silk Trade Seen," *New York Times* (21 October 1938); "A Blow to Japan," *Beaumont (Texas) Journal* (22 October 1938); "DuPont Makes New Material for Fine Hosiery: Expected to Replace Silk from Japan," *Chicago Tribune* (28 October 1938), all in Accession 500, Series II Part 2, Rutledge Papers 1930–1941, HML.

11. "Castor Oil, Coal Newest 'Silkworms' for Stockings," *Science News Letter* (1 October 1938): 212.

12. "Textiles: No. 2,130, 948," *Time* (3 October 1938): 47.

13. "Silk Stocking Sanctions," *New York World Telegram* (30 August 1938), Accession 500, Series II Part 2, Rutledge Papers 1930–1941, HML.

14. Lois W. Banner, *American Beauty* (New York: Knopf, 1983), 10, 75.

15. Robert C. Allen, *Horrible Prettiness: Burlesque and American Culture* (Chapel Hill: University of North Carolina Press, 1991), 81, 89.

16. Sarah A. Gordon, "Any Desired Length: Negotiating Gender Through Sports Clothing, 1870–1925," in *Beauty and Business: Commerce, Gender and Culture in Modern America*, ed. Philip Scranton (New York: Routledge, 2001), 24–51; Banner, *American Beauty*, 4–10, 154–67; James R. McGovern, "The American Woman's Pre-World War I Freedom in Manners and Morals," *Journal of American History* 55 (September 1968):

315–33; Elizabeth Ewing, *Dress and Undress: A History of Women's Underwear* (London: Batsford, 1978), 110.

17. Ewing, *Dress and Undress*, 113–55; Jill Fields, "Fighting the Corsetless Evil: Shaping Corsets and Culture, 1900–1930," in Scranton, *Beauty and Business*, 109–40.

18. Ewing, *Dress and Undress*, 140.

19. Hounshell and Smith, *Science and Corporate Strategy*, 260; Chemical Department, "Report to Executive Committee, for the year 1935, E. I. du Pont de Nemours & Company, Inc.," Accession 1784, DuPont Central Research and Development Department, Box 16, 1–2, HML.

20. Chemical Department, "Report to the Executive Committee for the Year 1936," Accession 1784, DuPont Central Research and Development Department, Box 16, HML.

21. G. P. Hoff, "Nylon as a Textile Fiber," presented at the Division of Industrial and Engineering Chemistry, American Chemical Society, Detroit, Michigan, 27 June1940, Accession 140, DuPont Public Affairs Department, Box 10, HML; E. K. Bolton, "Development of Nylon," *Industrial and Engineering Chemistry* 34 (January 1942): 53–58; A. G. Edison, "Let's Spin a Yarn," address before the Middle Atlantic Section of the A.S.E.E., 7 December 1946, Accession 500, Series II Part 2, Rutledge Scrapbook for Nylon 1947–1949, HML; also Hounshell and Smith, *Science and Corporate Strategy*, 258–59, 262–73.

22. E. K. Gladding to L. A. Yerkes, Rayon Department, 15 September 1937, Buffalo, New York, Accession 500, Series II Part 2, Preston Hoff Papers Box 963, HML.

23. G. P. Hoff to E. K. Gladding, "Objectives of Plant 66," 21 July 1939, Accession 500, Series II Part 2, Preston Hoff Papers, Box 969, HML.

24. T. C. Welling, "Office Trade Report: May Hosiery Mills" 30 January 1939, Accession 500, Series II Part 2, Preston Hoff Papers, Box 954, HML. See also R. A. Ramsdell, "Office Trade Report: Holeproof Hosiery Company," 14 December 1938; R. A. Ramsdell, "Office Trade Report: Vanity Fair Silk Mills," 26 January 1939; T. C. Welling, "Office Trade Report: Hanes Hosiery Mill Company," 1 February 1939, all in Accession 500, Series II Part 2, Preston Hoff Papers, Box 954, HML.

25. Charles Stine, "What Laboratories of Industry Are Doing for the World of Tomorrow: Chemicals and Textiles," Charles M. Stine, Vice President, E. I. duPont de Nemours & Company to be delivered before the New York Herald Tribune Eighth Annual Forum on Current Problems, Thursday, October 27, 1938 at New York World's Fair Grounds, Accession 500, Series II Part 2, Rutledge Papers 1930–1941, HML.

26. "Forum Closes 3-Day Session with Glimpse of Tomorrow's World at Fair Grounds," *New York Herald Tribune* (28 October 1938): 12.

27. D. A. Kelsey to B. M. May, 25 March 1938, Accession 500, Series II Part 2, Rutledge Papers 1930–1941, HML.

28. Charles H. Rutledge, "The Name Nylon and Some of Its Adventures," 20 June 1966, Accession 500, Series II Part 2, Rutledge Papers 1930–1941, HML.

29. George Lipsitz, "The Struggle for Hegemony," *Journal of American History* 75 (June 1988): 146–50.

30. For a detailed description of marketing's beginnings, see Susan Strasser, *Satisfaction Guaranteed: The Making of the American Mass Market* (New York: Random House, 1989).

31. Carolyn Goldstein, "Mediating Consumption: Home Economics and American Consumers, 1900–1940," Ph.D. dissertation, University of Delaware, 1994; Simone Weil Davis, *Living Up to the Ads: Gender Fictions of the 1920s* (Durham, N.C.: Duke University Press, 2000); Roland Marchand, *Advertising the American Dream: Making Way for Modernity, 1920–1940* (Berkeley: University of California Press, 1985).

32. Victoria de Grazia, "Empowering Women as Citizen-Consumers," in *The Sex of Things: Gender and Consumption in Historical Perspective*, ed. Victoria de Grazia with Ellen Furlough (Berkeley: University of California Press, 1996), 279.

33. Meikle, *American Plastic*,

34. "News Release," Public Relations Department, E. I. DuPont de Nemours and Company, 2 February 1947, Accession 140, DuPont Public Affairs Department, Box 48, HML.

35. "Dear Silk," *Time* (19 February 1940): 76–77.

36. News Release, 23 October 1939; "An Announcement About Nylon Hosiery," 23 October 1939, advertisement in Wilmington, Delaware, newspapers; "Scene at Wilmington, Delaware, Store During Sale of Nylon Hosiery," 25 October 1939, Accession 500, Series II Part 2, Rutledge Papers 1930–1941, HML.

37. News Release, 14 May 1940, Accession 500, Series II Part 2, Rutledge Papers 1930–1941, HML.

38. "Nylon," *Life* 8 (10 June 1940): 60; Bernice Bronner, "Report on Nylon Hosiery," *Good Housekeeping* 111 (August 1940): 106, 120.

39. News Release, 14 May 1940, Accession 500, Series II Part 2, Rutledge Papers 1930–1941, HML.

40. "Nylon Sellout," *Newsweek* (27 May 1940): 65–66.

41. "Stocking Panic," *Business Week* (9 August 1941): 24–25.

42. "Hosiery Woes," *Business Week* (7 February 1942): 40.

43. "A Woman Complains; An Editor Answers," *Business Week* (3 October 1942): 87.

44. "A Woman Complains; An Editor Answers, 87.

45. "We Borrowed Their 'Nylons' to Make Tires for the Navy," *Life* (3 May 1943), Accession 500, Series II Part 2, Rutledge Papers 1942–1946, HML.

46. "Nylon in Tires: Giving Good Service Under Severe Conditions," *Scientific American* (August 1943): 78; "Textiles Go to War," *American Photographer* (March 1944): 28–29.

47. Beatrice Oppenheim, "Post-War Jobs for Nylon," *New York Times Magazine* (5 November 1944): 37; see also "Nylon After the War," *Science News Letter* (9 January 1943): 19; "Nylon for Everything," *Time* (16 August 1943): 38–39; "Nylon Applications Will Spread into Many Post-War Fields," *Scientific American* (January 1945): 46.

48. David O. Woodbury, "Your Life Tomorrow," *Collier's* (5 June 1943): 48.

49. Accession 500, Series II Part 2, Rutledge Papers 1942–1946, HML.

50. Frank Bock, "Bootleg Nylons," *Reader's Digest* (February 1945): 66–68; see also "Bootleg Nylons," on Radio Reader's Digest over WABC and CBS networks, 25 March 1945; Denis Sneigr, "The Black Market Boys: Nylons Come High—They Aren't Nylons," *New York World Telegram* (27 March 1945), Accession 500, Series II Part 2, Rutledge Papers 1942–1946, HML.

51. Edith Efron, "Legs Are Bare Because They Can't Be Sheer," *New York Times Magazine* (24 June 1945): 17.

52. "News Release: Memorandum on Nylon," 22 August 1945, Accesssion 140, Du-Pont Public Affairs Department, Box 49, HML.

53. "1200 Cheer as Nylons March in," *Los Angeles News* (12 December 1945); "10,000 Jam Nylon Line: Two Hours in Snow Pays Off," *Syracuse Post Standard* (22 January 1946); Clarissa Start, "Nylons! Did You Say Nylons? How St. Louis Dealers Are Coping with This National Feminine Frenzy," *St. Louis Post Dispatch* (7 January 1946); "Screaming Mobs Rush Dayton's Nylon Sale: Men First to Buy," *Minneapolis Star Journal* (February 1946). See also "First on Store Counters in 3 Years—Nylon Stockings Go on Sale Here," *St. Paul Pioneer-Press* (28 October 1945); "Nylons, Says Flash, and What a Jam!" *Milwaukee Journal* (29 November 1945); "Shoppers Told to Take Nylons off Yule Lists," *New York Herald Tribune* (12 December 1945); Joan Younger, "Nylons? Chance of Getting Them About Same as Being Struck by Lightning," *Goshen (Indiana) News-Democrat* (12 December 1945); "Hose Counters Remain Bare as Demand Climbs," *Philadelphia Inquirer* (18 March 1946) Accession 500, Series II Part 2, Rutledge Papers 1942–1946, HML.

54. "Yesterday Macy's Sold 50,000 Pairs of Nylons," *New York Times* (6 February 1946), Accession 500, Series II Part 2, Rutledge Papers 1942–1946, HML.

55. Earl A. Dash, "Headaches of Selling Hard-to-Get Goods," *Women's Wear Daily* (6 March 1946); Donald L. Pratt, "Public Seen Revolting Against Hosiery Lines," *Women's Wear Daily* (12 April 1946); "That Nylon Nightmare," *Hosiery and Underwear Review* (March 1946); "Heaven Help Our Hosiery Buyer," *Hosiery and Underwear Review* (March 1946); William Cooper, "Nylon Mob, 40,000 Strong, Shrieks and Sways for Mile," *Pittsburgh Press* (13 June 1946), Accession 500, Series II Part 2, Rutledge Papers 1942–1946, HML.

56. Harry Lazarus, "Operation Nylon," *New York Times* (10 February 1946), Accession 500, Series II Part 2, Rutledge Papers 1942–1946, HML.

57. Gladys Parker, "Mopsy," *Halsey (Oregon) Review* (2 March 1946); see also "Side Glances," *Le Grande (Oregon) Observer* (14 March 1946); Dorothy Bond, "The Ladies" (22 April 1946); Mischa Richter, "Strictly Richter," King Features Syndicate (14 May 1946); Denys Wortman, "Everyday Movies," *New Yorker* (9 November 1946), Accesssion 500, Series II Part 2, Rutledge Papers 1942–1946, HML.

58. Tim Sims and Bill Zaboly, "Popeye," *Philadelphia Inquirer* (14 July 1946), Accesssion 500, Series II Part 2, Rutledge Papers 1942–1946, HML.

59. "Nylons? Anything'll Do! Hose, Please! Toes Freeze," *Chicago Daily News* (8 February 1946), Accession 500, Series II Part 2, Rutledge Papers 1942–1946, HML.

60. Both cartoons are marked 1946 with no other identifying information in Accession 500, Series II Part 2, Rutledge Papers 1942–1946, HML.

61. "Nylon Post-War Stockings," 23 April 1943, DuPont News Releases, Public Relations Department, Accession 500, Series II Part 2, Rutledge Papers 1942–1946, HML.

62. Harry T. Brundidge, "Name It and You Can Have It—It's Nylon," *Cosmopolitan Magazine* (May 1944), Accession 500, Series II Part 2, Rutledge Papers 1942–1946, HML.

63. "Press Bulletin," National Association of Hosiery Manufacturers, 6 February 1946.

64. "US Girls," cartoon, *Boston Post* (15 February 1946), Accession 500, Series II Part 2, Rutledge Papers 1942–1946, HML.

65. Harold Brayman to Herbert Nichols, Science Editor, *Christian Science Monitor* (19 February 1946), Accession 140, DuPont Public Affairs Department, Box 9, HML.

66. Mabel Greene, "Hosiery Firm's Head Is Gloomy," *New York Sun* (4 February 1946); "Hose Men See Bleak Future for Silk Stockings," *Women's Wear Daily* (3 May 1946): 18, Accession 500, Series II Part 2, Rutledge Papers 1942–1946, HML.

67. "Nylon Yarn Statement" by Warren A. Beh at the Ninth Hosiery Industry Conference, 29 April 1946, Accession 140, DuPont Public Affairs Department, Box 10, HML; see also Mabel Greene, "Hosiery Firm's Head Is Gloomy," *New York Sun* (4 February 1946), Accession 500, Series II Part 2, Rutledge Papers 1942–1946, HML.

68. "News Release," 6 February 1947, Accession 500, Series II Part 2, Rutledge Papers 1947–1949, HML; Warren A. Beh, "Nylon Yarn Prospects for '48," talk at the Hosiery Merchandising Forum, Waldorf-Astoria, New York, 4 February 1948, Accession 140, DuPont Public Affairs Department, Box 9, HML. See also John G. Zervas, "First Post-War Year in Hosiery Production," *Hosiery and Underwear Review* (March 1947): 165–67, Accession 500, Series II Part 2, Rutledge Papers 1947–1949, HML.

69. "What's New in DuPont Nylon: Nylon Promotion," March 1947, Accession 500, Series II Part 2, Rutledge Scrapbook for Nylon 1947–1949, HML.

70. "A Woman Complains; An Editor Answers"; Donald L. Pratt, "Public Seen Revolting Against Hosiery Lines," *Women's Wear Daily* (12 April 1946), Accession 500, Series II Part 2, Rutledge Papers 1942–1946, HML.

71. "McKinney Goes on the Air to Answer Kicks on Hose Quality," *Hosiery Industry Weekly* (28 February 1949), Accession 500, Series II Part 2, Rutledge Papers 1942–1946, HML.

72. W. E. Coughlin and Michael Drury, "The Truth About Nylon Stockings," *Good Housekeeping* 131 (September 1950): 60–61, 242–43.

73. "If It's Nylon It's Nicer," advertisements in *Women's Wear Daily, Daily News Record, Colliers, Life, Saturday Evening Post, Department Store Economist, Merchants Trade Journal, Knit Goods Weekly, Hosiery & Underwear Review, Corset & Underwear Review,* 1948, Accession 500, Series II Part 2, Rutledge Papers 1947–1949, HML.

74. "News About Nylon," advertisement appearing in *Life* (23 February 1948), *Saturday Evening Post* (7 February 1948), *Colliers* (21 February 1948), *Time* (16 February 1948), Accession 500, Series II Part 2, Rutledge Papers 1947–1949, HML.

75. "Nylon Gives You Something Extra," advertising campaign, 1948–49, Advertising Department, Accession 1803, Box 43, HML.

76. Judith Crist, "Nylon Industry Survey Shows Quality of Thread Has Improved," *New York Herald Tribune* (6 February 1949), Accession 140, DuPont Public Affairs Department, Box 9, HML.

77. Robert Prall, "Nylons Don't Last? Of Course Not!" *New York World-Telegram and Sun* (26 February 1951).

78. Sylvia F. Porter, "Nylon Stocking 'Plot'," *New York Post* (1 June 1954), Accession 500, Series II Part 2, Rutledge Papers 1950–1957, HML.

79. "Filmed in Nylon: Stocking News," *Vogue* 121 (1 March 1954): 66.

80. "Don't Crab About Nylon Stockings," *Kiplinger Magazine* 8 (April 1954): 17–18.

81. "Your Nylons," *National Business Woman* 36 (January 1957): 7.

82. "Helen Hennessy, "Be Kind to Nylons—They're Sheer Delight," *Birmingham Post-Herald* (12 May 1964), Accession 500, Series II Part 2, Rutledge Papers 1964–1965, HML.

83. Elizabeth C. Ramsay, "Playing a No-Run Game in Hosiery," *Good Housekeeping* 109 (October 1939): 180–81, 200; "Susan Takes Care of Her Stockings," *Good Housekeeping* 121 (October 1945): 95.

84. Margaret Davidson, "How Long Do Your Stockings Wear?" *Ladies Home Journal* 55 (August 1938): 67; "Keep Stocking Diaries; Life Stories of 253 Pairs," *Science News Letter* 6 (August 1938): 90; Ida A. Anders, "A Study of the Practices of a Selected Group of Employed Women in the Buying and Care of Hosiery," *Journal of Home Economics* 30 (October 1938): 554–55;"What Are Your Stocking Habits? A Stocking Questionnaire," *Ladies Home Journal* 56 (November 1939): 48.

85. "Is the Lady Getting the Run-Around on Hosiery? Or Is She Getting the Dope on Denier?" Advertisements appearing in *Daily News Record* (19 June 1951), (6 November 1951); *Women's Wear Daily* (20 July 1951), (16 October 1951), Accession 500, Series II Part 2, Rutledge Papers 1950–1957, HML; News Release, "Nylon Stocking Sound-Slide Film Available from the Du Pont Company," 15 January 1952, Accession 140, DuPont Public Affairs Department, Box 9, HML.

86. Coughlin and Drury, "The Truth About Nylon Stockings"; see also W. E. Coughlin, "What's Next in Hosiery?" *Good Housekeeping* 122 (April 1946): 98–99.

87. Earl Constantine, president of the National Association of Hosiery Manufacturers, "Observations on the Merchandising of Hosiery at the 4th Annual Hosiery Forum, Hotel Waldorf Astoria, New York, 9 January 1950"; Charles Rutledge to Arthur Godfrey, 2 November 1951, Accession 500, Series II Part 2, Rutledge Papers 1950–1957, HML; News Release, 8 January 1953, Accession 140, DuPont Public Affairs Department, Box 49, HML; C. H. Rutledge to G. S. Hoagland, "Growth of 15-Denier Yarn in Hosiery," 24 April 1953, Accession 140, DuPont Public Affairs Department, Box 9, HML.

88. J. K. Novins, "Consumer Is Heard from in Roper Hosiery Survey," *Hosiery and Underwear Review* (May 1950), Accession 500, Series II Part 2, Rutledge Papers 1950–1957, HML.

89. "Nylons," *Consumer Reports* 22 (August 1957): 356–59.

90. Joseph L. Nicholson, "Synthetics Preferred: The Revolution in Man-Made Fibers," *Harper's Magazine* (August 1941): 2432–51.

91. "Cheaper Nylons?" *Business Week* (12 April 1947).

92. C. H. Rutledge to G. S. Hoagland, "Growth of 15-Denier Yarn in Hosiery," 24 April 1953; News Release, 8 January 1953, Accession 140, DuPont Public Affairs Department, Box 49, HML.

93. On the Astor Place riot, see Peter George Buckley, "To the Opera House: Culture and Society in New York City, 1820–1860," Ph.D. dissertation, State University of New York, Stony Brook, 1984; Lawrence Levine, *Highbrow/Lowbrow: The Emergence of Cultural Hierarchy in America* (Cambridge, Mass.: Harvard University Press, 1988).

94. Beginning with John Kasson, *Civilizing the Machine: Technology and Republican Values in America, 1776–1900* (New York: Penguin, 1997) up to and including Steven Lubar and David W. Kingery, eds., *History from Things: Essays in Material Culture* (Washington, D.C.: Smithsonian Institution Press, 1993).

95. Steven Lubar, "Culture and Technological Design in the 19th Century Pin Industry: John Howe and the Howe Manufacturing Company," *Technology and Culture* 28 (1987): 253–82.

96. The literature on the culture of consumption is now huge. Two of my favorite definitions are contained in Michael Schudson, *Advertising, the Uneasy Persuasion* (New York: Basic Books, 1984) and Marchand, *Advertising the American Dream*.

97. For the agency of audience members, see John Fiske, *Reading the Popular* (Boston: Unwin Hyman, 1989); Fiske, *Understanding Popular Culture* (Boston: Unwin Hyman, 1989); and for a history of audiences, Richard Butsch, *The Making of American Audiences: From Stage to Television 1750–1990* (New York: Oxford University Press, 2000).

98. Dana Frank, *Purchasing Power: Consumer Organizing, Gender, and the Seattle Labor Movement, 1919–1929* (Cambridge: Cambridge University Press, 1994); Annelise Orleck, *Common Sense and a Little Fire: Women and Working-Class Politics in the United States, 1900–1965* (Chapel Hill: University of North Carolina Press, 1995).

99. For example, see Kathleen Franz, *Tinkering: Consumers Reinvent the Early Automobile* (Philadelphia: University of Pennsylvania Press, 2005).

100. Meikle, *American Plastic*, 128.

101. Meikle, *American Plastic*, 139.

CHAPTER 3. REORIENTATION AND ENTERTAINMENT IN OCCUPIED JAPAN

1. General Headquarters, Supreme Commander for the Allied Powers, "Theater and Motion Pictures," *History of the Nonmilitary Activities of the Occupation of Japan, 1945–1951* (Tokyo: Headquarters, 1951), 5: 30–31.

2. D. R. Nugent, Lt. Col., USMC, Chief, CIE Section to Charles Mayer, Central Motion Picture Exchange, 10 November 1950; Motion Pictures, Box 5155; Administrative Division; Civil Information and Education Section; Supreme Commander for the Allied Powers, Record Group 331; National Archives at College Park, MD, hereafter cited as CIE Section; SCAP, RG331; NACP.

3. John Dower, *Embracing Defeat: Japan in the Wake of World War II* (New York:

New Press, 1999), 23; For another description of the ways race complicated the Occupation, see Yukiko Koshiro, *Trans-Pacific Racisms and the U.S. Occupation of Japan* (New York: Columbia University Press, 1999). A useful overview of the scholarship on the Occupation and its pitfalls is Carol Gluck, "Entangling Illusions—Japanese and American Views of the Occupation," in *New Frontiers in American-East Asian Views of the Occupation*, ed. Warren Cohen (New York: Columbia University Press, 1983), 169–236.

4. For a discussion of the scholarly debate on this subject, see Rob Kroes, "American Empire and Cultural Imperialism: A View from the Receiving End," *Diplomatic History* 23 (Summer 1999): 463–77.

5. Miriam Silverberg, "Remembering Pearl Harbor, Forgetting Charlie Chaplin, and the Case of the Disappearing Western Woman: A Picture Story," *positions* 1 (1993): 24–76; thanks to Kerry Smith for calling this article to my attention and for all his help in my studies of Japan.

6. Silverberg, "Remembering Pearl Harbor," 61; see also Miriam Silverberg, "Constructing a New Cultural History of Prewar Japan," in *Japan in the World*, ed. Masao Miyosi and H. D. Harootunian (Durham, N.C.: Duke University Press, 1993), 115–43.

7. Donald Richie, "The Japanese Kiss," in Richie, *A Lateral View: Essays on Culture and Style in Contemporary Japan* (Berkeley, Calif.: Stone Bridge Press, 1992), 225.

8. On postwar literature and the Occupation, see Jay Rubin, "From Wholesomeness to Decadence: The Censorship of Literature Under the Allied Occupation," *Journal of Japanese Studies* 11 (Winter 1985): 71–103.

9. Dower, *Embracing Defeat*, 150.

10. Kyoko Hirano, *Mr. Smith Goes to Tokyo: Japanese Cinema Under the American Occupation, 1945–1952* (Washington, D.C.: Smithsonian Institution Press, 1992), 154–70.

11. For a brilliant description of the relationship between the American and Japanese film industries, see Donald Kirihara, *Patterns of Time: Mizoguchi and the 1930s* (Madison: University of Wisconsin Press, 1992), 39–58.

12. Hirano, *Mr. Smith Goes to Tokyo*, 27.

13. For some examples, see "Japanese Motion Pictures," edited translation, *Kinema Jumpo*, February 1948, translator, T. Omori; "The Advance of Imported Movies," edited translation, *Kinema Jumpo*, 15 April 1949, translator, K. Onishi; "Control on Import of Foreign Films and Japanese Pictures," edited translation, Helicopter Column, *Mainichi Shimbun*, 24 July 1951, all contained in Digests and Publications, Box 5235; Translation Unit; Executive Branch; Information Division; CIE Section; SCAP, RG331; NACP.

14. Emily S. Rosenberg, *Spreading the American Dream: American Economic and Cultural Expansion, 1890–1945* (New York: Hill and Wang, 1982), 36.

15. Edward G. Lowry, "Trade Follows the Film," *Saturday Evening Post* 198 (7 November 1925): 12; Paul Swann, "The Little State Department: Washington and Hollywood's Rhetoric of the Postwar Audience," in *Hollywood in Europe: Experiences of A Cultural Hegemony*, ed. David W. Ellwood and Rob Kroes (Amsterdam: VU University Press, 1994), 176–95.

16. For examples, see Kristin Thompson, *Exporting Entertainment: America in the*

World Film Market, 1907–1934 (London: British Film Institute, 1985), 111–17, 141; Ian Jarvie, *Hollywood's Overseas Campaign: The North Atlantic Movie Trade, 1920–1950* (New York: Cambridge University Press, 1992), 294; Kirihara, *Patterns of Time*, 43.

17. Lowry, "Trade Follows the Film"; for postwar European resistance to American films, see Sydney B. Self, "Movie Diplomacy," *Wall Street Journal* (16 August 1944).

18. Rosenberg, *Spreading the American Dream*, 100.

19. Robert Sklar, *Movie-Made America: A Cultural History of American Movies* (New York: Random House, 1994), 215–16.

20. Thomas Doherty, *Projections of War: Hollywood, American Culture and World War II* (New York: Columbia University Press, 1993), 5.

21. For an excellent account of OWI policy, see Clayton R. Koppes and Gregory D. Black, *Hollywood Goes to War: How Politics, Profits, and Propaganda Shaped World War II Movies* (New York: Free Press, 1987), particularly 66–67, 141–43.

22. For a reprint of the entire memo, see Jarvie, *Hollywood's Overseas Campaign*, 377–82.

23. Self, "Movie Diplomacy"; see also Herman A. Lowe, "Washington Discovers Hollywood," *American Mercury* 60 (April 1945): 407–14.

24. Ralph Willett, *The Americanization of Germany, 1945–1949* (New York: Routledge, 1989), 28–39.

25. Billy Wilder to Davidson Taylor, "Propaganda Through Entertainment," 16 August 1945, Headquarters, United States Forces, European Theater, Information Control Division, reprinted in Willett, *Americanization of Germany*, 40–44.

26. Robert Joseph, "Our Film Program in Germany: How Far Was It a Success?" *Hollywood Quarterly* 2 (January 1947): 122–30; Gladwin Hill, "Our Film Program in Germany: How Far Was It a Failure?" *Hollywood Quarterly* 2 (January 1947): 131–37. Historians have clearly outlined the Occupation's failures in using film as propaganda in Germany. See Heide Fehrenbach, *Cinema in Democratizing Germany: Reconstructing National Identity After Hitler* (Chapel Hill: University of North Carolina Press, 1995); Swann, "The Little State Department"; Hans Borcher, "Hollywood as Reeducator: The Role of Feature Films in U.S. Policies Directed at Postwar Germany," *Paedagogica Historica* 33 (1997); and Uta R. Poiger, *Jazz, Rock, and Rebels: Cold War Politics and American Culture in a Divided Germany* (Berkeley: University of California Press, 2000).

27. Thomas Guback, "Shaping the Film Business in Postwar Germany: The Role of the U.S. Film Industry and the U.S. State," in *The Hollywood Film Industry*, ed. Paul Kerr (New York: Routledge & Kegan Paul, 1986), 266–68.

28. *His Butler's Sister*, Dir. Frank Borzage, Perfs. Deanna Durbin, Franchot Tone, Pat O'Brien, Universal Pictures, 1943, videocassette, MCA Home Video, 1996; *Madame Curie*, Dir. Mervyn LeRoy, Perfs. Greer Garson, Walter Pidgeon, Metro-Goldwyn-Mayer, 1943, MGM/UA Home Video, 1992. On the early showing of *Madame Curie* see Makoto Hori and Takashi Abe, American Movie Culture Association to Supreme Commander Allied Forces, Japan, 1 June 1949, Motion Pictures, Box 5072, Administrative Division, CIE Section; SCAP, RG331; for a list of "features released to date" that has *His Butler's*

Sister as number 1 and *Madame Curie* as #2, see CIE to Chief, Civil Affairs Division, "Feature Films, Shorts and Documentaries," 18 June 1947; Motion Pictures 1947, Box 5063; Administrative Division; CIE Section; SCAP, RG331; on *Madame Curie*, see Dower, *Embracing Defeat*, 195.

29. Carol Gluck, "The Power of Culture," in *The Occupation of Japan: Arts and Culture*, ed. Thomas W. Burkman (Norfolk, Va.: MacArthur Foundation, 1988), 256.

30. Yole Granada, "Glamour Replaces Banzai," *United Nations World* 2 (February 1948): 28.

31. On film, see Hirano, *Mr. Smith Goes to Tokyo*; on radio, see Susan Smulyan, "Now It Can Be Told: The Influence of the United States Occupation on Japanese Radio," in *Radio Reader: Essays in the Cultural History of Radio*, ed. Michele Hilmes and Jason Loviglio (New York: Routledge, 2001), 301–17; on censorship of print media, see Jun Eto, "The Censorship Operation in Occupied Japan," in *Press Control Around the World*, ed. Jane Leftwich Curry and Joan R. Dassin (New York: Praeger, 1982), 235–53.

32. Theodore A. Wilson, "Selling America via the Silver Screen? Efforts to Manage the Projection of American Culture Abroad, 1942–1947" in *Here, There, and Everywhere: The Foreign Politics of American Popular Culture*, ed. Rheinhold Wagnleiter and Elaine Tyler May (Hanover, N.H.: University Press of New England, 2000), 83–99; for similar concerns voiced by a private citizen, see Harry Emerson Wildes, "Can Hollywood Win the Peace?" *Asia and the Americas* 46 (February 1946): 81–83.

33. *His Butler's Sister*, videocassette, MCA Home Video, 1996.

34. Dower, *Embracing Defeat*, 73.

35. For the way in which these economic ideas worked out in radio during the U.S. Occupation of Japan see Smulyan, "Now It Can Be Told," 301–17.

36. Irving Maas, Vice President and General Manager, Motion Picture Export Association to General Douglas MacArthur, Supreme Commander of the Allied Powers, 9 March 1951; Motion Pictures, Box 5088; Administrative Division; CIE Section; SCAP, RG331; NACP.

37. Iwasaki Akira, "The Occupied Screen," *Japan Quarterly* (July/September 1978): 303–4.

38. Marlene Mayo, "Psychological Disarmament: American Wartime Planning for the Education and Re-Education of Defeated Japan, 1943–1945," in *The Occupation of Japan*, ed. Burkman, 22–24.

39. Motion Picture Section, Department of the Army, Civil Affairs Division, New York Field Office to General Robert A. McClure, Chief, New York Field Office, "Progress Report of Motion Picture Section for the FY1948," 30 June 1948; Motion Pictures, 1948, Box 5066; Administrative Division; CIE Section; SCAP, RG331; NACP.

40. Mayo, "Psychological Disarmament," 91: Hirano noted that Nugent was the conservative successor to New Deal liberal Brigadier General Kermit Dykes, an NBC executive, who left in the spring of 1946, Hirano, *Mr. Smith Goes To Tokyo*, 8.

41. D. R. Nugent to Chief of Staff, Civil Information and Education Section, "Foreign Media Control," 16 September 1946, Records Section, Box 8521, Civil Censorship

Detachment, SCAP, RG331, NACP; on the placement of Motion Pictures in the CIE, see also Hirano, *Mr. Smith Goes to Tokyo*, 27.

42. D. R. Nugent, Chief, CIE Section to Mrs. Florence Baldwin, Napa High School Library, 25 November 1949; Motion Pictures, Box 5072; Administrative Division; CIE Section; SCAP, RG331; NACP.

43. CIE to CIC, Central Motion Picture Exchange, "Inquiry About CCD," 25 February 1948; Motion Pictures 1948, Box 5066; Administrative Division; CIE Section; SCAP, RG331; NACP; also Eto, "The Censorship Operation in Occupied Japan," 235–53.

44. WBP to Deputy Chief, Civil Intelligence Section, "Draft Circular 'Admission of Foreign Magazines, Books, Motion Pictures, News and Photo Services, etc. and Their Dissemination in Japan," 1 November 1946; Records Section, Box 8521; Civil Censorship Detachment; SCAP, RG331; NACP; further details about censorship by CCD and CIE can be found in Hirano, *Mr. Smith Goes to Tokyo*, 44–49.

45. CIE to CCD, "American Pictures Presented for Censoring by Japanese," 19 January 1948; Motion Pictures, 1948, Box 5066; Administrative Division; CIE Section; SCAP, RG331; NACP; CIE to CIC, Central Motion Picture Exchange, "Inquiry about CCD," 25 February 1948; Motion Pictures, 1948, Box 5066; Administrative Division; CIE Section; SCAP, RG331; NACP.

46. General Headquarters, *History of the Nonmilitary Activities*, 5: 24.

47. WAR to CINCFE, "Coupling of Feature Films and Documentaries," 26 April 1947; Motion Pictures, 1948, Box 5066; Administrative Division; CIE Section; SCAP, RG331; NACP.

48. CINFE to WDSCA, "Coupling Feature Films," 2 June 1947; Motion Pictures 1948, Box 5066; Administrative Division; CIE Section; SCAP, RG331; NACP.

49. D. R. Nugent, Chief, CIE Section to Brigadier General Robert A. McClure, Chief, Civil Affairs Division, 4 October 1948; Motion Pictures, 1948, Box 5066; Administrative Division; CIE Section; SCAP, RG331; NACP.

50. Quoted in Hirano, *Mr. Smith Goes to Tokyo*, 44–45.

51. Hirano, *Mr. Smith Goes to Tokyo*, 45.

52. Office of Military Government for Germany (U.S.), Motion Picture Branch, "Operation Reports," March 21, 1949, reprinted in David Holbrook Culbert, Richard E. Wood, and Lawrence H. Suid, eds., *Film and Propaganda in America: A Documentary History*, vol. 4, *1945 and After* (New York: Greenwood Press, 1990–1991), 81; for a description of the work of the MPEA see Guback, "Shaping the Film Business in Postwar Germany," 255, and Fehrenbach, *Cinema in Democratizing Germany*, 65.

53. CIE to G-1, "Clearance for Paramount Representative," 23 June 1947; Motion Pictures, 1947, Box 5062; Administrative Division; CIE Section; SCAP, RG331; NACP.

54. D. R. Nugent, Chief, CIE Section to Fair Trade Commission, "Motion Picture Export Association, 1 July 1949; Motion Pictures, Box 5072; Administrative Division; CIE Section; SCAP, RG331; NACP; see also Central Motion Picture Exchange, "License to Engage in Business in Japan," 27 May 1947; Motion Pictures, 1947, Box 5062; Administrative Division; CIE Section; SCAP, RG331; NACP.

55. Chief, CIE to Office of C-in-C, "Info on Charles Mayer," 12 October 1951; Motion Pictures, 1951, Box 5088; Administrative Division; CIE Section; SCAP, RG331; NACP.

56. The MPEA represented Columbia Pictures International Corporation, Loew's International Corporation, Paramount International Films, Inc., Republic Pictures international Corporation, RKO Radio Pictures, Inc., Twentieth Century-Fox International Corporation, United Artists Corporation, Universal International Films, Inc., and Warner Brothers Pictures International Corporation. See Irving Maas, Vice President and General Manager, Motion Picture Export Association, to General Douglas MacArthur, 9 March 1951; Supply Branch, Box 5233; Administrative Division; CIE Section; SCAP, RG331; NACP.

57. Charles Mayer to Lt. Col. D. R. Nugent, CIE, 12 April 1948, "Plagiarism of DARK VICTORY Story," Motion Pictures 1948, Box 5066; Administrative Division; CIE Section; SCAP, RG331; NACP; "Mayer Bans Newspaper Movie Critics from American Film Previews," edited translation, *Shimbun Kyokai Ho* 27 October (no year), translator, K. Morimoto; Digests and Publications, Box 5235; Translation Unit; Executive Branch; Information Division; CIE Section; SCAP, RG331; NACP; GHQ, SCAP to Irving Mass, Motion Picture Export Association; Supply Branch, Box 5233; Administrative Division; CIE Section; SCAP, RG331; NACP; Charles Mayer to Col. D. R. Nugent, 14 February 1950; Motion Pictures, Box 5081; Administrative Division; CIE Section; SCAP, RG331; NACP.

58. CIE to CS, "Proposed Radio to MPEA," 29 March 1949; Motion Pictures, Box 5072; Administrative Division; CIE Section; SCAP, RG331; NACP.

59. CIE to CD of S SCAP, "Check Sheet, Background Information on W-84531," 24 February 1949; Motion Pictures, Box 5072; Administrative Division; CIE Section; SCAP, RG331; NACP; see also D. R. Nugent to Chief of Staff, Civil Information and Education Section, "Foreign Media Control," 16 September 1946; Records Section, Box 8521; Civil Censorship Detachment, SCAP, RG331; NACP.

60. D.R.N., CIE, to Asst. Chief of Staff, G-2, "Control of Foreign Publications and Pictorial Productions in Japan," 9 July 1946; Records Section, 8521; Civil Censorship Detachment: SCAP, RG331; NCAP.

61. For the formal document which outlined CIE and CCD powers, see General Headquarters, Supreme Commander for the Allied Powers, "Circular No. 12: Admission of Foreign Magazines, Books, Motion Pictures, News and Photograph Services, Et Cetera, and Their Dissemination in Japan," 5 December 1946; Records Section, Box 8521; Civil Censorship Detachment; SCAP, RG331; NCAP; for the provisions for returning some funds to individual companies and the growing competitive natures of the Japanese film market see D. R. Nugent, Lt. Col., USMC, Chief, CIE Section to Charles Mayer, Central Motion Picture Exchange, 13 September 1948; Motion Pictures, 1948, Box 5066; Administrative Division; CIE Section; SCAP, RG331; NACP.

62. CIE to CS, "Proposed Radio to MPEA," 29 March 1949; Motion Pictures, Box 5072; Administrative Division; CIE Section; SCAP, RG331; NACP.

63. General Headquarters, Supreme Commander for the Allied Powers, "Circular No. 8: Admission and Dissemination of Foreign Magazines, Books, Motion Pictures, News and Photograph Services, Et Cetera, and Business Relating Thereto," 8 April 1950; Miscellaneous File, Box 1274; Legal Section; Administrative Division; CIE Section; SCAP, RG331; NACP.

64. D. R. Nugent, Lt. Col., USMC, Chief, CIE Section to Charles Mayer, Central Motion Picture Exchange, 10 February 1951; Motion Pictures, Box 5088; Administrative Division; CIE Section; SCAP, RG331; NACP.

65. Headquarters, Tokai-Hokuriku Mil Govt Region to CINCFE, GHQ, SCAP, Attn: CI&E Section, "American Films," 23 December 1947; Motion Pictures, 1947, Box 5062; Administrative Division; CIE Section; SCAP, RG331; NACP.

66. Copy of Letter from Dept. of the Army Civilian to C.I.&E. Section, 15 December 1947, 23 December 1947; Motion Pictures, 1947, Box 5062; Administrative Division; CIE Section; SCAP, RG331; NACP.

67. Robert A. McClure, Brigadier General, USA, Chief, New York Field Office to Lieutenant Colonel D. R. Nugent, Chief, Civil Information & Education Section, 30 September 1948; Motion Pictures, 1948, Box 5066; Administrative Division; CIE Section; SCAP, RG331; NACP.

68. Information Division, Civil Information and Education Section to Administrative Officer, Administrative Division, 24 December 1948; Motion Picture Branch, Box 5304; CIE Section; SCAP, RG331; NACP; on "Dallas" see D. R. Nugent, Lt. Col., USMC, Chief, CIE Section to Charles Mayer, Central Motion Picture Exchange, 28 August 1951; Motion Pictures, Box 5088; Administrative Division; CIE Section; SCAP, RG331; NACP.

69. D. R. Nugent, Lt. Col., USMC, Chief, CIE Section to Charles Mayer, Central Motion Picture Exchange, 4 November 1950; Motion Pictures, Box 5155; Administrative Division; CIE Section; SCAP, RG331; NACP.

70. G. K. Crew, Capt, WAC, Acting Chief, CIE to A. L. Caplan, 22 November 1950; Motion Pictures, Box 5155; Administrative Division; CIE Section; SCAP, RG331; NACP.

71. Robert M. Lury, Eagle Lion Classics, Inc. to Donald Brown, GHQ, SCAP, 30 March 1951; Motion Pictures, Box 5088; Administrative Division; CIE Section; SCAP, RG331; NACP; see also D. R. Nugent, Lt. Col, USMC, Chief, CIE Section to Edmund Goldman, Columbia Films, Lt, 21 November, 1951; Motion Pictures, 951, Box 5088; Administrative Division; CIE Section; SCAP, RG331; NACP.

72. D. R. Nugent, Lt. Col., USMC, Chief, CIE Section to Charles Mayer, Central Motion Picture Exchange, 28 August 1951; Motion Pictures, Box 5088; Administrative Division; CIE Section; SCAP, RG331; NACP.

73. J. E. Dagal, Warner Brothers, First National Pictures, Inc. to Charles Mayer, Central Motion Picture Exchange, 22 August 1951; Motion Pictures, Box 5088; Administrative Division; CIE Section; SCAP, RG331; NACP; see also Thomas L. Blakemore to Don Brown, Information Division, CIE Section, 20 July 1950; Motion Pictures, Box 5111;

Administration Division; CIE Section; SCAP, RG331; NACP; Charles Mayer, Central Motion Picture Exchange, to D. R. Nugent, Lt. Col., USMC, Chief, CIE Section, 31 October 1950; Motion Pictures, Box 5155; Administrative Division; CIE Section; SCAP, RG331; NACP.

74. D. R. Nugent, Lt. Col., USMC, Chief, CIE Section to Charles Mayer, MPEA, 17 May 1950; Motion Pictures, Box 5081; Administrative Division; CIE Section; SCAP, RG331; NACP.

75. Charles Mayer, Motion Picture Export Association to Lt. Col. D. R. Nugent, CI&E, 16 August 1951; Supply Branch, Box 5233; Administrative Division; CIE Section; SCAP, RG331; NACP; Extract from Letter from Mr. Maas, NY, Letter No. 512 dated August 8, 1951; Supply Branch, Box 5233; Administrative Division; CIE Section; SCAP, RG331; NACP.

76. Charles Mayer, Motion Picture Export Association to Lt. Col. D. R. Nugent, CI&E, 7 August 1951; Supply Branch, Box 5233; Administrative Division; CIE Section; SCAP, RG331; NACP.

77. D. R. Nugent, Lt. Col, USMC, Chief, CIE Section to Charles Mayer, Central Motion Picture Exchange, 4 October 1951; Supply Branch, Box 5233; Administrative Division; CIE Section; SCAP, RG331; NACP.

78. Irving Maas, Vice President and General Manager, Motion Picture Export Association to General Douglas MacArthur, 9 March 1951; Supply Branch, Box 5233; Administrative Division; CIE Section; SCAP, RG331; NACP.

79. Irving Maas, Vice-President and General Manager, Motion Picture Export Association to Brig. Gen. K. B. Bush, 30 April 1951, Supply Branch, Box 5233; Administrative Division; CIE Section; SCAP, RG331; NACP; Charles Mayer, Managing Director, Central Motion Picture Exchange of the Motion Picture Export Association, Inc. to Lt. Col D. R. Nugent, 8 September 1951; Supply Division, Box 5231; Administrative Division; CIE Section; SCAP, RG331; NACP; D. R. Nugent, Chief, CIE Section to Charles Mayer, Central Motion Picture Exchange, 26 September 1951; Motion Pictures, Box 5088; Administrative Division; CIE Section; SCAP, RG331; NACP.

80. "*Maru* Round-Table Discussion on Future of Japanese Motion Pictures," edited ranslation, *Maru*, June 1950, translator, K. Morimoto; Digests and Publications, Box 5235; Translation Unit; Executive Branch; Information Division; CIE Section; SCAP, RG331; NACP.

81. "Message of Lt. Col. D. R. Nugent, Chief of the Civil Information and Education Section, GHQ, SCAP, on the 10th Anniversary of the Daiei Motion Picture Company," 1 November 1951; Supply Branch, Box 5231; Administrative Division; CIE Section; SCAP, RG331; NACP; also in Motion Pictures, 1951, Box 5088; Administrative Division; CIE Section; SCAP, RG331; NACP.

82. ESS/FIB to CIE, "UKLM Position on Motion Picture Imports," 5 February 1951; Motion Pictures, Box 5088; Administrative Division; CIE Section; SCAP, RG331; NACP; see also General Headquarters, Supreme Commander for the Allied Powers, "Cir-

cular No. 12: Admission of Foreign Magazines, Books, Motion Pictures, News and Photograph Services, Et Cetera, and Their Dissemination in Japan," 5 December 1946; Records Section, Box 8521; Civil Censorship Detachment; SCAP, RG331; NACP; and General Headquarters, Supreme Commander for the Allied Powers, "Circular No. 8: Admission and Dissemination of Foreign Magazines, Books, Motion Pictures, News and Photograph Services, Et Cetera, and Business Relating Thereto," 8 April 1950; Miscellaneous File, Box 1274; Administrative Division; Legal Section; SCAP, RG331; NACP.

83. D. R. Nugent, Chief, CI&E Section to Norman Westwood, British Commonwealth Film Corporation, 6 December 1947; Motion Pictures, 1947, Box 5062; Administration Division; CIE Section; SCAP, RG331; NACP.

84. F. Chevalier, Syndicat d'Exportation des Films Français to Colonel D. R. Nugent, Chief, CIE Section, 4 April 1951; Motion Pictures, Box 5088; Administrative Division; CIE Section; SCAP, RG331; NACP.

85. United Kingdom Liaison Mission in Japan, British Embassy, Tokyo to Diplomatic Section of GHQ, SCAP, 23 January 1951, Motion Pictures, Box 5088, Administrative Division, CIE Section; SCAP, RG331; NACP.

86. CIE to ESS, Mr. D. Brown, 19 February 1951, Motion Pictures, Box 5088, Administrative Division, CIE Section; SCAP, RG331; NACP.

87. CIE to CS "Importation of Soviet Films," 20 September 1948, Motion Pictures, 1948, Box 5066, Administrative Division, CIE Section; SCAP, RG331; NACP.

88. CIE to DCS/SCAP, "Screening of Soviet Motion Pictures," Motion Pictures, Box 5096, Confidential Decimal File, Administration Division, CIE Section; SCAP, RG331; NACP.

89. For some examples see CIE to GS2, "Distribution of Russian Film," 19 November 1946, Motion Pictures, 1946, Box 5060, Administrative File, CIE Section; SCAP, RG331; NACP; K. Dehevyanko, Lieutenant General, Member, Allied Council for Japan from U.S.S.R., to Major General Mueller, HQ, SCAP, undated, Motion Pictures, 1947, Box 5062, Administrative Division, CIE Section; SCAP, RG331; NACP.

90. CIE to Deputy Chief of Staff, "Release of Soviet Films," 30 December 1950, Motion Pictures, Box 5096, Confidential Decimal File, Administrative Division, CIE Section; SCAP, RG331; NACP.

91. D. R. Nugent, Lt. Col., USMC, CIE to C/S, 9 May 1951, Supply Branch, Box 5231, Administrative Division, CIE Section; SCAP, RG331; NACP.

92. Norman Cousins, "The Free Ride, Part II," *Saturday Review of Literature* (28 January 1950): 21.

93. Norman Cousins, "The Free Ride, Part III," *Saturday Review of Literature* (4 February 1950): 22.

94. For a single example, see Mary Dudziak, *Cold War Civil Rights: Race and the Image of American Democracy* (Princeton, N.J.: Princeton University Press, 2000).

95. There has been much debate about the effect of Cold War politics on the Occupation. A good overview is Gluck, "Entangling Illusions."

CHAPTER 4. ADVERTISING NOVELS AS CULTURAL CRITIQUE: DRY MARTINIS, RARE STEAKS, AND WILLING WOMEN

1. I first became aware of these novels when reading Stephen Fox, *The Mirrormakers: A History of American Advertising and Its Creators* (New York: Vintage Books, 1985), 200–210. Fox does interesting readings of about half the novels that he sees as formulaic, as well as reflective of both life on Madison Avenue and 1950s life in general. For a list of novels examined here, see the Appendix at end of the chapter.

2. "The Drumbeatniks," *Time* 72 (10 November 1958): 104; see also Milton Moskowitz, "Novels of Past Decade Paint Lurid Ad World," *Advertising Age* (8 October 1956): 2, 96; William Hogan, "Glamor Novels—Some Faces in the Crowd," *San Francisco Chronicle* (14 October 1958): 33; Al Morgan, "Unhorsing a Heel," *Saturday Review* 41 (1 November 1958): 20; A.C. Spectorsky, "SR Runs Six Up the Flagpole," *Saturday Review* 41 (8 November 1958): 14–15; Ralph Vines, "Is It True What They Say About Admen?" *Advertising Age* 31 (11 July 1960): 104.

3. Roland Marchand, *Advertising the American Dream: Making Way for Modernity, 1920–1940* (Berkeley: University of California Press, 1985); Daniel Horowitz, *The Anxieties of Affluence: Critiques of American Consumer Culture, 1939–1979* (Amherst: University of Massachusetts Press, 2004).

4. On the best-seller list see Alice Payne Hackett, *Sixty Years of Best Sellers: 1895–1955* (New York: Bowker, 1956); on the total number of copies sold see Keith L. Justice, *Best-seller Index: All Books, Publisher's Weekly, and the New York Times Through 1990* (London: McFarland, 1998); the six books that appeared on the *New York Times* best-seller list were Frederic Wakeman, *The Hucksters* (New York: Rinehart, 1946), 58 weeks; Eric Hodgins, *Mr. Blandings Builds His Dream House* (New York: Simon and Schuster, 1946), 8 weeks; Herman Wouk, *Aurora Dawn* (New York: Doubleday, 1947), 4 weeks; Gerald Green, *The Last Angry Man* (New York: Charles Scribner's Sons, 1956), 52 weeks; Sloan Wilson, *The Man in the Gray Flannel Suit* (New York: Arbor House, 1955); Al Morgan, *The Great Man* (New York: E.P. Dutton, 1955), 6 weeks; on the use of best-seller lists to gauge popularity, see Laura J. Miller, "The Best-Seller List as Marketing Tool and Historical Fiction," *Book History* 3 (2000): 286–304.

5. "The Drumbeatniks," 104.

6. Thomas Frank, *The Conquest of Cool: Business Culture, Counterculture, and the Rise of Hip Consumerism* (Chicago: University of Chicago Press, 1997).

7. Horowitz, *The Anxieties of Affluence*, 4.

8. Kathy M. Newman, *Radio Active: Advertising and Consumer Activism, 1935–1947* (Berkeley: University of California Press, 2004).

9. Wakeman, *The Hucksters*, Jack Conway, dir., 1947.

10. Paul Lazarsfeld and Patricia Kendall, *Radio Listening in America* (New York: Prentice-Hall, 1948), 75.

11. Lazarsfeld and Kendall, *Radio Listening in America*, 77–79.

12. Herman Wouk, *Aurora Dawn* (1947; New York: Pocket Books, 1983), Preface. All references are to this reprint edition, which is still easily available.

13. John P. Marquand, *H. M. Pulham, Esquire* (Boston: Little, Brown, 1941). See also "Harvard '15," *Time* 37 (3 March 1941): 87–88 and Malcolm Cowley, "The Boston Story," *New Republic* 104 (3 March 1941): 314–15; Dorothy Hillyer, "Boston Legend and *The Right People*: Brilliant Novel That Explains Some Myths and Prejudices," *New York Herald Tribune Books* (23 February 1941): 1; "Boston and Maine—Light on Asia," *New Yorker* 17 (22 February 1941): 68, 70; J. Donald Adams, "The Portrait of a Bostonian," *New York Times Book Review* (23 February 1941): 1; Howard Mumford Jones, "Think Fast, Mr. Marquand," *Saturday Review of Literature* 23 (22 February 1941): 5; Mason Wade, "Three Novels," *Commonweal* 34 (2 May 1941): 39–40.

14. Dorothy Sayers, *Murder Must Advertise* (New York: Harcourt Brace, 1933); Janet Hitchman, *Such a Strange Lady: A Biography of Dorothy L. Sayers* (New York: Avon Books, 1975).

15. Edwin Lefevre, *H. R.* (New York: Harper & Brothers, 1915).

16. Daniel Pope, *The Making of Modern Advertising* (New York: Basic Books, 1983), 119.

17. Nathaniel C. Fowler, Jr., *Gumption: The Progressions of Newson New* (Boston: Small, Maynard, 1905), 242.

18. "Recent Fiction," *Dial* 57 (16 October 1914): 299–300; for other reviews see *Literary Digest* 50 (16 January 1915): 107; "The Clarion," *New York Times* 19 (11 October 1914): 431; Samuel Hopkins Adams, *The Clarion* (New York: Houghton Mifflin, 1914).

19. Adams, *The Clarion*, 258.

20. W. S. B., "A Battle for Principle," *Boston Evening Transcript* (23 September 1914): 20.

21. I take the term "advertising fictions" from the work of Jennifer Wicke, *Advertising Fictions: Literature, Advertisement, and Social Reading* (New York: Columbia University Press, 1988), although my use of it is much narrower than Wicke's wide-ranging exploration.

22. Harford Powel, Jr., *The Virgin Queene* (Boston: Little, Brown, 1928); for reviews see "The Virgin Queene," *Saturday Review of Literature* 4 (19 May 1928): 896; "Tongues in Cheeks," *New Republic* 55 (13 June 1928): 102; and "High-Hearted Spoofing," *New York Times Book Review* (22 April 1928): 8.

23. Simone Weil Davis, *Living Up to the Ads: Gender Fictions of the 1920s* (Durham, N.C.: Duke University Press, 2000), 69–70.

24. Amy Kaplan, *The Social Construction of American Realism* (Chicago: University of Chicago Press, 1988), 7.

25. Kaplan, *Social Construction of American Realism*, 9.

26. Kaplan, *Social Construction of American Realism*, 13.

27. Kaplan, *Social Construction of American Realism*, 159–60.

28. For a different view of "reality" versus media image in the advertising novels, see Lynda M. Maddox and Eric J. Zanot, "The Image of the Advertising Practitioner as Presented in the Mass Media, 1900–1972," *American Journalism* 2, 2 (Spring 1985): 117–29.

29. Spectorsky, "SR Runs Six Up the Flagpole," 14–15; for a brief note about the

advertising careers of James Kelly, Edward Stephens, Shepherd Mead, and Harold Livingston see "Books—Authors," *New York Times* (23 September 1958): 30.

30. Davis, *Living Up to the Ads*, 2, 14.

31. Kaplan, *Social Construction of American Realism*, 13.

32. *Nobody's Fool* had the same plot; a public relations firm found the most "common" man who would then endorse ideas and products. See Charles Yale Harrison, *Nobody's Fool* (New York: Henry Holt, 1948).

33. Robert Alan Aurthur, *The Glorification of Al Toolum* (New York: Rinehart, 1953), 77.

34. Green, *Last Angry Man*. In *Pax*, a PR firm uses a war hero to sell drugs and learns a lesson; Middleton Kiefer, *Pax* (New York: Random House, 1958). In *The Build Up Boys*, the chosen spokesman turns out to be evil and so teaches the young executive about life; Jeremy Kirk, *The Build-Up Boys* (New York: Charles Scribner's Sons, 1951). Morgan's *The Great Man* is told from the viewpoint of the honest man chosen to replace a beloved television host.

35. Green, *Last Angry Man*, 217. I dedicate this quote to my father, who agrees with the ideology it expresses.

36. James Kelly, "SR's Book of the Week: The Last Angry Man" *Saturday Review* 40 (2 February 1957): 12; for other reviews see Granville Hicks, "The Doctor Was Tough," *New York Times* (3 February 1957): 4; Fred Marsh, "TV and M.D. in a Big Novel" *New York Herald Tribune Book Review* (3 February 1957): 1, 8.

37. Green, *Last Angry Man*, 401.

38. Don Mankiewicz, "Average American," *New York Times* (19 April 1953): 25; Lee Rogow, "Offspring of the Big-Ad Men," *Saturday Review* 36 (13 June 1953): 20, 43.

39. Harold Livingston, *The Detroiters* (Boston: Houghton Mifflin, 1958), 258.

40. James Kelly, *The Insider* (New York: Henry Holt, 1958), 252.

41. Wolcott Gibbs, "The Big Boffola," *New Yorker* 22 (1 June 1946): 88.

42. Wilson, *Man in the Gray Flannel Suit*, Introduction.

43. Wilson, *Man in the Gray Flannel Suit*, 183.

44. Gerald Weales, "Life on Madison Avenue," *Commonweal* 62 (26 August 1955): 525–56; for other reviews, see Rose Feld, "Stepping out of Army Uniform into That of the Junior Executive," *New York Herald Tribune* (17 July 1955): 1; James Kelly, "Captive of the 5:31," *Saturday Review* 38 (23 July 1955): 8; Nora Magid, "The Gray Flannel Soul," *New Republic* 133 (8 August 1995): 19–20; *Catholic World* 181 (October 1955): 473–74.

45. Aurthur, *Glorification of Al Toolum*, 201.

46. For evil, emasculating female advertising executives see Matthew Peters, *The Joys She Chose* (New York: Dell, 1954); Robert Bruce, *Tina: The Story of a Hellcat* (New York: Lion, 1954); Kirk, *The Build-Up Boys*; and later, Jane Trahey, *Thursdays 'til 9* (New York: Harcourt Brace, 1980).

47. Robert L. Foreman, *The Hot Half Hour* (New York: Criterion Books, 1958), 11–12.

48. Al Morgan, "Unhorsing a Heel," *Saturday Review* 41 (1 November 1958): 20; for

other reviews of *The Insider* see David Dempsey, "Ad Alley Revisited," *New York Times* (19 October 1958): 57; Robert C. Healey, "Ad-Men's Quicksand Empire," *New York Herald Tribune Book Review* (2 November 1958): 9.

49. American Association of Advertising Agencies, *The Advertising Business and Its Career Opportunities* (New York: AAAA, 1956); Institute for Research, *Advertising as a Career* (Chicago: Institute for Research, 1952).

50. Harry P. Bridges, *Practical Advertising: A Comprehensive Guide to the Planning and Preparation of Modern Advertising in All of Its Phases* (New York: Rinehart, 1949), 775.

51. Marchand, *Advertising the American Dream*, 25–51; Michael Schudson, *Advertising, the Uneasy Persuasion* (New York: Basic Books, 1984), 44–89.

52. For a comparison to what happened in an earlier era, see Peggy Kreshel, "The 'Culture' of J. Walter Thompson, 1915–1925," *Public Relations Review* 16, 8 (Fall 1990): 80–93.

53. Many applicants before World War II described their planned or published novels, including Peregrin Acland to Stanley Resor, 6 February 1937, Box 1; Thayer Bancroft, January 1930, Box 1; Chester Carlan Application for Employment, 18 April 1928, Box 4; John Wiley, Application for Employment, 3 October 1923, all in Personnel Files. In the postwar period, among those who mentioned writing novels in their application essays were Emily Whitty (Mrs. Lambert), 5 April 1955; Virginia B. Moore, 17 March 1947; and Herbert L. King, 6 November 1946, all in Personnel Files. Many of the women described themselves as "writers" rather than novelists, among them Valerie Platt, 23 June 1952; Elizabeth Obey, 14 June 1956; Valerie Jones, 18 March 1960; Bergit Kiely, 9 May 1956; Lois Gaeta, 8 August 1955, Personnel Files. Among those copywriters described as writing novels in the company's internal newsletter were Cyril Chessex, 21 June 1954; Lionel Day, 4 April 1955; Gene d'Olive, 19 May 1958; Arnold Grisman, 23 December 1959; Walter A. O'Meara, 12 April 1948, all in *Thumbnail Sketches*, J. Walter Thompson Papers, John W. Hartman Center for Sales, Marketing and Advertising History, Rare Book, Manuscript, and Special Collection Library, Duke University (hereafter JWT Papers).

54. "How Well Do You Know Your JWT'ers?—Storrs Haynes," 25 February 1957, *Thumbnail Sketches*, JWT Papers.

55. Joseph Kaselow, "Along Madison Avenue with Kaselow: Meet the Happy Copywriter: No Frustrated Novelist Neff," *New York Herald Tribune* (7 August 1960): 9, in Richard Barclay Neff, Personnel Files, JWT Papers.

56. "How Well Do You Know Your JWT'ers?—Walter A. O'Meara," 12 April 1948, *Thumbnail Sketches*, JWT Papers.

57. Milton Moskowitz, "Novels of Past Decade Paint Lurid Ad World," *Advertising Age* (8 October 1956): 2, 96.

58. Ralph Vines, "Is It True What They Say About Admen?" *Advertising Age* 31 (11 July 1960): 104.

59. Vines, "Is It True What They Say About Admen?" 104.

60. James F. Kelly, "In Defense of Madison Avenue," *New York Times Magazine* (23 December 1956): 15ff., reprinted in *Advertising in America*, ed. Tyler Poyntz (New York: H.W. Wilson, 1959), 197.

61. Neil Jumonville, *Critical Crossings: The New York Intellectuals in Postwar America* (Berkeley: University of California Press, 1991), 3, 13.

62. Alan Wald, *The New York Intellectuals: The Rise and Decline of the Anti-Stalinist Left from the 1930s to the 1980s* (Chapel Hill: University of North Carolina Press, 1987), 222.

63. Michael Wreszin, *A Rebel in Defense of Tradition: The Life and Politics of Dwight McDonald* (New York: Basic Books, 1994), 287.

64. Dwight MacDonald, "A Theory of Mass Culture," in *Mass Culture: The Popular Arts in America*, ed. Bernard Rosenberg and David Manning White (New York: Free Press, 1957), 60.

65. MacDonald, "A Theory of Mass Culture," 62.

66. MacDonald, "A Theory of Mass Culture," 72.

67. Jumonville, *Critical Crossings*, 164.

68. H. H. Holmes, "Science and Fantasy," *New York Herald Tribune* (5 July 1953): 8.

69. Frederik Pohl and C. M. Kornbluth, *The Space Merchants* (New York: Ballantine Books, 1952), 5.

70. Pohl and Kornbluth, *Space Merchants*, 100.

71. Pohl and Kornbluth, *Space Merchants*, 19.

72. Frederik Pohl, *The Merchants' War* (New York: St. Martin's Press, 1984).

73. Andrew Ross, "Containing Culture in the Cold War," *Cultural Studies* 1 (October 1987): 328–48; James Burkhardt Gilbert, *Writers and Partisans: A History of Literary Radicalism in America* (New York: John Wiley, 1968), 217.

74. On the role of the intellectual in this time period, see Andrew Ross, "Containing Culture in the Cold War," *Cultural Studies* 1 (October 1987): 328–48.

75. Michael Denning, "New York Intellectuals," *Socialist Review* 88, 1 (January-March 1988): 147.

76. Michael Denning, *The Cultural Front: The Laboring of American Culture in the Twentieth Century* (New York: Verso, 1997).

77. Horowitz, *Anxieties of Affluence*, 1.

78. Leokum, *Please Send Me . . . A Novel* (London: Harper, 1946); Fielden Farrington, *The Big Noise* (New York: Crown, 1946): for a similarly evil hero who lacked military service during the war see the story of a marketing department at a grocery chain, J. Harvey Howells, *The Big Company Look* (New York: J. Harvey Howells, 1958).

79. "Books: Briefly Noted," *New Yorker* 22 (3 August 1946): 63.

80. Hobe Morrison, "Not Nice People," *Saturday Review of Literature* 29 (10 August 1946): 8; see also C. V. Terry, "Another Huckster's Whirl in the Golden Cage," *New York Times* (4 August 1946): 5.

81. Farrington, *The Big Noise.*

82. Farrington, *The Big Noise*, 258–59.

83. Leokum, *Please Send Me*, 310.

84. Edward Stephens, *A Twist of Lemon* (Garden City, N.Y.: Doubleday, 1958), 440.

85. Stephens, *A Twist of Lemon*, 332–33.

86. For very similar endings, see Green, *Last Angry Man*; Ian Gordon, *The Whip Hand* (New York: Crown, 1954) and, of course, Wouk, *Aurora Dawn.*

87. Vance Packard, *The Hidden Persuaders* (New York: David McKay, 1957), 266.

88. Packard, *Hidden Persuaders*, 258; see also Daniel Horowitz, *Vance Packard and American Social Criticism* (Chapel Hill: University of North Carolina Press, 1994).

89. Shepherd Mead, *The Big Ball of Wax: A Story of Tomorrow's Happy World* (New York: Avon Book Division, 1954), 242.

90. Mead, *Big Ball of Wax*, 21.

91. Mead, *Big Ball of Wax*, 153.

92. Horowitz, *Anxieties of Affluence*, 79–100.

93. David M. Potter, *People of Plenty: Economic Abundance and the American Character* (Chicago: University of Chicago Press, 1954), 175.

94. Potter, *People of Plenty*, 84, 188.

95. Potter, *People of Plenty*, 167.

96. Hodgins, *Mr. Blandings Builds His Dream House*, 14–15; for a similar passage see Green, *Last Angry Man*, 174.

97. Robert M. Gay, "Mr. Blandings Builds His Dream House," *Atlantic Monthly* 179 (February 1947): 138; for other reviews, see Richardson Wright, "A Huckster Builds a Country Home," *New York Herald Tribune Weekly Book Review* (26 December 1946): 6; Brooks Atkinson, "The Country Squire's Comeuppance," *New York Times* (29 December 1946): 5; Alistair Cooke, "No Joke, Son," *New Republic* 116 (27 January 1947): 116.

98. "How Well Do You Know Your JWT'ers?—Thomas J. Glynn," 16 September 1957; Leonard Hyde, 5 June 1950; see also Mildred Jesslund, 8 December 1947; David Lundstrom, 17 October 1949; C. C. Nash, 16 October 1950; Arthur "Bob" M. Jones, Jr., 26 November 1951; Philip Birch, 8 July 1957; Caroll Hudders, 15 July 1957; Woodrow Benoit, 20 January 1958; Sandy McLean, 25 August 1958, Biographical Information, *Thumbnail Sketches*, JWT Papers.

99. William Pfaff, "Blandings' Way," *Commonweal* 53 (24 November 1950): 179–80.

100. Eric Hodgins, *Blandings' Way* (New York: Simon and Schuster, 1950), 47, 172.

101. Pfaff, "Blandings' Way," 79–80.

102. *New Yorker* 26 (7 October 1950): 132; for other reviews see Nathanial Benchley, "In the Field of Current Fiction: Liberal Troubles," *New York Times* (8 October 1950): 32; "Connecticut Gamut," *Time* 56 (16 October 1950): 102.

103. Horowitz, *Anxieties of Affluence*, 11.

104. Lizabeth Cohen, *A Consumers' Republic: The Politics of Mass Consumption in Postwar America* (New York: Knopf, 2003), 11.

105. Thomas Newhouse, *The Beat Generation and the Popular Novel in the United States, 1945–1970* (Jefferson, N.C.: McFarland, 2000), 25.

106. Manuel Luis Martínez, *Countering the Counterculture: Rereading Postwar American Dissent from Jack Kerouac to Tomás Rivera* (Madison: University of Wisconsin Press, 2003), 9–10.

107. See Marchand, *Advertising the American Dream*, 25–51; Daniel Pope and Wil-

liam Toll, "We Tried Harder: Jews in American Advertising," *American Jewish History* 72, 1 (1982): 26–51.

108. George Panetta, *Viva Madison Avenue!* (New York: Harcourt, Brace, 1957), 6, 9.

109. Panetta, *Viva Madison Avenue!* 121.

110. Al Morgan, "Pair of Hustling Hucksters," *New York Herald Tribune Book Review* (28 April 1957): 10.

111. Gerald Carson, "Babes in the Big Business Jungle," *New York Times* (24 March 1957): 40; for other reviews, see Larry Wolters, "Humor Along Ad Row," *Chicago Sunday Tribune* (26 May 1957): 6; Martin Leven, "Buffoons from Madison Ave," *Saturday Review* 40 (13 April 1957): 48.

112. Frank, *The Conquest of Cool*, 9.

113. Shepherd Mead, *The Admen* (New York: Simon and Schuster, 1958), 250.

114. Mead, *Admen*, 37–38.

115. Frank, *Conquest of Cool*, 55.

116. Sammy R. Danna, "William Bernbach (August 13, 1911-October 2, 1982)," in *The Ad Men and Women: A Biographical Dictionary of Advertising*, ed. Edd Applegate (Westport, Conn.: Greenwood Press, 1994), 56–62; see also Pope and Toll, "We Tried Harder," 26–51.

117. Denis Higgins, *The Art of Writing Advertising: Conversations with Masters of the Craft* (Chicago: NTC Business Books, 1965), 15, 23.

118. Frank, *Conquest of Cool*, 55.

119. Jackson Lears discusses the uses of the term "creativity" in the lives of advertising agents in "The Ad Man and the Grand Inquisitor: Intimacy, Publicity, and the Managed Self in America, 1880–1940," in *Constructions of the Self*, ed. George Levine (New Brunswick, N.J.: Rutgers University Press, 1992), 107–41.

120. Livingston, *Detroiters*, 40.

121. Livingston, *Detroiters*, 64–65.

122. Livingston, *Detroiters*, 94.

123. Livingston, *Detroiters*, 150, 207.

124. Livingston, *Detroiters*, 330, 341; see also Meyer Levin, "2–1-0 Means Two in One," *New York Times Book Review* (19 October 1958): 58.

125. Elizabeth Peer, "Corporate Sex Wars," *Newsweek* (14 September 1981): 84; Anne Tolstoi Wallach, *Women's Work* (New York: New American Library, 1981); for other reviews, see Charlotte Curtis, "Many Tears," *New York Times Book Review* (6 September 1981): 10–11; V. S. Pritchett, *New Yorker* (12 October 1981); "How Well Do You Know Your JWT'ers?: Anne Tolstoi Foster," 28 October 1959, *Thumbnail Sketches*, JWT Papers.

126. Jack Dillon, *The Advertising Man* (New York: Harper's Magazine Press, 1972), 123.

127. Dillon, *Advertising Man*, 256.

128. Martin Levin, "New and Novel," *New York Times* (10 September 1972): BR40; see also Christopher Lehman-Haupt, "Fear and Loathing on Mad. Ave," *New York Times* (15 September 1972): 35.

129. Jack Dillon, "Commercials Can Be Fun, So Why Not?" *New York Times* (29 October 1972): F15.

CONCLUSION. STORIES OF *OTAKU* AND *DESIS*

1. Moye Ishimoto, "Anime in America and the American *Otaku*," senior thesis, Department of American Civilization, Brown University, May 2003, 46.

2. For a description of the scholarly controversy over whether imported Japanese popular culture is perceived as "foreign" and/or Japanese, see Anne Allison, "A Challenge to Hollywood? Japanese Character Goods Hit the US," *Japanese Studies* 20 (1 May 2000): 67–88; the two best studies of anime in the United States are Antonia Levi, *Samurai from Outer Space: Understanding Japanese Animation* (Chicago: Open Court, 1996) and Susan Napier, *Anime from Akira to Princess Mononoke: Experiencing Contemporary Japanese Animation* (New York: Palgrave, 2000).

3. For an example of a small, fan-run anime importer, see http://www.animeigo.com/ (accessed 3 August 2006).

4. A good explanation of the deal signed between Disney and Miyazaki's Studio Ghibli can be found at a fan website, http://nausicaa.net/miyazaki/disney/ (accessed 3 August 2006).

5. Amita Manghnani, "Rhythm Nation: South Asian America Performs Race Onstage," senior thesis, Department of American Civilization, Brown University, May 2006.

6. For similar studies see the excellent books by Sunaina Maira, *Desis in the House: Indian American Youth Culture in New York City* (Philadelphia: Temple University Press, 2002) and Sunita Mukhi, *Doing the Desi Thing: Performing Indianness in New York City* (New York: Garland, 2000).

INDEX

ACKNOWLEDGMENTS

I'd like to thank Robert Lee, Steven Lubar, Elliott Gorn, and Susan Douglas for reading parts of the manuscript and providing useful critiques with which I always argued and which I then accepted. For help with the manuscript in its entirety, I don't know how to begin to thank Rick Farrell. For assistance in the publishing process, I am indebted to Roy Rosensweig and to Robert Lockhart of the University of Pennsylvania Press. Terry Murphy explained to me that I had a book in my various projects and I'm grateful she convinced me that she was right.

I owe much to Marjorie McNinch at the Hagley Museum and Library and to Rosemary Cullen and Patrick Yott at the Brown University Libraries. I appreciated a fellowship at the John W. Hartmann Center for Sales, Advertising, and Marketing History, Duke University, to work in the J. Walter Thompson Papers.

Many student researchers helped along the way and I thank each of them. In particular, Tara Rodgers found the materials on which Chapter 1 is based and persuaded me to pay attention. For introducing me to their research on nylon, part of a different project, thanks to Carolyn Goldstein, Carlita Kosty, and Marilyn McClain.

Those I always think of, in *Star Trek* terms, as the "next generation" have provided ideas and support in extraordinary measure. My gratitude to Jane Gerhard, Kathy Franz, Mari Yoshihara, Briann Greenfield, Alex Russo, Themis Chronopoulos, Susanne Wiedemann, and all the graduate students in the Department of American Civilization, Brown University, who have been and are so wonderful and exasperating at the same time.

The transnational turn in American Studies brought me great new colleagues who listened to these chapters as papers all over the world. I'd like to acknowledge Collette Collomb-Boureau, Claudette Fillard, Helene Quanquin, Didier Aubert, France Jancene Jaigu, Franco LaPolla, Douglas Craig,

David Goodman, Takeshi Matsuda, Masako Notoji, Naoki Onishi, and Yujin Yaguchi.

For hosting me on research trips and/or collegiality and/or friendship beyond recounting, I want to thank Teresa Murphy, Joel Kuipers, Bruce Sinclair, Gail Cooper, Ed Hardy, Tamar Katz, Jim Egan, Kerry Smith, Robert Emlen, Brian Casey, Jennifer Wood, Paul Buhle, Mari Jo Buhle, Pat Malone, Judy Babbitts, Linda Pritchard, Gerry Frei, Lisa Smulyan, Michael Markowitz, Betsy Smulyan, Ted Haber, and Ruth and Harold Smulyan.